The Dark One Cometh

A Novel By
James Garnett

Dedication

I dedicate this book to my wife, Susan, who, after 11 years of listening to me gripe about how much I wanted to write a book, finally said:

"Enough! You want to write a book so badly? Go down and do it already!"

So she banished me to my writing area, which I had created in the laundry room of the basement, and brought me coffee and snacks throughout the creative process to provide nourishment and energy, until I finished.

Acknowledgment

I want to acknowledge my project manager, Benjamin Wilson, Iris, and her entire editing team at BookWave Publishing for all their tireless efforts to polish this manuscript.

Thanks to everyone. I am grateful.

About the Author

James L Garnett was born on October 5th, 1970, in Philadelphia, Pennsylvania, and currently resides in Hazleton, Pennsylvania. He earned a Bachelor's degree in Business Administration and a Master's degree in Human Resources Administration.

His writing journey began in 2001 when he penned The Dark One Cometh and submitted it—fresh off his laser jet printer—to a traditional horror publisher. The rejection that followed was devastating, and after shedding some very real tears, he shelved the manuscript with a broken heart. Decades later, while relocating his writing space from a basement laundry room to an upstairs vacant bedroom, he rediscovered the forgotten manuscript. Brushing off the dust, he reread it with fresh eyes and was impressed by what he found. As an avid horror reader and aspiring horror author, he thought to himself, "Wow, I would buy this book." Encouraged by that realization, he decided to resubmit it, and this time, The Dark One Cometh was accepted for publication by BookWave Publishing.

Outside of writing, he enjoys ATV riding and immersing himself in the horror genre. He currently has four other novels in various stages of development, including the sequel to The Dark One Cometh.

He has been married once—and to the same woman, Susan, since 1989. Together, they share three grown children, Michael, Valerie, and Destiny, and are proud grandparents to three grandchildren: Gaige, Ella, and Isabella.

Prologue

Space experts dubbed the arrival of the comet as the unrivaled event in human history.

Comet enthusiasts far and wide, wielding everything from telescopes to binoculars, came out to witness the phenomenon.

Shortly after it appeared in the night sky, the first spontaneous abortions began.

The comet stayed in Earth's orbit for a mere twenty-four hours, and for its duration, ravaged every pregnant woman, on every continent, until there were none.

Hospitals all over the globe are filled to capacity in major cities, small towns, and villages in every nation.

Chaos ruled as desperate husbands, boyfriends, fathers, mothers, friends, neighbors, or passersby tried in frantic desperation to get medical attention for the ailing women and unborn children.

Medical professionals were left helpless to save a single soul, mother or child.

There could be no question; every woman who had conceived in the days, weeks, or months prior to the comet mysteriously and simultaneously perished, dooming the fetus they carried.

It was as if the end had come, a generation decimated. Everyone (leader and losers alike) had been affected, if not by personal loss, then by acquaintance.

The aftermath left the human race reeling. For the first time ever, the world united to mourn.

Many believe the power generated by the anguish of the mourners could be detected in space.

Press releases and scientific speculation abound in the weeks after, but no one theory prevailed. The most prominent conclusion was that the comet emitted some unknown form of radiation highly toxic to pregnant women.

****

During the first few days of Annette's nausea, Marty and Annette dismissed her suffering as a passing stomach flu. But when days started to become more than a few days, they both knew it was time to see a doctor. They did not want to take any chances.

Marty was stuck on mandatory overtime, so he could not be there when she went to see the doctor. He was confident that this visit would get her tended to and back on speed.

His cell rang just as he was leaving the pet shop. Although he figured she might call, the timing could not have been worse. Fumbling with the stinking door and the box containing the cutest cross-eyed Siamese Kitten he had ever seen, he managed to retrieve the cell, recognize her number, and answer.

"Hello, my lil' sweetheart." The cat shifts awkwardly in the box.

"Marty, I'm still at the doctor."

"Is everything ok?" A steady silence causes him to check if the cell has lost signal. Sweetie, have I lost you?"

"I'm here, Martin."

Her tone made him uneasy, "Everything is ok, right?"

He stood dead in front of the doorway, noticing late that hurried customers wanted in, and stepped aside.

Her tone didn't sound right to him, "We were wrong, it's not a stomach flu, I'm pregnant."

Marty could have been leveled with a feather, "Honey, there has to be a mistake!" Years of trying, and a team of specialists had already confirmed. "Remember my low sperm count, and your hostile immune system?"

"Trust me, Marty, I am just as surprised. It's not a mistake, Dr. Sohon proved it with a sonogram. There's a baby in here with a heartbeat and all the essential parts. But hold on, she will confirm it."

Before he could object, Annette had the doc on the other end, "Yes, Martin, it's true." "I, too, am stunned by this, especially in light of the fact that nothing has changed with Annette's condition."

The kitten scurrying in the box snapped him back to reality, "I don't understand." "If nothing has changed, then how is this possible?"

"I can't offer an explanation, Mr. Sooner." "It is a miracle." Let us not worry about that right now. Count your blessings, there have been few reported pregnancies since the disaster last month. I have to go; there are other patients waiting to see me. Congratulations, Dad."

"Thank you, Doctor." Marty tried to sound appreciative, but still found it hard to believe.

Marty and Annette expressed their love for each other and raced home. Her love of the kitten was immediate, the moment she opened the box.

Just as he anticipated, and bought it simply to see the joy in her expression and take her mind off feeling ill for a little while. It seemed apparent that the cute little bugger was stressed out from being transported in the box. While extremely playful and affectionate in the pet store, its demeanor had changed drastically once Annette scooped it from the box. Ears back, it hissed and clawed her cheek, causing her to drop it as a reflex. The kitten quickly shot out of the room.

"Ooh, she's a little edgy," Annette proclaimed, rubbing her cheek. "Let's just give her a little time to adjust and unwind."

For the duration of a few weeks, Marty and Annette embraced each other with love and happily prepared for the addition to their family. Thankful their luck had changed.

Table of Contents

Chapter 1: Darkness Conceived

The shrill discharge of the overhead intercom slicing into the crisp night air did not catch Marty's attention. He was preoccupied with loading pallets onto the flatbed trailer while listening closely to the familiar voice of late-night DJ Donny B announcing the next thirty-minute string of hits about to play in his headphones. The announcement following the attention signal began filtering into his senses as a string of garbled sounds, not unlike a person speaking underwater. Marty halted his progress, pallet mid air, silencing the engine and sliding the earphones around his neck, listening intently, only to hear the tail end of the announcement.

If the announcement had been meant for him, another would follow, so with a slight shrug, he continued. A few minutes passed before the beep came again. This time, Marty was ready, turning off the propane-powered motor, to hear better, 'Marty Sooner phone call on extension 315', the sound of the announcement from the speaker mounted outside the factory reverberated through the night air.

The hair on Marty's arms stood on end, Oh no, he whispered, this can't be good, he was overwhelmed with an uneasy feeling that something was dreadfully wrong. Surely a phone call at 3 a.m. meant bad news of some sort. In the seven years since he began the graveyard shift at the factory, he had only ever received two phone calls. One bore the terrible revelation of his father's heart attack, the other that his brother had been involved in a fatal car wreck.

In a flash, Marty lowered the pallet to the ground, the whole time thinking of the worst-case scenarios; could there be something wrong with his mother, wife, or Sis? His heart beat rapidly as he drove the lift at an unsafe speed towards the entrance of the loading docks, barely avoiding stacks of pallets and guide rails along the way. Once parked outside the shipping office, he instinctively set the parking brake and fumbled with the rigging that secures the operator into the forklift safety cage. "Damn belt!" he shouted, struggling with the restraint system. He grew increasingly anxious with every passing second. Again, the beep of the overhead intercom sounded, causing him more distress, "Marty, Sooner you have a call holding on extension 315." Finally, the assembly of the harness was left loose, and Marty peeled the harness surrounding his body, thrusting himself from the confines of the safety cage, intent on revealing the dreadful news he knew to be forthcoming. Consumed by the struggle of the safety buckle, Marty did not realize his elbow remained slightly entangled within the strapping. As he leapt from the safety cage, the loose shoulder harness cinched tight around his bicep, shifting his bodyweight to the side, causing him to stumble awkwardly, flailing to regain his stability in a sideways half-run movement. His effort to regain steadiness was ineffective, for the inertia of his forward motion sent him hurling hard onto the floor, ripping a large hole through the knee of his jeans, scraping a painful gash in his flesh.

Marty grimaced, his breath hissing through his teeth in reaction to the searing pain of the fresh wound. Standing to inspect the damage, he became aware that his mishap was witnessed by a group of co-workers standing close by. He tried to ignore their howling and taunting laughter, making every effort to appear composed and unaffected, even though he could feel his face reddening from embarrassment. He paused at the entrance to the, the sound of his coworkers still reveling in the merriment of his awkward dismount caused his face to redden, and he could make out the voice of Dale (the biggest ball buster in the factory) howl, "We all saw that, youu clumsy fuckah!" He clenched his eyes tight, praying this not to be another doomed pregnancy for Annette," (his wife of five years). He flung open the door, dialing extension 315 before the flicker of the overhead lights fully illuminated the office. "Hello, this is Marty."

"Martin!" He immediately recognized his wife's trembling voice, "Annette, is there something wrong, honey?" "Yes, Martin, it's the baby." Marty felt the blood drain from his face as she spoke those words, "Oh no, Annette, not again!" He groaned, remembering the heartache that accompanied all the previous failed pregnancies. "No, Martin, it's not like that this time, the baby is moving a lot, and feels strong, really strong."

Marty breathed a sigh of relief, pushing the hair from his forehead and using his thumb and index finger to soothe his throbbing temples. He clenched his teeth, again hissing slightly while adjusting the ripped denim to better examine his stinging knee, "Geeze, Annette, you nearly gave me a heart attack!" "Why would you call me at work, this time of the morning, to tell me that the baby feels ok?" His relief was quickly replaced by feelings of annoyance, "You know, Annette, I nearly broke my neck trying to get off the lift to answer this call. I thought something was terribly wrong." Annette cut him off, "But Martin, I called to say there is something terribly wrong, the baby is"…her voice trailed off, straining to maintain her composure. Anxious to understand what is on her mind, Marty urged her to continue, "The baby is what, Annette?" She did not answer, and after a moment of silence, Marty asked sternly, "What is it you want to tell me?" "The baby is evil!" she blurted out in a forced, pitchy voice, "I can't believe I am finally admitting it!"

Marty's jaw dropped, a stunned expression consuming his face, "What!?"…his utter shock caused him to pause, shaking his head in disbelief; "Did you say, what I think I heard?" "You're joking, right?" "Hah, Hah, go ahead, tell me you're joking!"

Annette's response came firm and direct, "No Marty, I have never been more deadly serious." Growing angry Marty snapped, "What the hell are you talking about?" "Annette, do you hear what you're saying, and just how insane it sounds?" Annette had to make him understand, "I've been having the most horrible dreams, about the future, of horrible suffering and death." Her voice now trembling as if she were holding back tears "I'm convinced these dreams are visions of the horrifying future that awaits the world after this child arrives." "My God Annette, I can't believe my ears!" "Why are you talking like this?" "Martin, I know this sounds crazy, but I started feeling

3

this way even before the doctor confirmed I was pregnant." "Almost immediately after having the fertility procedure I could feel the evil taking root within me." "And with each passing day it gets stronger, I feel its cold essence, its darkness growing within me, feeding off me." "And it has been making me do things." Marty was confounded "Make you do what sort of things?" She sniffled lightly, "It made me stick a knitting needle in the wall socket." Her voice grew more frantic, along with the pace of her speech "I had no control of my arm!" "I didn't even realize it was happening at first." "I was on the couch watching my soaps and knitting while you were sleeping, and the next thing my arm kind of started feeling tingly, like when the circulation is cut off for a while." "And while I was sitting there looking at my hand as I holding the knitting needle, my arm started convulsing and going crazy, I couldn't control, or stop it from happening." I was really freaked out, and I slid from the couch onto my knees, because I didn't know what the hell was happening, when all of a sudden, all of a sudden!" She had to pause and gather herself, "All of a sudden my arm reared up over my head jamming the needle into the wall socket." "The shock was an unpleasant feeling for me, but I think the baby enjoyed it." "I don't think it was the shock...so much it enjoyed, but more the power it displayed over me."

Marty was floored by this conversation, struggling with how to respond, "Honey, just listen to me for a second, you have got to calm down, you probably just had an involuntary muscle spasm; you shouldn't get yourself so upset." "No, Marty, it's not just that; there's other stuff, and it's been worse. Last night I was having another dream, I woke up screaming, but I wasn't in bed." "I was standing at the dresser in our bedroom with one of the chocolate candies you bought me in my hand, and my mouth was full of them." "I had chocolate running all down my chin and the front of my night clothes!" "Annette, that sounds to me like you may have been sleepwalking." "No, Marty, it's more, I can feel it." Marty knew he had to remain rational and reason with her, "Annette, you have got to stop this crazy talk." "I've heard that when a woman is pregnant, her body goes through some

4

pretty crazy shit, and this is probably the cause." "You are just overreacting because of all the hormones." "Just calm yourself and go back to bed. If you get some rest, you will feel better." Annette cut in, "I'm afraid to sleep, it has more control when I am sleeping." "Get yourself a glass of warm milk; it will help you calm down." Looking through the window of the shipping office, Marty noticed the truck driver he had been loading was looking impatient, tapping his finger on his wristwatch, and motioning for Marty. He talked softly, mellowing the tone of his voice to comfort her. "Listen, sweetie, I don't mean to cut you short, but I am in the process of loading a truck, and I have to get back to work." "Ok, Marty, I'll do that. I'm sorry to scare you." "Ok, Annette, I'll see you in a couple of hours when I get home. Goodbye, I love you." "I love you, Marty. Bye."

After hanging up, he stood still for a moment reflecting on the phone call. Shaking his head and rubbing the back of his very tense neck, he turned off the light and went back to work. The remaining hours of his shift seemed just too far away, and the phone call from his wife left Marty with a very uneasy feeling that something was very wrong. "She's acting crazy like this because of the hormonal changes, that's all it is", became his consolation for the remaining hours of his shift, but did little to ease his growing apprehension.

Martin was first in line at the time clock at the end of the shift, punching out and rushing to his car, tossing his lunch pail, jacket, and safety glasses on the back seat, and jumping into the driver's seat, fumbling with his keys hastily. "Come on, God dammit!" He shouted at himself, struggling to align the key properly in the ignition. Once he got the key right, it was just a matter of seconds before the engine raced and the transmission was in drive, lurching the car forward, cutting right into the path of the line of co-workers that had already gotten their vehicles in motion. BEEEP.....a horn screamed, and Marty could see Jack, a line worker, raising his hands, yelling out the window, 'stupid fuck!' Waiving his hands in the air, Marty said, 'Sorry", and in a flash, he was in a line of vehicles waiting to exit the parking lot of the plant. He began assessing the line of cars in front of him, exiting the parking lot slowly. "Oh man, this is just perfect!" he yelled while slapping the dashboard after noticing the long line of cars waiting to exit the industrial park. In his haste to leave, he forgot that there is always a major bottleneck of cars exiting the industrial park. Most of the factories all have shifts that start and end at the same time. Marty usually departs about 15 minutes after the end of his shift to avoid the frustration of being trapped in the bottleneck. If a person is not lucky enough to get into one of the pole positions exiting the lot, it ends up becoming a blood sport of darting into any gap that might open up in the line of cars.

As the line of cars in front of him began creeping their way into the bottleneck, Marty contemplated whether he should exit by way of the bottleneck at entrance one or race down to one of the entrances that exist farther down in the park. Alternatively, he envisioned throwing caution to the wind and attempting to cross the quarry that ran parallel to the industrial park. "Yeah, I could cut out all the waiting if I just detoured through the quarry," he said aloud to himself. The line in front of him lessened by another car. "Time is running out, Marty, you have to make a decision quickly," again speaking aloud as if his alter ego was sitting invisibly in the seat right next to him. "Think, think," he began tapping his finger on his forehead. "The quarry could possibly save you some time." He envisioned that instead of turning left into the bottleneck, he could make a right and take a small left toward the dirt entrance of the quarry, spinning his tires around each turn. He imagined (with all the vividness that most any teenage boy fantasizes about driving fast and furiously), roaring onto the dirt road, a trail of dust flying behind him, the sound of pebbles and dirt glancing off the underside and quarter panels, the wind in his hair, his machine responding perfectly to the expertise of his command. "Yeah, yeah," he was beginning to really enjoy the fantasy. Another car darted into the single-file bottleneck, just one more in front of him now. He envisioned ripping through the quarry in time enough to get ahead of the first person who had left the plant. Then, for some reason, he starts considering the worst-case scenario, "Oh my God, I could just imagine ripping something major off the bottom of the car." His vision included a ripped off oil pan, and the loud rapping of the engine as it quickly loses oil. Or the loss of his exhaust system, and how ridiculous he would feel pulling in front of the house with a car louder than a freight train. Or even if he ran over something sharp, puncturing a tire, "Ooh, that wouldn't be good," he said, contorting his face as he imagined feeling like a complete idiot as he discovers his spare tire is out of air. He would have to roll the full-size spare a mile and a half to the nearest service station to fill it up, and then roll it back to change it. "Then I wouldn't get home until dusk," he said with a low groan. He had a quick vision of Annette standing behind the door, slapping a rolling pin in her hand, annoyed, waiting to pounce. Or even worse, he imagined flying down the dirt quarry road straight into the path of a huge dump truck, crushing him to death. The last scenario was enough for him to play it safe and enter the bottleneck.

The ride home went quickly, within ten minutes, Marty was parking in front of the quaint two-bedroom home he and Annette shared. He was sure to be quiet as he slipped the key in the lock on the front door,, as it was 7:20 a.m., and if Annette were he would not want to disturb her. Upon entering the living room, he glanced around to see nothing out of the ordinary; the strong morning sun came peeking through the cracks in the drawn curtains. Heading to the kitchen, he stopped dead in his tracks, astonished at the sight that lay before him. "Oh God!" he whispered. "What the hell?" The kitchen was in a state of disarray, the refrigerator door ajar, eggs broken on the floor, the milk carton crushed with a puddle of milk, and random patterns of footprints on the linoleum floor. "Annette," he called out, immediately regretting it, because an intruder may still be there. He grabbed a long knife from the butcher block on the counter. His mind was gripped by the fear of what he had yet to discover in the house. He began making his way down the hall towards the bedroom as he crept closer towards the partially open door. He could hear a faint sound, almost a gurgling, but he could not quite tell what it was. "What is that noise?" He wondered, his mind racing. He paused about two feet from the door to listen. He distinctly heard gurgling and grunting. Marty reached forward and pushed the door open to notice the sight of his wife crouching in the middle of their bed with her back to him. "Annette?" he asked as he rounded the far side of the bed. The sight of his wife made him shudder, and he dropped the knife so that it stuck blade-first in the floor. She was crouched in the middle of the bed, holding the bloody carcass of the kitten he had brought home a few days ago. She was very intent on what she was doing, completely oblivious to his presence. Bloody fur lined her face and shoulder-length brown hair. "Annette," he said, raising his voice and grabbing her shoulders. "What are you doing?" She looked up at him and uttered a sound unintelligible, and not in a tone of voice Marty had ever heard her use before; it reminded him of an infant's voice. "Annette," he said again, shaking her slightly. She immediately closed her eyes and went limp, dropping the kitten. He reacted quickly to ease her down. Once on her back, she immediately began screaming and crying out, "Nooooo!" Tears were streaming down her cheeks. Again, Marty shook her. "Annette, honey, what's wrong?" Annette's eyes shot open, and she sat straight up in the bed, knocking Marty off balance backwards into the wall. She was still wailing and crying. "Marty?" She asked as if she had not seen him before. She was breathing heavy and obviously very upset. "I was dreaming, a terrible dream, about the baby, about the horrible things he's done," she sobbed. Marty remained in the position he had fallen, staring at his wife; a look of mixed shock and terror was his expression, wondering what to expect next. She looked down at her hands in disbelief, then pulled her nightgown straight, revealing the bloodied carcass of the kitten hidden in the folds. She leapt to her feet in the middle of the bed. "What the hell is that?" she shrieked. "Oh, Marty, I don't understand what is going on!" Marty stood up, still dazed and not knowing how to process what he had just witnessed. "You mean you don't remember what you were just doing?" His voice rang with disbelief. "No, I don't," she said.

"Honey, you were just eating that!" Gagging, she bolted from the room. Marty could hear her throwing up in the bathroom a moment later. He went to her; she had flushed and pulled herself into the fetal position on the floor. "Marty, something is seriously wrong here," she began to rock slightly, staring blankly, void of any expression. "I can feel it in the very core of my being, an icy, vile presence growing within me."Her voice remained unwavering and calm. Marty felt an urgency to gain some sense of normalcy, "Annette, we will make an emergency appointment with the Doctor today." "Let the Doctor examine you and try to explain what you are going through." "Ok?" "Come on, let's get you cleaned up, and I will call the Doctor to see if we can get in right away, first thing if possible." He reached over, lightly caressing her slimy-coated hand. "Yeah, Marty, that's a good idea," she agreed in a monotone voice.

Chapter 2: Losing Control

After seeing that Annette had gotten safely into the shower, Marty immediately called the fertility doctor he and Annette had been using. Since it was before office hours, the answering service paged the doctor to have her return Marty's phone call. Marty waited nervously for the phone to ring, contemplating how he could tell the doctor what was happening with his wife without making her sound like a complete nut. He shook his head, thinking there would be no easy way to explain the events of the past 10 hours.

He thought it best to immediately clean up and started by grabbing a trash bag to place the kitten into. "We didn't even give you a name yet," he spoke to the lifeless little thing as he placed it in the bag. He then headed for the kitchen, cleaning up the mess of eggshells and tossing them into the trash. "Eww, what a mess," he grimaced, tossing the crushed half-gallon milk carton in the trash. He grabbed the roll of paper towels and began ripping them off three at a time, covering the most obvious clusters of mess. The first ring startled him, and as he tried to pick it up, the phone slipped from his grip onto the floor, skidding right through a gooey pile of slime. "Oh sure, add insult to injury!" He whined, picking up the cordless phone. "Hello." "This is Doctor Sohon returning an emergency page for Martin Sooner." The woman's voice rang in his ear with the familiar Middle Eastern accent. "Yes, Doctor Sohon, thank you for returning my call so promptly." The doctor wasted no time in getting right to the point: "What is it I can help you with?" Marty fidgeted nervously as he started to speak, "I need to make an emergency appointment in your office as soon as possible." The doctor's concern became obvious: "Martin, if your wife is in need of emergency medical treatment, promptly take her to the nearest hospital; do not wait to make an appointment at my office." "No, Doctor, it's nothing like that. Physically, she seems fine; it's the way she's been acting, very strange, and I would like you to examine her." Trying to determine the extent of the emergency, she probed further, "Explain what you mean by acting strange." "I'd rather not discuss it until I get her in your office," he said, trying to remain aloof. "Well then, Martin, bring her to my office. I will be arriving around 8:30, and I will examine her first thing, before any other appointments." Breathing a sigh of relief, Marty thanked the doctor, confirming that she should expect them soon.

After hanging up, Marty went back into the bedroom to see how Annette was progressing with her clean-up. He entered their bedroom to find Annette sitting on their bed with a towel wrapped around her body, maintaining the blank, numb look. Behind her was Annette's lap dog, Popsicle, chewing on what remained of a steak Annette had dropped while rummaging in the refrigerator. "Popsicle!" Marty yelled. "Give me that!" He started towards her, at which point she started chewing even more vigorously and began growling. He approached the dog, knowing full well that if he just reached to grab the raw meat, she would probably bite him. Popsicle was not particularly vicious, but Annette had had the dog longer than she had known Marty, and even though the dog had become tolerant of his presence, when it came to food, she remained defensive. He knew it would take some firm coaxing for her to give it up. "Popsicle," he said slowly and sternly. "Give me that meat," he maintained the sternness of his tone. He started by rubbing the back of her head, then moved to cover her eyes. The dog growled again. "Popsicle, give me that meat," he said again, maintaining the tone. With one hand covering her eyes, he moved the other hand, grabbing the bone. Popsicle tightened her grip on the meat, attempting to stop her meal from being pillaged. Marty tugged on the bone, uncovering her eyes to get a grip with both hands. In about three seconds, the tug of war ends with Popsicle scampering under the bed, hiding to consume the little piece of meat she was able to escape with. "Damn dog!"

Throughout his struggle with Popsicle, Annette remained motionless; she did not even turn to look at what was happening. Marty approached her, still holding the bone of the steak. "I sure was looking forward to cooking these beauties on the grill for dinner tonight," he said with an air of disappointment. "Annette, I made the appointment for the first thing after the office opens up this morning." "Have you thought about what you want to wear?" The look on Annette's face changed, which indicated to Marty that what he said made contact. "Yeah, Marty," she said, standing up. "Um, I will wear this black shirt and stretch pants," she said as she made her way to the closet. Even with being pregnant and having a big belly, Annette remained adamant that she did not want to get huge and preferred to wear black because she considers it to be slimming.

Marty goes to the bathroom to check his appearance; he had not looked in the mirror since before leaving for work the night before. He is not impressed with his reflection, but knows there is not enough time to shower. He imagines with displeasure that he will have to endure looks of distaste at his appearance from the patients and staff of the doctor's office. As he is ready to walk out of the bathroom, Annette walks by the open door. He is walking right behind her with his head down, inspecting his clothing for any obvious flaws, like an open zipper, when she stops dead in front of him, gasping slightly. Unaware that she stopped, she slams into her. "What?" He asks, pointing to the mess only half-way cleaned up on the kitchen floor. Popsicle apparently discovered the mess as well, and was eagerly lapping the linoleum floor in delight..."Popsicle!" "Damn dog!" He yells, darting past Annette. "I almost forgot about this." Popsicle's tongue hits sonic speed as Marty nears; she emits a faint growl, burping as he whisks her up and away from the mess. "I'm going to have to lock her up until we get back from the Doctors," he said, passing Annette once again, shoving Popsicle into the nursery, and shutting the door. "Did Popsicle do that?" She asked in a stunned tone. Marty was surprised by her question. "Annette, do you honestly think Popsicle is capable of opening the refrigerator door and getting out the milk, eggs, and steaks?" And maybe she brought the steaks in to share them with you while you slept. His tone turned slightly sarcastic, at which point Annette turned to him and said, "Your sarcasm is duly noted." She watched as he walked by, "If I can't remember being responsible for this mess, she was the only other living soul in the house." Marty recognized his wife's defensive posture and suggested that they leave the mess until after returning from the doctor's office. "Fine, let's go," she said as she headed for the front door.

Within minutes, they arrived at the doctor's office. The secretary, who had seen them countless times before, was aware they were on their way in and immediately led them to an examining room. Within a minute, the office nurse came in to conduct the usual blood pressure and weight check, assuring them the doctor would be with them in a few minutes. The couple was alone about a minute in the examining room before the doctor entered, "Hello, Mr. and Mrs. Sooner, how is Annette today?" Marty felt reluctant to recount the full-blown version of what Annette had told him over the phone. He began by telling the doctor, "I am concerned because my wife has been sleepwalking, eating abnormally, and having disturbing dreams." "I wanted to have you examine her to ensure everything is going ok with the baby, to help set our minds at ease."

The Doctor asked Annette a series of routine questions to establish whether she had ever had symptoms of this sort. Annette made a concentrated effort not to become upset as she explained what was going on, "Doctor, these symptoms have only begun since the time we conceived." Doctor Sohon jotted notes in a file as Annette shared her concerns, "Should we be worried?" The doctor smiled slightly as she looked up from the file she was writing in, "Probably not." "There have been documented cases of people sleepwalking that date back to the earliest medical journals." "Sometimes these people have been observed carrying out a whole array of tasks, cooking, gardening, and pool cleaning." "Those who sleepwalk rarely have any memory of doing it." "Apparently, when a person sleepwalks, they are only functioning on a small portion of the brain that is in overdrive." "The rest of their brain functions as it does when the person is sleeping." "The overactive portion of

13

the brain causes them to start a random task." "In most cases, they just make a mess, go back to bed, and wake up to the mess they have no recollection of making."

Just as the doctor appeared to be ending, Annette interrupted, "What could be causing this?" She began to shine a pen light in Annette's pupil, "Have you been sleeping normally?" Annette blinked as she moved to the other eye, "Not really, I have been having recurring nightmares that wake me up several times a night." Doctor Sohon replaced the light in the pocket of her jacket, "Disturbances in your normal sleep pattern may be a possible cause. "REM sleep is very important in resetting the internal mechanisms of the brain, and elevated activity during sleep, such as recurring nightmares, could cause a disruption." "Sleepwalking has been attributed to a variety of sources ranging from stress to hormones," she explained. "Both stress and hormones could be a factor in your sleepwalking." "After all, you have made it into the second trimester; you are probably anxious since this is the first pregnancy you have carried so long." "Plus, your hormones are raging."

What the doctor described sounded reasonable to Marty. She did not seem alarmed by what he had said about Annette's strange behavior, and even performed a routine ultrasound on her while explaining. She noted that the ultrasound imaging indicated the baby was developing well, and according to measurements, was quite large for a fetus sixteen weeks along.

Annette appeared relaxed as she listened to what the Doctor was saying. Marty even made a silent mental note of how this news must be comforting to her. It certainly was setting his mind at ease; in fact, it was exactly what he had hoped to hear. Annette cleared her throat, indicating she was about to speak, "But Doctor, I haven't always been sleeping when this happened." Marty rolled his eyes, "Oh no!" He could feel himself screaming in his head; his temples began throbbing. On the drive to the Doctor's office, Marty had tried to convince Annette not to say anything that sounded crazy. There was a brief pause. "So you have been conscious at times?" The Doctor asked without

14

changing her tone of voice. "Tell me what you are speaking of." Annette recounted to the doctor the tale of the knitting needle and the electrical outlet she called Marty about. She maintained her composure throughout her voice, never wavering. "Over the past couple of weeks, I have been doing things that I can't explain," she said. Her breathing accelerated. "It's hard to put in plain words, but it feels like there's someone inside my head and my body sharing everything I experience." She raised her body and propped it on one arm, "I know this sounds crazy, but I know it's the baby", her voice lowering to a whisper. "It takes control of my body, kind of jumps in, and interrupts what I'm doing without warning." Marty reached for his wife's hand, "Honey, don't get yourself upset again." Annette continued, paying no attention to his subtle plea, "A couple of days ago, I started the stove to heat water for tea, and just as I turned from the stove, I involuntarily lurched back and reached for the flame." Annette was beginning to feel self-conscious about what she was saying; she saw in her mind's eye the reaction the Doctor could have if she told the tale of how she was really feeling. "It was only for a second, and my hand pulled back once it felt the heat, " her voice trailed off as she was at once showing signs of distress.

Doctor Sohon, taking notice of this, stood from her stool and gestured for Annette to lie back and relax. "This feeling of a loss of control in your life probably has a lot to do with the changes your body is going through while it accommodates the pregnancy." "You said there's someone in your body sharing everything you experience, and you are right, it is your baby." Her voice was soothing and direct. "I am going to order a few routine tests for you." "What you have described to me doesn't sound like anything to become overly alarmed by, but we do want to be sure." "As I said before, she continued, physically everything appears to be satisfactory, and even better than we had hoped possible." "You and the baby have responded well to the fertility treatment, and I'm sure the tests will help calm your fears." "All right, Doctor," Annette sniffled in reply.

15

With that, the Doctor turned and retrieved a sterile cloth for Annette to help clean off the gel smeared on her rounded belly. Doctor Sohon concluded that she would arrange for the time and date of the tests, and someone from her office would be in contact for confirmation of the appointment.

Before she turned to exit the examination room, the Doctor placed a hand on Annette's shoulder and said, "Promise me you will try not to worry. I realize this is all new to you, but worry and stress will only make things more difficult." Annette nodded her head in agreement, "I will, Doctor, I promise." Doctor Sohon turned to Marty, "I want you to make sure she gets as much bed rest as possible. She is exhibiting some signs of physical exhaustion, which is not uncommon in pregnant women during the first and second trimester." "But with her being such a high-risk pregnancy, we don't want to take any unnecessary chances." " Will do, Doc," he said, nodding his head and giving a double thumbs-up response, trying to create the illusion of enthusiasm. The Doctor then briefly explained they would be coming to the office for visits much more frequently over the course of the coming weeks, before she left the examination room.

Once the Doctor was out of the room, Marty breathed a sigh of relief and made the gesture of wiping pretend sweat from his forehead. He feared that if Annette had gotten hysterical again about visions of the future and her evil baby theory, the outcome of the visit might have been different. They collected her purse and headed to the waiting room, where Marty handed the receptionist his insurance card. The receptionist confirmed that someone from the office would contact them with the time and date of the tests the Doctor had requested, and they left as quietly as they entered.

Annette and Marty hardly talked as they drove home; she had developed a sense of being let down by her husband when he did not believe what she knew to be real. In addition, not being able to share all the details with the doctor only added to her frustration. Marty could sense his wife's displeasure. "What's wrong, Annette?" "You mad at me for something?" She had been leaning her head against the car window as he drove. He reached over and began rubbing her shoulder, "Come on, babe, don't be mad." He made smoochey kissing sounds, "I wuv yewww!" Her anger subsided as she turned to him, "I guess I can't be mad at you, I know what I said last night on the phone makes me sound stark raving mad." "But it's the truth." "Do you think I would make this up after all we have been through over the last five years to conceive this baby?" Marty felt the need to defend himself. "Now come on, Annette, if you had gone and told that Doctor that you feel the child you are carrying is evil and out to do the world harm, she would have you evaluated by a psychiatrist." "But as it is, you told her about feeling out of control at times and she attributed it to being pregnant; just like I thought she would." "Plus, the doctor was able to explain the probability of your sleepwalking." "And she has even offered to set up those tests to set your mind at ease." "Honey, please… let's think positively, there is nothing wrong with you or the baby."

Although she was irritated, she knew ultimately he was right, "Yeah, maybe the tests will give us some better answers, thanks, honey." She leaned towards him, giving him a little peck on the cheek. The break in her mood gave Marty a little boost, "See, sweetie, everything will be fine." he wrapped his right arm around her and pulled her close to him as he drove.

They were home within a few minutes. As the car stopped up in front of the house, they both turned to each other at the same time and said the same thing simultaneously, "Ooh, I have to pee!" A roar of laughter from both of them followed. Soon, Annette was weak, squeezing her legs together, saying, "Don't make me laugh, I'll pee my pants right here!" For Marty, a combination of drowsiness coupled with the discomfort of a full bladder caused him to become giddy, "Oh, now that wouldn't be good, imagine how it would smell in here on a hot summer day", he mused. They both laughed as he described his vision of her laughing and peeing, and laughing some more and peeing some more, quickly flooding the cab of the car with yellow liquid, and how the news would report their bodies being discovered. He put the transmission in park, and they sat there for a moment heaving with laughter together. Regaining some composure, Marty playfully shoved Annette's shoulder, "We had better get into the house before Murphy's Law kicks in." "You know how it goes, we're out here joking about stinky pee on the car seat, then it happens for real." "I'll be out here sopping up pee with a disgruntled look on my face." A part of him that believed the reality of what he was saying wasn't far-fetched, "Imagine for real driving to work each day, the smell never really leaving, grumbling to myself, good job dickhead; you just had to make her laugh until she peed."

That being said, he yanked the key from the ignition as she heaved herself from the car, heading for the front door. Marty raced around the car and ran to catch up to his wife, who was scurrying through the front gate and up the yard. He caught up to her right about the time she reached the stairs to the porch. In a flash, they were both up the few stairs and standing at the front door. "You know, my dear, if this were most any other time, I would trample you in a race to the latrine, but considering your delicate status, I'll let you pee, my lil petunia." He wrapped his arms around her, kissing her neck. Annette pranced a little in place, "Yeah, yeah, that's mighty noble of you; come on, unlock the door, I really have to piss".......she breathed through her teeth and pranced again...."Bad!" Marty fumbled with the key in the lock, and within about 30 seconds, the front door flung open. Annette tossed her purse on the sofa and made a beeline for the bathroom, with Marty close behind. Popsicle had begun whining and scratching at the nursery room door the moment they stepped onto the porch, and wasted no time howling loudly to announce her displeasure with being confined. "Damn dog", Marty thought, remembering the events earlier in the morning. Annette did not bother to close the bathroom door since her bladder was screaming with an unwavering urgency to be evacuated. Marty passed the bathroom door, catching a glimpse of Annette preparing to lift the toilet seat in his peripheral vision. His intent to check if Popsicle had caused any destruction in the

18

nursery was sidetracked when a weird sound from the bathroom stopped him in his tracks. He backed up, peering into the bathroom, "What the hell was that?" Believing would have another opportunity to poke a joke at Annette's way. What he witnessed took the wind out of his sails. Annette stood bent over the toilet, right hand still on the uplifted toilet lid, staring at the blue water in the bowl. She staggered forward in a jerking movement, and a line of drool spilled from her lip. Suddenly, she plunged her left hand into the water, splashing repeatedly, the whole time gurgling a happy, almost gleeful infant sound. She fell down on her knees, her head slumped slightly forward and to the side, placing her right hand on the floor next to the toilet. She continued splashing her left hand repeatedly in the toilet water (which was stained blue by the drop in cleaning puck), soaking her hair, face, clothing, wall, and toilet roll hanging on the wall to her left. "Marty!" Annette's scream mixed simultaneously in an eerie combination with a gleeful voice coming out of her mouth. Marty stood there, paralyzed with a mixture of disbelief and horror at the sight playing out before him. Annette remained kneeling there; only her right eye was visible to him, as her left hand continued to splash wildly in the water, causing her body to jerk and lurch violently. She reached towards him with her right arm, causing her body to slump to the floor, and began clawing in Marty's direction, "Help me!" The voice coming out of her mouth turned from gleeful to a miserable-sounding, temper tantrum-laden screech. Annette's left hand continued to reach frantically for the bowl. She kicked off from the wall, sliding her body towards him. Marty noticed in added disbelief that Annette lost control of her bladder and began urinating through her clothes onto the floor. She did not seem to notice as she continued reaching her right hand in his direction. Her left hand continued to reach towards the toilet as she slid her body with her legs towards him.

Marty, feeling the urgency to help his wife, entered the bathroom and grabbed her by the right arm, dragging her across the floor towards the bathroom entrance. As he did this, he noticed Annette's right eye was focused directly on him, but her left eye was pointed in the direction her left arm was reaching. Marty lost his footing, slipping in Annette's urine, and repositioned his legs to use the sink cabinet for leverage. He pushed once more until he dragged Annette another leg's length across the tile floor, his back coming to rest precisely at the entrance to the bathroom. Just as quickly and unexpectedly as she began acting out, the episode was over. Suddenly, her left hand dropped to the floor, and her left eye faced forward to fully focus on Marty's direction. The two of them sat in that position for a few seconds, gasping, trying to internalize what they had just been part of.

The sound of Popsicle scratching at the nursery door and whining, which had been drowned by the commotion, suddenly came rushing in. "Damn dog", Marty whispered in a chuckling voice, rolling his eyes and wiping his sweaty forehead with the sleeve of his shirt. Standing, he reached out to her, "Come on, let's get you cleaned up." She reached up, accepting his help to get her on her feet.

"You cannot seriously tell me you are going to ignore what just happened in here," Annette snapped at Marty. "Indeed, I have never been pregnant before, but I have heard a lot about it from other women and television shows." "Not one time have I ever heard that it's a normal part of pregnancy to lose control of parts of your body!" She moved a step closer to him, holding out her urine-soaked clothing, "Have you?" Marty stood there in front of her, raised his palms to face the ceiling, "I dunno, it may be possible," he said, shaking his head and dropping his facial expression. "Get fucking real, Martin!" She yelled loudly. "This is not normal!" "I could not stop my hand from splashing in the goddamn toilet!" "It was like some other force was controlling my hand, and I was only able to see out of my right eye!" "Did you hear that horrible sound coming out of my mouth?" "Have you ever heard me sound like that in the past five years we have been married?" Her voice was ringing with annoyance.

Marty had not slept in about eighteen hours and was beginning to run short on patience. "What do you want me to say?" He began raising his voice in a heated response, "We just came back from the doctor's office within the hour." "She just told us she is going to order tests to ensure that everything is going fine with the baby." "We are going to have to wait this thing out to see the results of the tests." "Can we please, please just clean up the bathroom and kitchen so that I can get some rest?" "Remember, I have work tonight?"

Annette recoiled a bit. After all, what was it going to accomplish standing there arguing with Marty over this? Waiting for the test seemed a reasonable request; they might reveal a condition that could be controllable. "I'm sorry to have snapped at you like that, Martin." " I realize there is nothing you can do, and considering how you were informed this was going on, you have been great." Her apology sounded sincere and immediately softened his mood, "Oh, Annette, I should not have yelled at you just now." "You have been going through a lot that you kept quiet about, and the last couple of hours alone have been sheer hell for me." "I can't imagine what it must be like for you, actually experiencing it."

The entire time the argument was going on, Annette never left the bathroom, and Marty remained in the doorway. She looked down at her urine-soaked clothes, grabbed hold of her long black shirt, "You know when you first pee on yourself, it comes out pretty warm, maybe even a little bit hot". "But when you sit in it for a while, ooh, does it cool down quick? I'm freezing," She said, attempting to lighten the mood, and began dancing back and forth from one foot to the other. "Come on, man; can't you take a hint?" "Move it, move it, out of the way, slowpoke." By now, she was moving in his direction, waving her hands to shoo him out of the way.

Marty moved aside, and Annette scurried past him, down the hall, and into their bedroom, closing the door behind her. Once again, he heard the familiar sound of Popsicle scratching at the nursery door and whining to be let out. Marty was reluctant to open the door, fearing the destruction he might find on the other side. Popsicle had been Annette's dog since before they met and had become very attached to her. She pretty much follows Annette everywhere she goes. If Annette leaves the house for any length of time, the dog suffers from separation anxiety. When left alone, she is notorious for tearing stuff to shreds, chewing things to unusable condition, being the sole participant of a poopathon, or any combination of the three. Her favorite target has been the garbage can; Marty has convinced himself that Popsicle (or Poop-sicle as he calls her when trying to get on Annette's nerves) is out to make a statement that leaves maximum impact and little doubt that she is pissed royally for Annette's absence.

He has many a foul memory of home after a night out with Annette, only to have the misfortune of stepping directly onto a strategically placed load of dog poop by the door. Popsicle always covered all the bases when she used the poopathon tactic. She would place several piles strategically at the front and back doors, scattering them about to ensure whoever first was bound to step into her foul surprise. For some reason, somebody always just happened to be him. Marty was convinced that the dog knew he would be coming in the door first. He often wondered how the dog managed to produce that volume of poop for those occasions. He became convinced that she has an internal poop factory with the ability to increase production when demand goes up.

Marty cracked open the nursery room door. In the five years since he and Annette were married, he has become accustomed to taking it slow when dealing with Popsicle, for he has to be prepared for anything. "Popsicle, back off, " he said, waiving his arm to shoo her from the door. She's a crafty little bugger that he believed would lay booby traps for him if she had opposable thumbs. She took a few steps back and sat her butt down. Marty was not disarmed by her attempt to placate him; he was ready for anything. "Now stay," he commanded as he opened the door enough for him to stick his head through. At first glance, and to his astonishment, there were no immediate signs of visible destruction. "This can't be," he said, opening the door further to examine the other side of the crib. At that moment, Popsicle seized her opportunity to escape. Like a bullet, she darted in between his legs, down the hall, and right into the open bathroom door. Marty reached to stop her getaway, but was not nearly fast enough. She ran top speed into the bathroom and was sniffing and licking at the puddle of urine left behind by Annette. Marty was in hot pursuit and entered the bathroom within the span of a second. "Oh, you gross little mutt!" He gagged once, then again, grabbing her and holding her at arm's length, immediately heading for the back door. "You are going to have to stay outside until these messes are cleaned up. Popsicle squirmed in a rebellious and vain attempt to free herself from his grip. There was no use; he had a firm hold on her, so she gave up and slumped, hanging her head and paws in almost dead weight.

Marty opened the door and connected the rope lead to Popsicle's collar, "There, enjoy some fresh air for a while." Turning from the door, he was startled to see Annette standing very close behind him. Her sudden presence took him off guard, so much so that he stumbled in two steps forward and screamed, waiving his hands, unable to hide that she had startled him, "AAAHHH!" "Are you trying to kill me?" Annette chuckled, reveling in the satisfaction and victorious feeling of catching him off guard. She had changed into one of his shirts, which came down to the top of her thigh. "Oh, sure, get my shirt all pissy smellin'!" She squinted her eyes and crossed her arms while shifting her body onto one leg, "What are you doing to my little girl?"

Marty, still stinging from the embarrassment of being startled and screaming like a girl, replied, "Not what I would like to be doing to her, the little demon pig!" He raised a balled fist, shook it, and pulled his lips back, exposing his teeth, mimicking anger. "It's precisely what I'll do to you if you ever sneak up on me like that again." "Wicked woman!" He added for effect.

They both chuckled lightly, and she gave him the, ha ha, gotcha look. "We had better get started on this cleanup," Annette suggested. Marty groaned, "Yeah, I know, I'm really dreading this." Annette thought about which mess she would like to take charge of cleaning up. She considered which mess would be easier, "The pee would probably be the easiest mess to dispose of," she thought. But then, she wondered if that was such a good idea; would she be trading the luxury of an easy way out, only to suffer through having to redo what Marty had not cleaned up properly? She thought about the stench that would fill the kitchen after a few days. The flies, airborne bacteria, pestilence, and eventually death could develop if the mess had not been cleaned up as it should be. That was enough for her to make a decision, "I'll take the kitchen, you take the bath."

Marty, happy the light at the end of the tunnel was near, nodded his head in agreement and walked wearily towards the bathroom. If he were going to get sleep, he had to get past this final obstacle. He entered the bathroom, went straight to the closet, grabbed three bath towels, and, with no hesitation, tossed them on the puddle. Annette, already in the kitchen, continued with the task Martin had started before they left for the Doctor's office. They finished about the same time, Marty using a rag and detergent, Annette employing the mop and bucket.

After they cleaned up, it was growing later in the afternoon. Marty had been up for over twenty-four hours, and he had to make the choice to either eat or sleep. Marty chose sleep. He walked to the kitchen, where his wife was throwing the final wet paper towel from her cleanup into the trash. "Annette, I am beat, I really need to lie down." She turned to face the pitiful sight of a man standing behind her, "Oh, honey, you look so tired." "Go ahead, lie down." "I am feeling a little tired, too. Maybe I'll come in and nap with you in a little bit." "But first I want to jump in for a really quick shower so I don't stink up the bed."

Making his way down the hall into their bedroom, Marty's limbs and eyelids were very heavy. Getting dressed into sleeping clothes did not cross his mind; instead, he collapsed into an exhausted heap on top of the bed, unconcerned with the dried blood and leftover uncooked steak around him, ominous reminders of the morning's appalling start. He drifted into a deep slumber within minutes.

Chapter 3: A Veiled Threat

Marty's eyes flicker open. The bedroom is shrouded in darkness, no sun filtering through the drawn blinds. It feels like it has only been a few minutes since falling asleep, but the lack of sunlight makes him wonder how much time has actually passed. He is curious about what time it actually is and attempts to turn his head to look at the alarm clock on the nightstand. He is frozen in place, paralyzed, only able to move his eyes. A wave of panic washes over him as he tries to speak out. Although his voice is screaming in his head, nothing comes out of his mouth. He lay there looking frantically about, unable to focus on anything familiar in the room, his heart pounding rapidly.

He detects a low, distant sound. At first, it is indescribable, but it intensifies, gradually coming closer and becoming more audible. Eventually, Marty can distinguish the muffled sound of voices. It's Annette's voice, talking with some guy. But they do seem to be in the same room with him. It seems as if they are speaking from behind a closed door or wall, all the while coming closer and getting louder. The volume of their voices increases to the point that it seems like they are right next to the bed, but still strangely muffled.

A blinding burst of light floods the room. He remains utterly still, frozen in place. As Marty's eyes adjust, he can make out the familiar face of his wife peering down at him. Tears stream down her cheeks and drip onto his hands, which are folded together on his chest. He remains frozen in position, unable to move or speak. Behind the silhouette of his wife's head, he notices the lining of a casket lid. The revelation that he is inside the casket they are peering into roars ominously into his thoughts. The person behind her gently grasps Annette's shoulder, easing her back from the casket, then reaches over and closes the lid. Marty's mind reels; he braces himself to scream with all his force. No sound comes out.

"I'm not dead, I'm not dead, Annette, please, please don't leave me," he pleads in silent desperation.

As the lid closes, Marty imagines the events he will miss dying so young. He envisions the joyousness of Annette giving birth, the baby walking its first steps, the first tooth, the first day of school, learning to ride a bike, and driving lessons. He feels sad and empty as he contemplates missing these milestones.

The lid closes with an echoing crash, leaving Marty, once again, in total darkness. His mind races to figure out what is going on and how to stop it. If this means the end for him, he is not ready.

He could hear activity around him just as the casket started moving and vibrating; he assumed his body was being transported to the cemetery. Marty's skin crawls; he is mortified at the idea of being buried alive. Surely, someone made a terrible mistake.

To his right, Marty distinguished the outline of a dark figure lurking in the shadows, just beyond the confines of the casket sidewall, with eyes glowing ember red, gazing upon him. Sensing the sheer power in its presence, Marty gains enough movement, muttering, "Who's there?".

"Don't you recognize your own flesh and blood?" The figure crackles in response.

The casket continues clanking and banging, jolting Marty slightly. He hears muffled male voices outside, unable to distinguish what is being said. "Help me," Marty pleads with the shadowy figure.

The sound of the casket being slid across metal rollers resounds within the compartment, bumping to a sudden halt. The unmistakable sound of a heavy metal door closing and latching follows. Marty knows the pallbearers have loaded his casket into the hearse.

He gains the ability to turn his head fully towards the dark figure, directing its unwavering gaze at him. Outside the casket, Marty hears a faint hissing sound, a quick, 'whoosh', resembling the noise their barbecue grill makes the moment the propane ignites. Within seconds, he feels an intense increase in air temperature.

The seals of the casket begin melting to reveal a white hot, intense heat. The lid of the casket bursts into flames. "I am being cremated!" "They're burning me and I'm not dead!" He screams at the top of his voice.

"Help me, please!" his arms respond.

"Father, don't forsake me," the figure beckons again.

The lid to the casket is completely engulfed in flames. Shards of burning material fall on his face and neck, singeing his skin.

He pounds with both hands on the sides of the casket. The intense heat blisters and peels the skin of his hands. In desperation, he pushes upward with his hands and legs, hoping for some chance the burning lid would give way. It won't budge. He pounds upwards for all he was worth, catching the sleeves of his jacket, and pant legs aflame.

"Someone, please help me, he wails, realizing that his voice is being drowned out by the roaring flames of the cremation chamber. The flames spread quickly, engulfing his entire body, leaving him writhing and screaming in pain.

Marty bolts straight up, clutching his chest, dripping with perspiration, and breathing rapidly.

"I was dreaming, he thought, staring down at his legs. Looking around reveals he is not in the familiar bedroom; instead, he sits at the intersection of two separate roads. On one, he sees a city burning and hears torturous screams in the distance from that direction.

At the foot of this road sits a limousine, engine idling. The back passenger side door opens.

"All this can be yours." An eerie voice spills out, engulfing him. "Just give me what I want."

A short distance on the road to his right, he sees an image of himself lying in the casket. Annette, looking gaunt and withdrawn, cries as she gazes upon his corpse. The sound of her wailing mixes with a distant ringing sound piercing all around him. Marty is aware of Annette's sorrow and wishes he could ease her pain. The ringing is louder now. Marty is rising, floating up above the two paths, looking down on them; he still hears Annette's sobs. All around him, the ringing grows louder.

Marty continues floating up into darkness, the two roads below him become smaller, and eventually disappear. The ringing grows louder and sounds closer to him each time. The light fades away, leaving him shrouded in blackness. The ringing, which had been coming in regular intervals, ceases abruptly. Carefully, he feels around to see if there is anything surrounding him, but there is nothing. The ringing begins again, this time he recognizes it is his home phone, but the tone drags on longer than he is used to. He concentrates on the sound, reaching towards it into the blackness. His hand brushes something hard; he pulls back, startled by its sudden presence. The ringing trails off again, leaving behind a diminishing echo.

Marty reaches into the blackness again, and curiosity takes the place of fear. Whatever it is in front of him is much closer now. He has drifted to within just a few inches without realizing it. His eyes adjust to the darkness enough for him to distinguish that he is hovering above horizontal rows of uniform wooden planks lying about eight inches apart from each other. This is familiar to him; he realized he was in the attic of their home. Now that he has some grasp on his location, he maneuvers his body along the floor planks, towards the drop-down door and fold-down ladder. The spring-loaded door gives way with a creak, and Marty (still floating) slips through the opening, guiding himself in the direction of their bedroom. As he enters their room, he is astonished to see himself still lying in bed. The ringing begins again as he floats towards his side of the bed. Instead of landing on the floor next to his motionless body, he sinks as if the floor is liquid, unable to halt his motion, as the walls melt away. As he sinks, he now sees that he is still next to himself, lying on the bed, but both lie at the fork of the two roads. A haunting voice echoes from all around him,

"Do not forsake me."

He is sinking faster and panics, reaching frantically, trying to hoist his body onto the bed. It doesn't work, and he slips further into the abyss. He unwittingly snatches hold of his mortal wrist. In his dream state, Marty feels the tight grasp he has taken on his mortal wrist. This slows his descent momentarily, and then his dream self and still slumbering mortal self both begin sliding from the bed. Now engulfed to his shoulders, he knows that if both his mortal and dream selves sink, they will be lost forever, and he will never wake. Just then, he lets go and continues frantically clawing at the sheets in a vain attempt to stop from sinking. His head disappears, then his elbows.

Marty bolts straight up in the bed, wincing from pain in his wrist; the fresh imprint from being grasped so tightly remains on his flesh, a vivid physical reminder of the dream still evident. Dripping with perspiration and breathing heavily, he searches around the room as if he were expecting to find someone else present.

The phone rings again, it is the same sound that drove him nuts in his dream, but now it is very real, and not in the same room, unfortunately. It's driving him nuts in a dream, now it's very real, but it's ringing, begging to be answered.

 In the dim light, he notices Annette is snuggling tight, her arm draped over his stomach.

She has one eyelid closed tight; the other is open, appears black, and is fixed upon him. She is twitching and groaning low. He wonders if she is dreaming. RING… the phone sounds off again. Marty picks Annette's hand from his stomach, laying it on her side, and he gets out of bed, leaving the room to answer the phone.

Marty picks up the receiver of the phone, "Hello." It is Doctor Sohon calling to confirm a time to meet her at the local general hospital the next morning.

"Mr. Sooner, is there something wrong?" The Doctor's voice indicates she has picked up his distress. Marty covers the mouthpiece for a couple of seconds while gaining his composure.

"No, Doctor, don't worry…I, um, stubbed my toe running to the phone." The time of the appointment is set for 10:00 a.m., and Marty scribbles the time and place of the appointment on the magnetic dry-erase board on the refrigerator.

"All right, Doctor, thank you for calling back so promptly. See you then," he says before hanging up. He stands there, leaning against the refrigerator, rubbing his chin, feeling stupefied, pondering his terrifying new experience. It was unlike any dream he had ever had before. This was so real, like he was actually physically experiencing it; the sounds and sights were so realistic, he actually felt the heat from the fire and the pain of being burned. He has an unsettling feeling that this dream is more than just a dream. Instead, he feels it is a vision, just as Annette had described to him on the phone the night before. He is shaken to the core, reeling, perspiration still dripping from his face, silently freaking out. He is convinced that it has some veiled meaning, something sinister he does not quite understand.

He feels awful for Annette and wonders if this is what she has been experiencing. During their phone dialogue the night before, she indicated her visions had been occurring at increasing intervals, becoming more intense each time.

"How could she have kept this to herself for so long?" This single experience left him feeling profoundly disturbed. He is sure some sort of basic internal instinct is warning him of impending doom and gloom. Suddenly, something cold grips onto his shoulder, his blood runs cold as ice as it drains from his face. His heart leaps in his chest, and he yelps, startled, and whips around to reveal Annette there. He stumbles backward, losing his balance, crashing backward into kitchen chairs, knocking them over, and moving the table as he fumbles clumsily. The sharp blow from a toppled chair leg abruptly forces the air from his lungs. He doubles over, gasping and grabbing his side, unable to regain his breath. What he sees is too much for him to comprehend. Annette hangs suspended, hovering about four inches from the floor. Her left eye was open, the color resembling a black marble, and her left hand was reaching and clawing in his direction; her right hand and leg were slumped, swaying in a motion similar to when an unconscious person is being carried.

Her mouth is open and unmoving as the words, "Don't forsake me," hiss forth in the familiar voice Marty recognizes from his vision. Annette hung there for about another second before floating towards him, her left hand still reaching and clawing vigorously.

"Don't forsake me, Father," hisses from her unmoving lips again.

Marty, still gasping to catch his breath, is unnerved the moment his wife's body starts towards him. His stocking slips on the linoleum as he tries to gain his footing. His thoughts are clouded by fear; he feels like a cornered animal scurrying to escape capture by a predator. The chair that he knocked over is still located behind him, hampering his movement. He pushes it out of the way with all his might, noticing as he turns that the back door is merely feet from where he had tumbled to the floor. He moves quickly towards it as Annette's body tilts horizontally, and flies at him, crashing hard onto his back, knocking him unconscious to the floor.

She is jarred to consciousness by the impact of her body crashing onto Marty's back; he lay under her, not stirring. She raises her upper body onto the length of her outstretched arms. She feels fuzzy, shaking her head and blinking her eyes to get better focus. She has no idea what has happened or how she has gotten into the kitchen on top of her husband. The last thing she recalls is lying next to him in bed as he slept.

She pushed herself up, crouching alongside him, touching his shoulder gently. She noticed that he was gasping for breath, "Marty," she shook his limp, gasping form. Although he had been knocked unconscious, he was still out of breath from the kitchen chair that had hit him during his stumble backwards.

"Marty," she raised her voice, hoping for a response, "What's wrong?" He does not respond, taking short, labored breaths.

Her mind races around the possibility of what must be going on with him. Could he be having a heart attack? Did he get drunk and pass out here? Should she get help?

She stands, "Don't panic, Annette," she says aloud. "Try to get him up, she scurries to the sink, maybe a little water will help." Opening a cabinet door, she grabs a cup, filling it with water. She rushes to his motionless body, calling his name and shoving his butt with her foot, noticing that his labored breathing had stopped. Not wanting to waste time, she aligns the cup with his head and pours about a quarter of the contents onto the back of his head and neck.

Immediately, Marty bolts up, yelling, "What the hell?", scurrying to his feet. He looks back to see Annette standing there.

"Marty, are you ok?" She asks, readying for a retreat, not sure what is about to happen.

HE feels anxious, but does not remember instantly why. "Yeah, Annette," he replies, regaining his composure. He leans forward, groaning while rubbing his pounding temples with his thumbs.

"Have you been drinking?" She asks him as if she is about to scold him.

Annoyed with the inference of her pointed question, Marty snaps back, "Of course not!"

"Well, what is all this?" She began pointing around the kitchen at the moved table and the scattered chairs.

Marty picks his aching head from his hands, looking around, remembering what had happened in there just moments before. He is not sure what to say, now that she is awake, and is expecting an explanation. He does not think the truth is the best option at the moment and stammers…" um, well, you see." He looks around the room, noticing the appointment time he had written down. "I got up to answer the phone; it was the doctor confirming your appointment time," pointing towards the refrigerator. "After I hung up, I tripped on a Popsicle and must have knocked the chairs over." "Now I've got one fierce headache, I must have whacked my head when I tripped." Damn dog, he adds for believability.

At that moment, Popsicle sauntered into the kitchen, her toenails clicking against the linoleum, stopping her advance short of where Annette stood. Promptly plopping her chubby butt down, and pulling her ears back, wildly wagging the phantom stub of her tail.

"Aw, look at her, she is saying sorry, Daddy." Annette always overcompensates for the pooch and once again rushes to her defense. She is unaware that Marty made it up, and the dog responded because she heard her name, and associated them being in the kitchen with her first love: food. Just about the moment Annette reaches down to scratch her affectionately, Popsicle realizes there is no food, snorts, gets up, and meanders her way out of the kitchen, having lost the initial zip and curiosity she entered with.

Annette snickers, "She's cute!"

Marty notices Annette's knee has been knocked open, and blood is trickling down her shin. "Do we have anything for a headache?" He asks, pointing to her leg, "Your knee is bleeding."

Annette looks down, but is not able to see her legs at all because her belly is in the way, and her nightshirt balloons out, hiding her lower body. She shifts her weight onto one leg and sticks her leg out to get a better view. "Hmm, so it is," she sounds genuinely surprised.

Marty continues curiously, "How did you get hurt?" He stands erect as she guides him to the kitchen cabinet containing the pain reliever.

Annette's voice changes, "It's the weirdest thing, I'm not sure." "In fact, I don't remember walking into the kitchen to help you; it's like I suddenly woke up here on the floor, wondering why you are here and how I got here."

"Martin, I am so confused. I feel like I was dreaming the most horrible dream."

Marty struggles to open the child-resistant cap on the bottle, which always seems to give him trouble. His head pounds as he turns and hands the bottle to Annette, "Help me with this, please?"

Effortlessly popping the top off, she shakes two pills into her hand, offering them his way along with the water she had used to wake him. He put the pills in his mouth, taking a sip to wash them down, groaning as he tossed his head back to swallow.

Leaning to glance over Annette's shoulder to get a better look at the time display of the microwave, "Oh shit, it's 9:11 pm." "I don't think I can handle work tonight. I'd better call in sick."

Marty prides himself on his commitment to his job, so his conscience bothers him as he commented. He thinks about how his absence might affect his co-workers, and how he hates when the same thing is sprung on him. But then his thoughts shift to his wife, and what impact his leaving her alone for the evening might have. He hesitates not a second longer.

He starts for the phone, dialing the number to the plant, offering his excuse for not coming in for his shift. The second shift supervisor says he will give the message to the third shift supervisor.

The foreman adds, "I'll have to go out onto the production floor to let Brent Culkner know he will have to pull a mandatory twelve-hour shift."

35

Marty knows this is the guilt tactic his employer often uses, and counters, "I know this is short notice, but I rarely call off, and I am calling off because I don't think I will make it through the shift." He says this, suggesting to the foreman that it is still early enough to call the first shift shipping person to come in at 4:00 am, without ruining his sleep.

The guilt tactic used by the supervisor works to some degree, but Marty consoles his guilt by reassuring himself that even if he does go into work, he probably will not be very productive, continuously thinking over the events of the day.

After hanging up the phone, Marty regrets his decision to skip work; he hates leaving his co-workers high and dry. Watching his wife tend to her wounded knee reinforces his final decision to stay home. He imagines the incredible sorrow and guilt he will feel afterwards if anything happens to Annette in his absence. This thought helps ease his remorse somewhat; plus, he reassures himself that missing work will never become a habit.

Displaying affection, Marty approaches Annette, wrapping his arms around her waist; her belly shifts under the presence of his grasp, and a cold chill runs through him.

"Ooh, you made the baby jump!" She was immersed in bending, with her foot on a chair, cleaning the dried blood from her wounded leg and shin, when she noticed him moving quietly behind her. "I can't believe it, you never call off, Mr. perfect attendance." "So what's the occasion?"

Marty figures it's best not to share what had happened to him; he wants to digest it, wrap his mind around it, before helping to confirm Annette's sneaking suspicion about the baby. However, standing with his arms around her, he knows down to his soul that what she said is true.

"I don't know, I think Popsicle may have knocked me out of my senses when she tripped me." "Besides, I still have a killer headache. I want to rest tonight."

36

She turns around to face him, "Don't get me wrong, it's ok with me, you never take any time off work, and besides, it will be nice to have you home at night for a change." "It is nice to be able to lie next to you and snuggle once again," she said, squeezing him tighter.

They decide it's best to go straight to bed. Marty lay awake for hours, unable to sleep, trying hard to make some sense of the situation. Annette is sleeping soundly about thirty minutes after lying down. She twitches and moans, and he keeps a close eye on her, suspecting she might get up and start moving around. Each time he shakes her, waking her momentarily.

Marty thinks long and hard about what happened to him since Annette's phone call at work the night before. He wonders if it is a possibility that they are sharing the same delusion. Maybe what is happening is being caused by something in the air they are breathing. The tests the Doctor will run might help clear up the mystery. He figures it is best to wait for the test results.

"Yeah," he convinces himself not to jump to any conclusions without having the test results. He needs to remain rational about the situation. Nevertheless, how will he bring it up to the doctor? The doctor is going to think they both are going crazy. 10:00 am seems so far off; he has to think of his action plan.

He lay awake for a long time, in part trying to come up with some enlightening explanation for what happened, but mostly he lay there because he was terrified of falling to sleep, afraid of dreaming, afraid of the dark figure looming in the shadows. Truly terrified of any consequence there may be if he is not in control.

The rest of their time in the hospital seemed to crawl at turtle pace; Annette endured numerous pokes with needles drawing blood, and amniotic fluid. Marty could not be present for many of the tests, so much of his time was spent aimlessly channel surfing.

About 3:15 pm, Annette emerged with the nurse pushing her in the wheelchair for the final time. She raised her hands up as a show of utter disgust, "Finally finished, and not a minute too soon." The nurse pushed her over to the bed, where Annette seemed all too eager to get on her feet, "I swear if I had to endure one more prick today, I would lose my sanity." She pointed at Marty's groin as they passed him sitting on the chair, "And that means you too."

The nurse instructed Annette to buzz the nurses' station after she was dressed, and she would return to escort her to check out. With all she had endured, Annette was growing short on patience and just shook her head yes and waved, mouthing 'bye' to the nurse. Annette wasted no time, clicked off the television, and began changing from her hospital garb into her street clothes. "I can't wait to get out of here. I hate hospitals and tests." She was dressed within a couple of minutes, and ringing the nurse station, the nurse appeared and said their Doctor had been summoned to another emergency, but she would be contacting them soon. This news made both happy, for it had been a long day, and they were anxious to get out of there.

Chapter 4: Show Me a Sign

Marty and Annette cover their eyes to block the sun as they search for their car in the enormous parking lot. He spots a reminder: "We parked in that direction." He points, looking back to make sure she is following his lead.

Annette grabs his hand, a move she knows he dislikes. He squirms his hand somewhat, but she squeezes tighter, "Don't you try to get away from me.

He rolls his eyes, sighing slightly, "Why do you always have to do that? It's such a girly thing for a dude to be holding hands."

She pulls his hand, causing him to lean backwards, craning her neck upward and puckering for a kiss.

He is happy to oblige.

After receiving his welcome kiss, she answers, "Because you're my husband and I love you."

Marty loves any opportunity to kid with her, and he knows where this is leading. "No, what's the real reason?"

She giggles, using the evil little monkey laugh he loves. "Eee, eee, eee!" "Because I know it drives you crazy."

Marty can't be coy; he loves to kid with her. He shakes his hand from her firm grip, trotting ahead. "You are a vile wench! Now you have to walk! Hah hah, walking wench!"

Annette dangles the car keys briefly in the air. "Can't get far without these, dickhead!"

He circles behind her. "I should push you into the mud," he said, grabbing her by both shoulders and shoving playfully.

She shrieks in delight, laughing, "Don't you dare," turning to face him, "Or you're coming down with me," she grabs the front of his shirt with both hands.

They laugh together for a second as she turns, heading towards the car. "I'm starving. Can we get something to eat?"

39

Marty wasn't quite out of his goofing around yet, "Sure, whatcha making us?"

They reach their respective sides of the car.

Annette tilts her glasses. "You don't honestly think I am cooking now, do you?"

Ah, yet another opportunity for him to break-em off on her, "Oh, I only buy take out for people who are nice to me," he chuckles arrogantly. "Who here in our presence has been nice to me?" He rubs his chin, looking toward the sky. "Umm…not Annette…now I've been nice to me. It's settled, I'll treat myself to take out, and all the nasty people can watch me eat; they can salivate."

Annette bends over, disappearing from view for but a moment, and quickly stands up straight again, showing a stone. "I'll throw a rock at you, buddy! Now let's get it in the car. I am really hungry."

Marty pretends to protect his face. "Ok, Ok, tough girl, geeze, don't hesitate, just whip out the big guns right from the start."

He unlocks the driver's door, jumps in, and reaches to pop the passenger side lock.

Annette drops the rock to the ground, happily entering the passenger side.

Not long after, he races their vehicle to life and rolls down the electric windows to alleviate the stifling heat. "Any place you're especially hungry for?"

She contemplates for a second, slouching as she rests her elbow on her knee. "How about that old-fashioned silver diner that resembles a train car?"

Marty ponders. "I know which one you're thinking. I haven't been there since I was a kid." He pauses, thinking back. "Actually, I was only there once with my mom and dad. I must have been about thirteen. I was screwing around."

Annette interrupts, "That doesn't surprise me."

"Oh, hah hah, Smartass! "That doesn't surprise me. That doesn't surprise me," he says, contorting his face and mocking her with a voice he knows annoys her.

"Anyway, as I tried to say, before I was so rudely interrupted. I was antagonizing my brother while we all sat in a booth at the same restaurant we were heading to. My antics went awry when I accidentally spilled an entire milkshake all over my mother and father. They were pretty pissed off." "I made matters worse as my dad yelled at me; his eyes were all bulging and crazy looking, and he still had milkshake dripping from his chin. I involuntarily burst out laughing! I couldn't help myself; our shenanigans leading up to the spill were still vivid and fresh in my memory. He chuckles, remembering, "My old man probably considered offing me right there. Too many witnesses, and he wouldn't be able to make it look like an accident. Ah, the memories."

Marty slows, believing he recognizes the road leading to the diner. " Am I going the right way?" Annette's mind is awash with thought, so his question does not connect. He reaches over, waving his hand over her unblinking eyes, "Hey, are you in there?"

She shakes her head, blinking, "I'm sorry, did you say something?"

He pulls over, not wanting to pass the road. "Is this the right road to the diner?"

She nods, "Yeah, you're going the right way." "Best milkshakes I've had yet."

Marty turns onto the road towards the diner, "I'm pissed that Dr. Sohon betrayed our confidentiality today. But I think it was cool of her to cover our tracks today. She could have easily told those dudes we were right there. Her butt is probably on the line in a big way."

Annette turns to face him, "I don't think it was truly her intention to cover our tracks."

He shrugs, "She probably felt bad because we were right there the moment those government thugs stormed in. I know I wouldn't want to be in the presence of a trusting couple that I betrayed the moment their captors arrive."

She reaches over, touching his shoulder. "It wasn't her decision at all. I convinced her to help us out."

He nuzzles his cheek to her hand, "Well, of course, sweetie. That, coupled with my badgering about her breach of the doctor-patient trust. That bitch! I still can't believe she sold us out!" Marty stops at a flashing railroad crossing. He knows she has something on her mind. "Honey, what's up?

Annette draws closer, whispering, I can cause certain things to happen."

Marty looks at her, not sure what she is getting to, "Like what kind of things?"

She continues, "It's hard to explain. Something I've noticed subtly throughout my life. But since the pregnancy, it is very strong, I can't ignore it."

The train horn blasts a short distance away as it bears down on the intersection. He fixes on her, "Give me an example of what you are talking about."

Annette rubs her belly, looking down. "It's especially prevalent when this kid gets worked up." She looks at him, "I'm convinced it knows what I am talking about."

He snatches her hands, pulling her gaze towards him. He is very serious. "Annette, you have to stop talking like this!"

She meets his stare squarely. "You want to run the car into the path of the oncoming train, right?"

He rolls his eyes, "Yeah, sure, Annette, that would be great for the finish."

She pulls her hand away, placing it on the knee of his gas pedal leg. "Go ahead, pull into the path of the train."

Without hesitation, his foot tromps the accelerator to the floor. The acrid smell of burning rubber engulfs them, pouring in the windows. He steps hard on the brake, his voice comes in a fevered pitch, "What the fuck!" He presses harder on the brake. The car inches closer to the tracks, the nose sliding under the wooden barrier. The continuous clank from the barrier's warning signal combines with the air horn from the train until the sounds are deafening. He knows the impact of mashing steel will soon follow. And although he wants and tries to stop, his foot remains relentlessly pressing the accelerator to the floor. The air horn blazes, then fades as the engine roars by. The wooden barricade bumps against the windshield and scrapes towards the roof as their car jerks closer to the speeding train. He blurts out in a panicked yelp, "Annette, stop it! We'll be killed!"

She removes her hand from his thigh, "All right then, stop."

His foot responds immediately, releasing the gas pedal. The car squeals to a halt with the clanking barricade resting on the roof. He shifts the transmission into reverse, backing away to a safe distance, angrily thrusting the gear shift into park, and turning off the engine. He faces her with a look of frantic fury in his eyes, "Don't ever do anything like that again!" He draws a deep breath as he, lying his head back onto the headrest, says, "My heart is in my throat." He glances at the rear-view mirror to see if anyone is behind them. Much to his disbelief and relief, there are no other cars around. He looks down at his crotch, "God dammit, Annette, I pissed myself, thanks."

Annette turns, staring blankly out her window. She notices the plume of blue smoke floating away on the distant breeze, "Marty traffic is coming this way, we should be getting onto the diner."

Marty peers into the rear-view mirror to see a line of headlights approaching from behind. He fires up the rattling engine and lurches the car into motion, hoping to outpace the traffic.

Annette turns from the window, her voice sounding dull, "Tie your outer shirt around your waist; that will hide the wet spot."

Marty nods in agreement, "Good idea."

She slams her balled fists into her thighs, "I wanted to give you a realistic glimpse of what I am about to describe, because I know it is going to sound like complete madness."

The parking lot and glowing diner sign are visible a short distance away. A flick of the turn signal switch, and soon the car is parked and the engine off.

Marty turns to her, "Ok, Annette, you have my full attention."

She points to his button-down, "Tie that around your waist, before we go inside."

He grabs the shirt, tying a knot around his waist with the sleeves, and arranging them to cover any sign of wetness.

"As I said before, for as long as I can remember, I have always felt like I possess an out-of-the-ordinary sense of perception. It's hard to describe, and that is why I have never mentioned it in the past." She struggles to find the words, "It's nothing very defined, or even barely noticeable; like knowing something is going to happen beforehand. I have dreamt of events before they happen, or can tell what someone is going to say before they say it. Her frustration builds with every word, uneasy with sharing her thoughts. None of this was important before I became pregnant, but now this perception has become incredibly sharpened. I think it comes from the power generated from this one." She points towards her belly.

The high afternoon sun blazes in, prompting her to roll down her window. "Come on, let's get in before I burst into flames."

They simultaneously pop their doors open and head towards the entrance of the diner, not giving a second thought to leaving the windows open for air.

Marty checks his pockets, realizing he didn't get the keys from the ignition. "Shit, I forgot the keys in the car." He dismisses it, "No one will steal that old heap."

He pulls open the door, waving for her to enter. Once inside, they stop by a sign reading 'please wait to be seated'. Within a short time, they were warmly greeted by a waitress, who led them to a booth where they sat across from each other.

Annette arranges her purse, grabbing a napkin from the dispenser, "Whew, that's better," dabbing her forehead.

The waitress walks up to the table, "You two ready to order?"

Both Annette and Marty have an urge for the steaks they never had the opportunity to eat. Marty leads, "I'll have a grilled porterhouse; rare."

Annette taps her laminated menu on the table, "Sounds yummy, I'll have the same."

The waitress jots their order onto a tablet, "Salad or fries?"

Marty hates rabbit food, "Fries for me."

Annette gathers his menu and hands them to the server. "Salad, please, with a side order of French dressing."

The waitress starts to exit, but turns, assuring them she will be back.

Annette leans in, talking low, "This kid possesses a vast power that I can't even begin to describe, and I feel it continuously growing stronger." "My being able to suggest you pull into the path of the train is a small example of the power I feel growing within me." Her eyes narrow, "You see, my suggestion became more of a command you couldn't ignore. I meant it to manipulate your brain to control your foot, making you do something completely unreasonable, downright suicidal, and you couldn't stop it."

His eyes dart nervously around the diner, "That was very fucked up."

She peers back over both shoulders, lowering her voice to a whisper so that no one behind her could eavesdrop. "I am able to channel it whenever the baby becomes uneasy." She caresses her belly, "Even now, it senses what I am saying. I can feel it coursing through me like an electric current." She reaches across the table, laying her hands over his. He jumps, feeling what she describes, but does not resist her grasp.

She continues, "I can sense people's thoughts. "How do you think I knew something was up with Doctor Sohon?" When I touched her hand, I knew the agents were coming for us. Even though she didn't know it for sure, she had a strong feeling about it. Then how do I convince her not to rat us out? And you with the train. She feels guilty for making him feel this way. "I had to use the train as an extreme example to prove what I am telling you is real, and not my imagination."

Marty pulls back from her, leaving her hands flat on the table; the terror of the train is still so fresh and excruciating to relive. He waits in silent angst for what Annette is about to say.

Her eyes glaze over, and her bottom lip quivers, "Marty, you have no idea how I hate to say this, but..." her voice trails off. She clears her throat as a tear wells up, streaming down her face. "I think we have to end this now before it's too late."

Marty's heart sinks, he lays his head onto Annette's hands, "Please don't ask me to do this. He keeps his face down, resting his forehead on her hands, "Too late for what?"

Annette feels his warm tears drip onto the back of her hand. Her heart aches so much, but she knows they need to finally come to terms with what has to be done. "Before it's too late to stop this baby from coming into this world." "We have to end this before it gets so powerful that we are helpless to take any action. If we wait much longer, it will be too late."

Marty knows with every fiber of his being that everything Annette says is true. Still, he can't accept it. After all they had been through, trying and hoping and praying without success for five long years to conceive. This baby is the last thing left to complete them. "Annette, I know what you are driving at, but I just can't."

Their waitress approaches the table, dispensing napkins and silverware, noticing Annette is upset. "Honey, is everything ok?"

Annette is so intent on her interaction with Marty that she has not noticed her approach. She wipes the tears from her face, "Oh yes, everything is fine."

The waitress makes small talk, doing her best to work them for a larger tip, "I see you are expecting, did you find out what you are having yet?"

Annette sheepishly looks at her stomach, "Umm, no, we didn't."

The waitress continues, "You are way stronger than I was. I just had to know." As she talks, she plops napkins, reaches for silverware tucked in her apron, and arranges their salad bowls. "Your meals will be here in a few minutes." She nudges them both, Come on, you two, cheer up, everything will work out."

Annette tries to fake a smile, "Thanks."

Marty had picked up his head after the waitress was gone, revealing his glazed, red, bloodshot eyes. A pained expression was evident on his face. "I can't believe you want to abort this baby!"

He said the words that she refused to utter, "Yes, Marty, that is what I am thinking." She grabs her stomach, doubling over slightly, "Oh, it knows."

Marty reaches for her hand, desperate for anything that might sway her. "But what about the tests?" "What if these feelings are being caused by something else?"

Annette stands, slamming her fist onto the table, causing both their steak knives and forks to fly point-first, sticking into the ceiling. "Damn it, stop talking about those frigging tests!"

The diner goes silent, and all eyes are on the couple.

Annette's face reddens, "Sorry folks, don't mind us, we're newlyweds." She playfully cups her hands to her mouth, raising her eyebrows.

After a few odd expressions from customers and workers, the conversation in the diner regains a deafening decibel.

Annette sits, glancing at the utensils protruding from the ceiling above her. She lowers her voice to a whisper. Without the roar, the whisper makes an impact. "Fuck that Doctor, those tests, and fuck you if you want to continue to disown this!" She points at him, "You can't deny what happened in the car; no test can provide answers as to why I can do that."

Marty leans forward, placing his elbows on the table and burying his face in his hands, sighing heavily, "But what if you're wrong, Annette?" "What if you are ruining our only shot at children?" "This is the farthest you have ever maintained a pregnancy. If you abort this child, chances are pretty good that you will never have another." Marty parts his hands to the sides of his cheeks, still visibly upset. "Plus, Doctor Sohon will almost certainly never offer us any further fertility help if you abort this pregnancy early." "And really, could you blame her?" "Also bear in mind that your recent outbursts in the Doctor's office may affect our ability to adopt as well." "I don't want to die a lonely childless old man."

He reaches for her hands, "I've always dreamed of a family, a whole family including a child to love and guide, someone to carry on our values." Marty crosses his arms, "I'm sorry, Annette, I just can't, and won't agree to this."

The waitress rushes to their table, "There you are, two medium rare porterhouse with a complimentary salad bar." She looks at their setting, puzzled, "I thought I brought you two forks and knives."

Marty points towards the utensils sticking to the ceiling, and the waitress follows his lead. How the hell?" She stops, raising her hand, and rolling her eyes, "Never mind, I don't want to know, I'll be back in a minute with new ones for you."

Annette sits silently, the wind stolen from her sails. After all the proof she has provided to convince him, he still refuses to admit there is something bizarre about this pregnancy, not easily explained away with conventional thinking or tests.

Although Marty appeared outwardly to be trying to influence Annette's decision, in the end, he knew she was facing reality. Internally, he had a battle of indecision and contradiction raging; he knew that if he confirmed that he, too, had experienced unexplainable visions and an out-of-body occurrence, paired with the train incident, that would be all she needed to reach the inevitable conclusion.

Marty felt the need to reason away all doubt, "Honey, what you are considering could have some sizeable repercussions, not just now, but after we pass on. I know we are not the most spiritual couple on the planet, but I do believe in God, and I especially believe in the first commandment 'Thou shalt not kill'." "In my opinion, that is exactly what you are suggesting we do." "Have you honestly considered the consequences?" He continued, "I'm not so sure I want to take that chance." "Plus, imagine the nagging guilt you would feel for the rest of your days, the what if I made a mistake feeling." "Will you be able to cope with that?" "I'm not certain I can."

The waitress returns, handing each of them a new set of silverware, "Now let's and keep them on the table this time." She moves on to cleaning the table next to them.

Annette feels uncomfortable with the waitress being so close, so she carves the fat from her steak. "Looks good."

Marty picks up on her non-verbal cue, slicing into his slab of meat, "Ooh yeah, we haven't eaten a good grilled steak in a dog's age. Annette looks up from her plate. He winks at her, "But Popsicle sure has."

Marty and Annette are about half done with their steaks by the time the waitress finishes clearing and wiping the table. Once she's not within hearing range, Annette continues, "But what if I am right, Marty?" "What if we do exactly what you are suggesting, and just let this come to pass?" "Don't you think there will be consequences once we lapse into death for turning a blind eye, especially since we have been warned?" "At that point, denying what you know will not work."

Marty holds his ground, "And what is wrong with doing nothing?" "What if we let it come to pass?" He slices off another piece of steak and pops it into his mouth, speaking as he chews, "There has been no clear sign that it is our responsibility to take any action; maybe we are not supposed to interfere."

Annette interrupts, "If you knew the visions of massive death, pain, and torture, I've experienced."

Marty motions, rolling his hand to hurry her to finish what she is saying, signifying that he needs to say something, "Don't you think since we have been given such vivid visions and warnings, that we should have been given a clear indication that we must do something to stop it?" "I haven't gotten a single sign from God telling me to end anything." "Have you?" "Did you ever stop to think that maybe God wants this to happen?" He certainly has been allowing some out-of-the-ordinary stuff to go on."

Annette suddenly stops in the midst of cutting a piece of meat, glaring up at him, "What did you just say?"

Marty feels self-assured that he might be winning the argument, but he didn't move, just stared at her for a moment, perplexed. "What?"

She leans in. "You just said that we have been given such vivid visions and warnings." "You never told me that you had had any visions."

50

Marty stammers, realizing that he has slipped up. "Umm," he pauses for what seems an eternity. He is caught off guard and lacks a quick response.

Annette rolls her hand to hurry his response, just as he had a moment before. "Let's have it."

He has to break the silence, "Shit, all right, I had a vision last night too." He is furious having carelessly left the cat out of the bag, but flabbergasted that she noticed it with such ease.

Her voice comes as a harsh, angry whisper, "You bastard, why didn't you share this with me before now?"

Marty quickly shifts mental gears to defend himself. "Listen, Annette, don't start with me, I didn't tell you because I didn't want to add to your stress, or mine." "Like I've been telling you since yesterday, I want to wait for the results of the tests," he said, tapping his fork on the plate after each word. Tests that you abruptly changed your mind about seeing through. How do I know that the shared visions aren't being caused by some vapors we are breathing at our house?" "I would rather exhaust every worst-case scenario before I jump to any hasty conclusions."

Annette holds her ground, "So you mean to tell me that you are just going to turn a blind eye to this situation?" "Even with the knowledge you own?"

Marty still has the piece of meat in his mouth, draws a breath to snap a heated response, leaning in to confront her. "Yes, if that's the way you want to look at it, then fine." He is clearly aggravated, and his face reddens as he starts to choke on the piece of steak that slipped into his airway. He holds up a finger to signal he needs a moment, as he tries to clear the piece of meat lodged in his throat.

Annette chuckles, pointing her finger close to his nose, "See, God is punishing you." Her demeanor quickly changes as Marty grabs his throat, throwing his head backwards, his face turning a scary beet red, "Marty, are you ok?"

He shakes his head forcefully, indicating he is not.

She exits her side of the booth, rushing to his side. She grabs the back of his neck, shoving him forward, and pounds on his back. It doesn't work, and he starts thrashing and gasping for breath.

The diner is silent, once again, every occupant now looking at them. A man occupying a booth close by stands and approaches them. "Miss, I know CPR and the Heimlich maneuver, let me help." By now, Marty's face has taken a bluish pallor, his hands and arms are reddened, and prominent veins are noticeable about his temples and neck.

Annette shrieks, "My God, he's dying, please help him!" She steps clear so the man can gain access to Marty.

The stranger sits, grabbing Marty around the waist, drawing him closer. Then the man stands, sliding Marty to the seat's edge and heaves his body upward, leaving his butt dangling inches above the seat. Marty's labored attempts to breathe quit, and he goes limp in the stranger's embrace. The man rounds his fist, placing it to the base of Marty's diaphragm, thrusting hard into his airless ribcage. Marty remains limp in his grasp.

Annette is frozen in horror, "Oh my God, I think he's dead!" "It didn't work, try again!"

The good Samaritan thrust his balled fist into Marty's abdomen, three times in a row, perspiring from the frenzied action. Marty is unresponsive, a dead weight in his arms.

Annette's heart beats so hard she feels it in her temples and neck. She pleads, "Breathe, Marty, breathe!"

Marty's dead weight and awkward position in the booth have worn on his would-be reviver. The man slides him from the booth, laying him awkwardly in the aisle, and quickly kneels over him, thrusting his fists once, twice, and a third time forcefully into Marty's abdomen, with no response.

Tears well up and spill down Annette's cheeks, "Oh please Marty, please don't die on me." She kneels, grabbing his hand tight, feeling helpless.

The good Samaritan plunges his fist three more times into Marty's stomach, launching the half-chewed piece of steak onto the floor. Marty gasps for life-saving air into his lungs. Marty's skin sheds its angry red color, returning to a human appearance.

The patrons of the diner surround the three of them sprawled haphazardly in the aisle. Marty opens his eyes, feeling better, and he extends his hand towards a waitress in the crowd, "Check, please."

A roar of laughter fills the diner, and the stranger who helped save his life rises to his feet.

Annette embraces him, tugging his neck down and kissing his cheek, "Thank you so much!

The man is obviously perspired and worn from the experience. "Don't give it a second thought, darling, it's the reason I take the trainin." He turns, parting the crowd, and his wife silently greets him with a gentle rub between his shoulder blades. They resume their original seating arrangement and continue their meal and each other's company.

Annette kneels, hugging Marty tight; "You scared the shit out of me, I thought you were gone."

Marty feels the sting of embarrassment as the other patrons of the diner look at them while returning to their seats. Annette helps him to his feet, and they return to their seat facing each other. He caresses her hand, "My life flashed before my eyes just now; it was pretty scary." He looks down at his half-eaten steak, the original appeal lost, and he pushes the plate aside. "I think I have had enough of that for one day."

Annette feels the same, "Yeah, I've lost my appetite too. We should have the leftovers wrapped and take a special treat home for Popsicle."

"Yeah, he agrees with a worn nod of his head. "She would love to devour a couple of bones from the steaks.

Chapter 5: Peril Thwarted

Marty catches the attention of a waitress passing their table, "Miss, can you please wrap our leftovers and give us the check.

She digs into her smock, producing a small booklet, rips out a copy of the bill for their meal, and places it on the table with some mints on top. She reaches over, grabbing both of their plates, "I will be right back with your take-out bags," and abruptly turns, heading towards the swinging double doors.

Marty cups his hand over his mouth, whispering to Annette, "I think she will be glad to see us leave." He flips the bill over to view the damage, and after looking, he turns it so that Annette can see.

She gasps, widening her eyes, "Thirty-four dollars?" "Wow, and that is before the tip."

He chuckles coyly, "Nah ahh, only seventeen dollars if you take off your half; plus tip, of course."

She throws her rolled-up napkin, hitting him in the face, "It didn't take you long to get back to yourself."

The waitress appears a short time later, handing them their bagged leftovers. "Have a nice day."

Marty suspects he does not have enough cash. "Do you take credit cards?"

She points towards the cashier in the middle of the diner, "Just take your bill to her." She bends closer, "You can tell her the additional amount for the tip, and she can add that to your balance."

Marty offers her an affirmation nod; he knew a tip hint couldn't be far off. "Actually, I was going to leave your tip in cash here on the table."

"Oh, whichever way you choose will be fine," her final stab at cordiality as she walks away.

Annette reaches for his hand, pulling his attention from the exiting waitress. Honey, please think over what we were discussing earlier." She rushes to speak before he can cut her off. "Your choking may have been the sign you were looking for. It was pretty ironic how you started right as you were speaking of God giving you a clear sign to act. She tugs him close, Do you agree?"

Marty rolls his eyes, feeling annoyed, "All right, Annette! His voice lowers, indicating his agitation. This conversation ends here. I have had enough for one day." He slides out of the booth. "I need to put this to rest."

A booming male voice erupts from the front of the diner, "Listen up!" Two masked gunmen, one of medium height and stocky build, holding a shotgun, the other tall and slender, holding a handgun. They stormed in through the entrance of the diner, pointing their weapons at the patrons and workers.

Marty turns to Annette, who looks very stunned. "What the hell is going on?"

The masked man with the handgun commands, "Everyone, face forward and keep your hands on top of the tables where I can see them, and no one gets hurt!" He motions to the other gunman, "You go and round up all the fucking crew from the back, let's go hustle, hustle, hustle!"

His accomplice burst through the swinging doors, and the sounds of people being herded, ordered, and rushed against their will filled the air. Every ear listens, and all flinch simultaneously, heaving a gasp of alarm as a single muffled gunshot resonates from behind the doors, followed by the double click of his shotgun being re-pumped. Stifled screams and the voice of the thug commanding them out towards the main section of the diner fill the air.

The employees in the kitchen were all busy with some task as the gunman rushed in. His presence does not immediately catch all their attention. A man wearing a stained apron is about to

55

redirect the gunman back to the customer area, but stops, takes notice of the gun, and backs away. The robber moves into the kitchen, and some female workers begin gasping and herding together.

Two young men working at a sink and dish conveyor are too preoccupied with clowning around, laughing, and spraying water at each other to notice what is happening, even as the robber rushes towards them. The teen spraying water at his blond coworker notices the masked gun-wielding goon approaching. He freezes, his eyes widen in disbelief, and panic washes over him.

The blond dishwasher holds a large knife he is about to load into a basket full of utensils on the conveyor. He looks over his shoulder in the direction his friend is staring. "What's up?" He is taken by surprise and turns to face the approaching robber.

The masked man believes the knife will be used in an act of bravado meant to ward him off. He pulls the trigger, the gun recoils as shrapnel from both barrels rips into the young man's abdomen. The force from the round sends the teen stumbling backwards onto the sink stacked with dishes. The knife flies from his grasp, skidding to the foot of his attacker. He grabs his stomach, gawking in horror at the wound in disbelief; there is blood, but no pain. He tries to regain traction and reaches wildly for anything to help him up. He bangs the spray nozzle, which emits a spurt of hot water, steady enough to wet his hair and shirt. The impact of his body has broken several dishes, as he thrashes, fragments bite deep gashes in his flesh. He rests, grimacing as all the fresh wounds throb. A crimson trickle appears from his nostril, streaming around his lips, dripping from his chin. A mixture of blood and water flows into the drain.

He gazes, glassy-eyed, at his coworker. "Todd, please help me up." His gurgling voice pleads as he reaches for help.

The robber moves through the cloud of blue smoke discharged from the gun, charging Todd just as he instinctively moves to aid Larry.

Before Todd could reach Larry, the gunman was upon him, shoving so forcefully that he was knocked off balance, stumbling back a few steps.

The robber draws closer to the teen, "Unless you want to end up like your buddy here, he gestures in Larry's direction, don't try to be a hero."

Todd resists, defiantly, and feelings of helplessness and rage overcome him. Tears form in his eyes, and he is about to charge as the gunman rushes him, pinning the lad by his throat against the wall with the stock of the gun. "Don't even think of fucking with me, boy! You got me?"

Todd struggles to alleviate the pressure of the gun pressing hard on his windpipe. "Yes" is all he can manage.

The gunman smiles, revealing a set of rotting teeth, "I figured you would agree." He releases his stronghold on the boy, shoving him towards his huddled co-workers. "Let's go, move it all of you!"

Larry struggles briefly, wincing as more dishes break beneath his weight. The final seconds of his earthly existence were quickly passing. "Todd?" He labors to look towards the commotion. "Todd, are you there?"

Todd hears his buddy and looks over, but can't help.

Larry struggles, reaching a weak hand in their direction. "Todd? His breathing is labored. "Todd? I'm so cold. Everything is getting dark." His voice weakens to a whisper as the final moments expire. "Please don't leave me here alone." His body settles limp onto the dishes, his head leaning sideways, with eyes that become a distant stare, and blood continues to stream from his nose as death swoops in to claim him. The sprayer stops discharging water upon his lifeless, crumpled body.

The robber shoves Todd into the huddling mass, "Everyone out!"

They begin moving from the kitchen through the doors into the dining area.

The blast sends a wave of panic through every occupant of the diner. The gunman keeping guard of those in the dining area flinches at the sound of the blast. "Everyone, stay right where you are, and remain calm."

As the kitchen employees file through the entrance, the voice of their captor grows in intensity to those in the main dining area.

Annette is able to see what is going on through the little square windows in the doors at the entrance of the kitchen. Marty nudges her leg with his foot from under the table and whispers, "Don't provoke them."

Larry's murderer grabs hold of Todd's shoulder, forcing him to turn, then yanks him close by grabbing a fistful of cloth from his chest. "When we get out there, you are going to lie face down and keep your hands and feet spread where I can see them." His voice rings vehemently, and his lips part, displaying those darkly discolored teeth, "You got me, Todd?" The gunman wants to provoke a confrontation as he presses his face very close to his frightened hostage. His vile hot breath reeks of alcohol; he is so close that his words puff the young man's hair. Wretched-smelling spit shower from the goon's mouth further added to the degradation of the teenager.

The gunman presses the barrel of the shortened shotgun against the side of a young man's neck, and the freshly discharged weapon sizzles as it touches his perspiring skin. "You know, Todd…I could blow your fucking head off right now."

Todd winces and squirms to escape the painful burn of the barrel, "Yes, I understand."

The gunman continues, "You don't want to try to be a hero like your buddy, Larry back there, right?" He presses the barrel harder under Todd's chin, lifting him up a little further off the floor onto the balls of his feet.

Todd's voice blurts out, sounding frightened and submissive, "No, no, sir, you won't get any trouble from me!"

The gunman yells, "Blam! You're dead!", attempting to further brutalize the teen as he shoves the gun up, causing his head to thump against the window. "Good, Todd, that's what I want to hear. I had a feeling you would be cooperative." He smiles arrogantly, enjoying his newfound power. He releases Todd, pointing the gun towards the rest of the crowd. "That goes for all of you. Once we get you through these doors, you are to find a spot in the open and lie face down, keeping your hands and legs where I can see them." The gunman positions himself so he can see if he is missing any stragglers, "If any of you fuck around with me, I'll shoot you dead."

The gunman motions for his captives to continue, "Now let's take this nice and easy, no sudden moves, don't do nothing stupid, and no one gets shot. If everyone cooperates, we will be gone in a little while, and you will never see us again."

Todd exits swinging doors, warily walking backwards with his hands in the air. Once on the open floor of the diner, he quickly lies down, slightly spreading his hands and legs, submissively as commanded. Soon after, the rest of the diner's kitchen crew and wait staff were through the doors and on the floor like they had been instructed.

The slender gunman who hung back in the main part of the diner rushes his accomplice as he emerges through the swinging doors, "What the fuck went on back there? I heard a shot." He looks at his partner in crime, not noticing he is uninjured. What did you do?"

The stocky gunman with the shotgun points towards Todd. "A young jock, kinda like this dick here, pulled a knife on me, and I shot him dead."

The slender robber with the handgun is visibly upset. "We agreed there would be no bloodshed. We get in quick, get the cash and wallets, and get out. Now you've fucked everything up by killing someone. We could get the death sentence for this, you asshole!"

His hefty accomplice turns on him, grabbing him by the front of his jacket, screaming in his face, "Shut the fuck up, man!" "You knew there was a possibility someone could get killed doing this! We have to keep going according to our plan. Don't worry about the dead jock! We can still rob the diner, get the purses, wallets, and jewelry, and get out quickly. If we stay one step ahead of the law, there's no problem." He releases his partner, shoving him backward slightly.

The robber holding the handgun shakes his head in disgust, "At least they haven't seen our faces." He produces a sack from his coat pocket. "You really fucked up big time, man." He unrolls the sack, then flaps it through the air to open it fully, and looks around, addressing everyone in the diner. "Listen carefully, everyone. I am going to pass this sack around. I want you to surrender all of your jewelry and wallets, and empty your purses into them. And don't think of holding out because we are going to check each of you." He points towards his accomplice, "It's pretty obvious to see, you don't want to mess with this guy."

The robber with the shotgun yells, "Who's in charge of this grease pit?"

An older man lying on the floor speaks up, "I own the restaurant."

Both robbers approach the owner, heaving him to his knees. The hefty thug presses the barrel to his neck. "Do you want to be a brave man today?"

The owner's voice cracks, sounding desperate, "No, just take whatever it is you want and leave."

They make him stand. The slender, taller robber presses his revolver to the owner's temple. "Open the register."

The owner obeys by popping the register drawer open, then stands back, placing his hands in the air. "There you are, take it all."

Both thieves reach greedily into the register, pulling the entire cash drawer out and dumping it into the sack. After they pillage the register, the stocky assailant turns on the owner, pressing the shotgun into his belly. "Take me to your safe."

The owner bluffs, "I don't have anything else to take. I'm cleaned out."

Both burglars stare at him, unconvinced. The dream of wrongful wealth gained, their aim.

The stocky criminal points the sawed-off barrel in his face. "I'll blow your fucking head off, pressing the squared barrel into the owner's flesh.

Not wanting to be totally fleeced, the owner tries to bluff, "What's in the register is all the cash on the premises."

The slender bandit leans close to the owner, "I think you are holding out on us."

His hefty cohort shoves the barrel to the owner's chin. "That's not a good idea. You better cooperate, or someone's gonna get hurt!"

The tension in the diner rises as patrons plead with the owner to cooperate. "A woman's voice sounds over the others, "God dammit, Clarence, give them what they want before someone else gets hurt or killed."

The hooligan with the shotgun grabs him, dragging him to the woman who spoke up, "Yeah, Clarence," he sneers, "Give me what I want, or she's gonna get hurt!" She flinches, yelling, "Oh God, Oh God!" As the shotgun bumps against the back of her head.

Clarence submissively tries to ease the gun from her. "Please stop! I'm sorry! The safe is in my office, you can take it all!" He thumbs over his shoulder. "No one else needs to get hurt. Just follow me, and this is over."

The slender gunman interjects, "I'll go with him to empty the safe, and you stay out here to finish getting the rest of the valuables from everyone."

The plump, aggressive thug stops, obviously accustomed to taking orders from his partner, "Ok, you go, I'll keep watch out here."

The trim villain pokes his revolver into Clarence's ribs, "Ok, Mr., let's get this over with." They start making their way to the office when the robber stops them, "Hold up for a second, Clarence." He walks back over to the outspoken woman, Ma'am, what's your name?"

"Isabelle."

He urges her to her feet. "Isabelle, I want you to come with us, to make sure Clarence will continue to cooperate." He extends a hand to help her up.

Wanting to keep the robbery on track, he urges the fifty-something, outspoken woman to her feet.

Clarence points with a shaky hand, an inevitable side effect of his advanced age, "My office is down that hall."

As he passes his cohort, he whispers, "Try not to hurt anyone else."

Clarence leads the way, heading towards the kitchen. The thin burglar has Isabelle by the elbow and urges her to follow. The owner parts the swinging doors, and the three exit the dining area.

Once through the doors, they see Larry's crumpled corpse; blood still coursing from his nose. Clarence stops.

Isabelle reacts with a hushed, "Oh my God, Clarence, Larry's dead!" Then breathes heavily, as if about to mourn.

A Clarence motions towards Larry's remains, then reaches back for Isabelle's hand. "I want you to be fully aware that your quest for easy cash has done more than loot my diner. You've robbed this bright, funny, respectable young man of his future.

Clarence spins around to face his captor, "Why? I have to know why you are doing this. What could be so important? Can a quick fix, or easy cash, be worth the price you are going to pay?"

The slender bandit pulls Isabelle close, pointing the revolver at her temple. "Listen up, old man. I just want out. So let's get this over with."

She whimpers, feeling the cold steel pressed into her skull. "Please, Clarence, please. Give him what he wants."

Clarence backs off. "Whoa, there is no need for anyone else to get hurt. Please, stop pointing the gun her way. I won't give you any more trouble. My office is right over there." He motions to a door a little way from them, "Follow me."

Clarence reaches into his pocket, and the robber's voice booms in panic, "Keep your hands where I can see them."

He complies, "The door is locked and I have to get the keys from my pocket."

The robber is fidgety and releases Isabelle, "I'll get them." He probes the owner's jacket pocket, pulling out a ring with numerous keys. He hands them to Clarence, "I can't take any chances."

He struggles to steady the tremor, then unlocks the office door and flips the light switch, and sits at his desk. He sits and rolls the office chair to the safe, "It takes me a little while to get the combination."

The robber motions for Isabelle to enter the office, and she sits in a chair close to her husband. His anxiety grows with each passing second, "Come on, old man, pick up the pace!" He commands, diverting his attention back and forth from the office to the kitchen entrance. He sees his accomplice through the windows, moving around the dining area.

Noise in the office draws his attention. Clarence has the safe open and is rummaging inside. "Back off, I'll take it from here." He alone will decide the contents to be pilfered.

Clarence submissively vacates one arm from the safe, raising it in the air while bracing himself with the other still inside. He faces his captor, "Here you go." He sits up, withdrawing his other hand, revealing a revolver clasped in his fist. He aims and fires, glancing a round across the robber's masked scalp, peeling back a sizeable flap of flesh and material exposing his skull.

In reaction, the robber squeezes off several rounds. A single shot rips into Clarence's eye socket and exits the back of his head, showering blood and skull fragments onto the wall.

Isabelle recoils and screams hysterically.

The robber turned murderer staggers, clutching his gaping wound, as blood gushes down into the eye holes of his mask.

Isabelle heaves herself onto her husband's limp body and pulls him tight, "No, Clarence, it can't end this way! You're my better half. We're in it together to the end."

She shakes him as if to rouse him and reverse his demise. "Clarence." Then speaks in a firm, but pleading tone, "Clarence, get up god dammit!" His weight slumps lifelessly, and she wails in grief.

She pries the revolver from his fist, hell bent on avenging her slain husband. "Die, you low-life piece of shit!"

The round comes so close he hears it wiz by his ear, and it ricochets several times around the office.

The thief staggers and fires, the round punches through her throat, coating Clarence, adding to his blood and skull fragments on the wall. She convulses violently on his lap, and the chair shifts as she slumps lifeless to the floor. Blood from both victims seeps onto the white floor.

Blood coursing from the wound stings his eyes. He snatches a red bandanna from the desk, applying pressure to stem the flow. His vision narrows from the sharp pain, "Fuck that hurts!"

He is startled by his masked image reflecting from a mirror on the wall. He moves the bandanna, and is nauseous as he grimaces at the sizeable flap of scalp clinging to the blood-soaked bandanna. He applies pressure to the wound again, and a seething wave of agony results: "Fuck, that hurts!" The wound requires medical attention, but that is not an option.

The blood from his scalp wound soaked through his mask, running down his forehead, dripping from the end of his nose. He looked frantically around the office for something to soak up the blood that gushed from his head wound, and spotted a red handkerchief on the top of Clarence's desk. He grabbed it and turned towards a small mirror that hung on the wall. The sight of his open, bloody scalp made him feel woozy. He staggered slightly and felt his stomach churn. He never could stand the sight of blood, especially his own. He closed his eyes to gain his composure. After steadying himself, he pushed the peeled back scalp back into place and put pressure with the handkerchief in an attempt to slow the bleeding, "Fuck that hurts!" He clenched his jaw, breathing in deeply as he applied pressure, "That's going to need stitches!"

The armed robber, who did not intend to kill anyone, was now responsible for the deaths of two innocent people. His mind raced; he had to think of some way out of this. They would never get away with this crime; there were far too many witnesses in the diner. "Oh shit!" his voice hysterical, "We will get the chair." His mind was reeling, trying to figure out a way out. He rushed towards the safe, rolling Clarence on his office chair out of the way, his wife's body slid partially off, but remained for the most part where she slumped on his lap. The wounded robber gazed into the open safe, rummaged through its contents, and removed a small, neatly banded assortment of money. "See, Clarence, it would have been much easier to just give me this." he reached behind him, showing the money bundle to the deceased, while he continued hastily probing the safe for anything of value.

He stood and glanced around the office, checking if there was anything left to steal. Finding nothing, he exited the office, closing the door behind him without looking back. He stood on the other side of the door for a short time, thinking about what their next move would have to be. They would have no choice; they would have to kill everyone in the diner and torch the place to cover the evidence.

After Clarence, his wife, and the gunman had left the crowd of patrons and employees to open the safe, the rotten-toothed gunman loomed over them, demanding they keep quiet and stay still. He instructed Todd, the dishwasher, to take the sack, collect the wallets, and have the women dump their purses. An eerie hush was present as they tried their best to obey his command. Everyone could hear the four gunshots that echoed down the hall, and the atmosphere in the diner quickly changed from stifled calm to subdued hysteria. Everyone's heart was racing. Marty and Annette still sat in the booth they had shared during their meal, facing each other. He whispered everyone's growing fear, "They're going to kill us."

The wounded gunman emerged alone from the hall and tossed the contents of the safe to his co-conspirator. "Did you get everyone's valuables?" Without a word, the shotgun-wielding bandit caught the bundle of money that had been thrown to him and, after stuffing it into the sack, nodded and jingled the sack to signify his task was complete. "Yo man, what happened back there? I heard gunshots." It was a question that was inevitable, and the bloody scalp wound he was nursing spoke volumes, "The old man was hiding a gun in the safe, and caught me off guard, " he said as he passed by his accomplice heading towards the entrance of the diner.

The bandit that had been posing as a sentry over the patrons and employees in the diner was not satisfied with that answer and was hungry for details: "Where did he shoot you?" "Are you hurt badly?" "Hey man, where you goin'?" The wounded gunman was not in any sort of mood to discuss his part in the demise of the husband and wife. "Just wait right here, I'll be right back, I've got a plan to get us out of this." As ordered, the subordinate criminal turned his attention back to guarding the conduct of the patrons, for he knew the pair had been in some pretty sticky situations in the past, and each time his partner had concocted a strategy to keep them liberated.

Once the wounded thief instructed his henchman to stay put for a minute, he exited the diner, heading for their getaway car and popping the trunk, and after rummaging around a little bit, returned a short time later with a medium-sized square cardboard box.

In the time it had taken the wounded gunman to walk down the hall from the office to the public part of the diner, he had formulated the plan in his mind of what they were going to do. He turned the box upside down, emptying the contents on the table of a vacant booth, revealing it was filled with pairs of handcuffs and shackles. "Ok, listen up, people, we are going to cuff all of you together, so we can have plenty of time to make our escape."

As he walked around passing out the pairs of handcuffs, he tried to justify to his own conscious what was about to happen. He lessened the difficulty he normally would have faced when considering taking another person's life, but he thought it had to be done; it was out of his hands now. In the past, he had controlled the situation better; more than once, he had calmed his rotten-toothed accomplice from severely hurting people, and until now had been fairly successful. Nevertheless, this time things were different; there was no way he could allow himself to risk the death sentence for a simple diner robbery gone awry. His unintended killing of Clarence and his wife had forced this new course of action.

As he passed out the handcuffs, he fought a fierce internal battle. Sure, he thought, even with the death of Larry the dishwasher, he could have saved his butt by testifying against his accomplice; he probably would have ended up with a ten-year sentence out of the ordeal, possibly even time off for good behavior.

He knew that in order to make all the people in the diner follow his command, he was going to have to create the illusion that their lives were going to be spared. During the quick formulation of his plan, he noted that neither of them had brought much in the way of ammunition, so unless they were able to harvest everyone's complete cooperation, opening fire on the semi-crowded diner would not work. People would scamper and escape as the two gunmen reloaded, assuming they even had enough ammunition. The wounded gunman did not want to leave any witnesses behind to tell what happened.

Neither he nor his accomplice had the cold-blooded instinct to execute the patrons and employees one at a time. That manner would be far too grizzly; he hated the sight of blood and knew he would not have the guts to see the whole thing through. He and his accomplice came to the diner with the motive of robbery, but because of circumstances beyond his control, he had to leave the diner as a murderous thief.

There were far too many flaws in the opening fire on their captives; it would leave a trail of evidence that would be easier for the authorities to track them. Plus, they would have to shoot with the precision of a skilled marksman, killing everyone with a single bullet, assuming they even had enough ammunition, and he didn't want to leave anything to chance or circumstance; he wanted to control the outcome of this disastrous day.

As he passed the handcuffs, he instructed, "I want everyone to put one cuff on a hand, then cuff yourself to the person sitting next to you."

He had to cover his tracks, and he considered his new plan a stroke of genius created out of necessity. This plan definitely included the death of every person in the diner. He would have them shackle themselves together, instructing his accomplice to make sure they are all secured together, arm to arm, employee to customer, forming a chain of people. Then he would have his accomplice cuff them from both ends of that human chain, securing it to the solidly enclosed footrests that are part of the stools permanently mounted by the counter.

As his oafish counterpart accomplished this task, he planned to slip into the kitchen, being sure to feel bad for the dead lad that had been so callously gunned down. He would proceed to push the gas stove into an awkward position, such as to stretch the flexible conduit that connects the stove to the natural gas pipeline. From there, he would snap the conduit from the pipe, creating the appearance that it had been separated as a result of the noticeable struggle that had ensued in the kitchen. The outcome would be aimed at filling the diner with highly flammable natural gas.

He would then re-enter the main portion of the diner, no one aware of his murderous plot. He planned to wait for the perfect opportunity to sneak up behind his unsuspecting partner, where he would sedate his simple associate with the liquid chloroform he had slipped into his pocket when retrieving the box of handcuffs from the trunk. He planned to soak a rag with the chloroform in the kitchen before moving the stove and breaking the gas supply line. After ensuring his crude colleague was immobilized, he would turn his attention to a random male diner, pouncing on him with the sedative-soaked rag.

He would hold the other captives at bay with his pistol while he instructed the last person left on the chain to remove the handcuff from the anesthetized diner, and replace the now unoccupied cuff on the footrest. At that point, he would drag the immobilized diner to the side of his slumbering cohort. He felt a twinge of shame at the devious manner of his plan, but felt there was no other possible alternative but to sacrifice his partner in crime.

He would explain to his terrorized captives that he was giving them an opportunity to regain their freedom, but had to make sure he would be able to safely make his escape. All this would be explained while placing his revolver in the immobilized patron's hand. In greater detail, he would explain to the chained individuals that the immobilized patron would awaken first, a few full minutes before his ruffian partner. Once awake, the patron would have to opportunity to pass the key to the cuffs off to them so they could free themselves, and then they could secure their bullying captor before he wakes up.

69

In his ultimate plan, he imagined himself walking away from the diner, and just as he suspected would come to play, the patrons and employees would be watching both men as they lay motionless, anticipating, sweating, hoping that his story was true. The slumbering diner may possibly even awake before his soon-to-be-deceased cohort, adding to their hopes of rescue from the hellish day they had lived to that point.

Little would they suspect that as soon as any automated appliance from the kitchen rumbled to life, the arc of electricity would ignite the kitchen, which by then would have most assuredly filled with explosive levels of combustible gas, shattering the diner to bits, and unfortunately killing everyone inside.

He felt confident that he would not have to be deeply worried that there was little chance of prosecution by law enforcement because they would assume that the two free men killed in the accidental explosion were the robbers inadvertently caught in the blast. The blast, of course, was the unavoidable result of the fracas that had occurred in the kitchen when the dishwasher was gunned down. The investigators would conclude that the gas line on the stove must have been severed, and no one, not even the robbers, suspected it.

The surviving robber, of course, planned to get as far away from the scene as possible, changing his life for the better, never entertaining a life of crime again. He would become an average citizen working in some menial job for the rest of his days.

The injured robber passed a set of handcuffs in front of Annette and Marty and moved on to the next occupied booth. Marty grabbed the restraints immediately, complying with the gunman's request by fitting one cuff, not too snugly, around his right wrist and clicking it until they were locked comfortably into place. He looked up at Annette, thinking she, too, would be all too happy to comply as well. She sat there with her arms by her side and her head bowed down with her eyes closed. Marty's heart rate increased. He did not want to make any waves and inflame either of his captors. He nudged her under the table with his foot, but she remained in that position. Slowly, everyone in the diner was complying with the gunman's request, except Annette, who remained frozen in place with her head bowed and eyes closed tightly.

Marty tried to remain as expressionless as possible and did not even move his mouth as he leaned slightly towards her and began to whisper as quietly as he could, "Annette, what are you doing? Come on." She did not budge. Marty reached his cuffed hand across the table, "Come on, Annette, give me your hand."

Like a viscous chained guard dog charges a trespasser, the robber who killed Larry stormed towards the booth Marty and Annette occupied, screaming and causing the already anxiety-laden captives to jump to attention, "What's the fucking hold up here?" Marty began to stand, motioning with his hands, in some attempt to diffuse the situation, "Ok, sir, we will cooperate..." His sentence was cut short as the gunman lunged at him, beating him on the head with the butt of his sawed-off shotgun. The blow caught Marty off guard, knocking him unconscious, causing his body to fly backwards onto the seat of their booth. A hemorrhaging gash appeared on his forehead, the immediate result of the viscous blow he had received.

The savage raised his gun over the top of Marty's unconscious frame, clearly about to pummel him again with the weapon. Annette maintained her position with her eyes closed, never even looking up, as her husband was brutally attacked. The wounded gunman turned around, being distracted from passing out the wrist restraints by his partner's dash across the restaurant towards Marty and Annette. He was not quick enough to react until the thugs' gun stock bludgeoned Marty the first time, and reached them in time enough to interfere with the next blow, "Stop!" He yelled just about the time he reached them. By this time, his partner already had the gun raised over his head and was about to set into motion a severe beating that could have severely injured or killed Marty.

The injured gunman threw his hand up to block the progress of the blow about to be inflicted on Marty's limp body, "What the hell is wrong with you, man?" The violent gunman looked somewhat surprised by his partner's interference, "These two aren't putting the cuffs on like you ordered." The injured gunman remained with his hands on the shotgun as he urged his partner, making direct eye contact, "Put the gun down," and they both lowered the weapon back down to waist level.

The injured gunman turned his head to look at Marty, "He has a cuff on his wrist, what the hell did you hit him for?" His voice reached a fevered pitch, but he knew he would have to maintain his demeanor so that the plan he had set into motion would not spiral out of control. Marty continued to lie motionless, and Annette, too, maintained her position, head bowed, eyes shut. The subordinate criminal took heed to his partner's verbal cues and calmed his temper, pointing a finger in Marty's direction, "I just heard him saying something about putting the cuffs on, and I thought he was refusing to follow your orders."

This latest twist played perfectly into the plot the mastermind had planned; now he would not have to subdue and sedate a random male diner. His victim lay unconscious to his right. He placed a hand on his partner's shoulder, "It's ok, we all make mistakes from time to time." "Now go and make sure all the people continue to join their cuffs, wrist to wrist, until they are all linked up. I'll take care of these two." He turned his back to Annette, as he wrapped his arm around the shoulder of his trusting helper, "You secure them to the footrests on the stools. I've got some work to do in the kitchen. When I come out, we will be leaving here."

Patting his shoulder and shoving him towards the crowd of waiting patrons, the wounded criminal turned his attention to the now unconscious Marty. He removed the handcuff and approached Annette, who defiantly remained with her head down and her eyes closed. He had the set of handcuffs in his hand as he stretched his arm to offer them to her, "Come on, young lady, all this is almost over, how about you put these on one wrist and join the rest of the people over here." Annette's response was a simple, firm, "No."

This response caught her captor off guard, "Excuse me?" The tone of his voice mirrored the surprise he felt, "Did you just tell me no?" Annette remained without emotion as she repeated herself, "I said no." He turned to address his partner, who had departed the three and was heading towards the crowd of people that were being cooperative, "Hey Fitzy, get this, the pregnant lady here is refusing to work with us." He winced internally, having slipped up by using his specific name, but did not show any external reaction. The delinquent, now only known as Fitzy, continued toward the end of the line of people shackled together, "See, I told you they weren't following your orders." The leader of the duo, still holding pressure on his scalp, moved closer to Annette as he spoke, dried blood streams lined to the eye and nose openings of his mask, "Listen, lady, don't make this any harder than it has to be. If you go with the flow here, this entire horrific ordeal will be over." "Now we can make this easy or difficult, all I have to do is give the animal there the ok, and he will be all over you and your man lying there in a heartbeat." "So what do you say, can we work together?"

For the first time since Marty had tried to urge her cooperation, Annette opened her eyes, fixing her them on the nameless brigand, "Fuck off, low life!" This unexpected outburst left him flabbergasted, and instantly aggravated him because he was making the extra effort to soothe his would-be victim. He took pride in his ability to manipulate people, and it infuriated him to be unsuccessful: "Listen up bitch, you're going to cooperate and put the fucking cuffs on, or else!" Annette's gaze did not waver, "Or else what, you weasel?" "You don't scare me," she immediately followed by spitting directly in his face.

That action was instantly followed by a hard slap across the face from the once docile gunman, causing Annette to turn her head to the side with a sudden, violent jerk. A raised welt began to appear on her cheek within seconds of the blow. Annette's head remained in that position, and she grabbed her stomach, lurching forward slightly, as the presence inside her was hurled into a state of distress, "What are you going to do, shoot me?" "Like you shot those two in the back office?"

The gunman bolted straight up, his mind flying in a furious rage. He reached, grabbing Annette by the wrist to drag her from the seat of the booth, "You bitch, you have given me no other choice than to force your cooperation." She resisted to some degree, digging her feet in for traction and holding onto the table for a stronghold. It was a few seconds before he was able to begin overpowering her, dragging her struggling frame across the seat. After losing her grip on the table, she turned and started striking him frantically over again on the face, shoulders, and top of the head. She landed a blow right on top of the scalp wound he had recently managed to stop from bleeding, causing him to recoil and release his grip on her wrist.

He immediately backed away, grabbing the top of his head. Intense pain throbbed across his scalp, and a trickle of fresh blood ran between his fingers and down the front of his mask. There was no way he could ignore the intense searing pain he felt; his breath hissed between his clenched teeth. The pain was so intense for an instant that he thought he would lose consciousness, for now the wound hurt worse than when first inflicted. Fitzy kept a close eye from a distance, continuing with the task of subduing the others as he had been assigned. Annette seized the break in the struggle to back all the way to the innermost corner of the booth, tucking her body under the table.

The injured gunman forced himself to regain his composure, "Fuck!" he screamed as he stomped his foot three hard times, "Get a grip, don't lose it", he struggled to reclaim some sanity during the tense moment. Once numbed to the intense pain of his throbbing scalp, the lead gunman approached the table, crouching to address Annette once again using his most soothing voice, "There's nothing to be afraid of." he reached under the table in an attempt to help coax her out, "Take my hand, everything will be all right." She refused to acknowledge his renewed attempt to reason, not even offering a verbal response.

"That's it!" Annette's would-be assassin had reached his breaking point; violence towards her was now more than just a possibility. He released the pressure from his aching wound, reaching under the table and grabbing her leg, "Hey Fitz, what do you say we take turns fucking this bitch?" Heaving backwards with the might of an infuriated man, Annette's petite frame did not offer much resistance as her body began sliding across the tile floor with ease that surprised her and the aggressor. She kicked him once quickly with her free foot in a vain attempt to resist, but stopped after a single kick, unsuccessfully trying to gain traction instead.

Try as she might, resistance was futile as he yanked her wriggling frame from under the table. He released his grip from her ankle momentarily to gain better leverage and pull her away from anything she could get a grip on. Once sure she was firmly under his control, he kicked her viscously hard in the ribs, knocking the wind from her lungs, and fracturing several ribs with an audible cracking sound, "You bitch did you think you were just going to get away with giving me such a hard time?" Annette, her heart racing, realized fully the consequences of her resistance, which may mean her death. The child in her womb remained in constant motion, causing her stomach to churn and sway visibly even to her adversary.

He reached down, grabbing two handfuls of her hair with the intention of pulling her to her feet, "Now you're going to do exactly what I say from here on out." As he got his stronghold on her locks, she reacted by reaching for his head, ripping the facemask off, revealing his unfamiliar face to her. The scalp flap from his gunfight was clearly visible; he immediately released his grip from her hair, for a shearing pain once again resulted from the wound being disturbed. He stood straight up, but kept his composure. He visibly winced from the pain reaching towards the top of his head, his breath hissed sharply through his clenched teeth. But even with the intense pain he felt, he kept his thoughts somewhat under control, for he did not want to look back at anyone for fear of being identified. "Now you're dead", he pointed at her, his voice calm and concise, as he reached towards the mask, stripping it back from her. He stood straight once again and began replacing the mask to re-conceal his face.

In the blink of an eye, a blasting sound erupted behind her aggressor, jolting his body violently. A gaping bloody hole erupted from his chest, and blood and tissue sprayed Annette's upper body, face, and hair. The gunman looked down in disbelief, placing a hand over the bloody wound, rolling the blood around his gloved fingers. A look of complete surprise ruled his expression; he had been staggered, caught off guard, completely unaware of whatever had taken place to cause his injury. Screams from those who witnessed the event could be heard filling the diner. The gunman remained standing only for a couple of seconds before falling face forward, dead weight on top of Annette, who raised her knees in involuntary reaction to his obvious fatal descent, unintentionally minimizing any injury she may have received from his corpse plunging on top of her. Using her legs, Annette abruptly shoved the dead man's carcass to the side, still wheezing for breath and grimacing from the pain she felt, having not recovered from the kick the fallen man had inflicted on her just moments before.

After pushing herself completely free from the spot where the dead gunman lay, Annette promptly turned her attention from her attacker to the man now looming before her. Much to her surprise, it was his accomplice, Fitzy, who had fired the fatal shot, instantly killing his partner. He stood motionless, staring straight ahead, a hypnotized expression on his face. His hands clenched the shotgun that had inflicted the fatal wound on his partner. He remained motionless, except for extending his right arm, pointing a finger toward Annette, "Do not forsake me, Mother." The words were pronounced in a long-drawn-out manner, resembling a loud whisper.

Fitzy moved forward a single step, never breaking his gaze from Annette as he bent down, removing the handgun from his associate's grip. Without uttering another word, he stood and began raising the pistol in Annette's direction. She reacted by throwing her arms up, covering her face, fully anticipating the round to be fired in her direction, her belly lurching and heaving visibly under her clothing. He hesitated for a second as he aimed the pistol towards Annette, but continued to point the pistol at his own face, held it in that position for a second, before he pulled the trigger. The pistol discharged with an echoing crack, firing a fatal bullet that pierced his face through his cheekbone. Blood immediately exited the hole, forming a steady stream over the surface of his mask and down the length of his body.

Annette flinched at the sound of the gunshot, but felt somewhat surprised when she did not feel anything impact her. She moved her arm from across her eye to discover Fitzy still standing motionless with the gun still pointed towards his own mug, a slight cloud of blue smoke lingered around him.

He stood there swaying slightly, blood collecting in a pool around his feet, seemingly unaffected by the shot, his expression locked, void of any emotion, mouth open, exposing his decayed grimace for a prolonged period of time, before his eyes rolled back, revealing complete white. He plummeted backwards, hitting the tile floor with a dull-sounding thud, followed by his feet slightly raising and falling back to the floor before slumping sideways in an unnatural, grotesque position.

The patrons of the diner collectively flinched and gasped as the drama played out for all of them to witness. Annette lingered on the floor for a short time before she completely came to the realization that both of the would-be robbers now lay crumpled dead in piles around her, the blood from their wounds creeping ever closer to her position. It couldn't be so, Annette could hear the phrase Fitzy had uttered echoing again and again in her head, the same phrase she had heard many times prior in her visions. She covered her ears and closed her eyes tightly, and began screaming, "No, no, no, she couldn't bear hearing it any longer. She got to her feet reeling, feeling in a fog, unable to make sense or even comprehend what had just happened. Stumbling slightly sideways to avoid stepping in the wave of blood that rolled towards her feet, Annette felt numb, cold, disconnected as she headed towards the entrance of the diner. She barely comprehended a voice as she walked, sounding distant, "Lady, where are you going? Get us the keys for these handcuffs."

She pushed her way through the exit of the diner and entered the driver's side of their car, turned the ignition over, and roared top speed from the parking lot, heading back down the road her Marty and she had traveled when entering the diner. She had no idea where she was going or how to get there; she just drove. Within minutes, she blazed over the railroad tracks, they had crossed earlier and squealed around the turn as she exited the dirt road. She remained oblivious to the blaze and wail of sirens rising behind her on the horizon as police cars turned onto the diner road about a half-mile behind her. She pressed the gas pedal, increasing her speed slightly.

Chapter 6: It Has Been Foretold

Annette's thoughts remained a swirling quagmire of choppy reflection as she drove, barely able to keep her composure enough to obey traffic laws, her eyes filled with tears as she drove through town. Once on the outskirts of town, she really began losing her restraint and pulled off the road into an empty lot and commenced heaving and sobbing heavily with her head down on the steering wheel, unable to shake the horror of what she had just experienced at the diner.

In the quick formulation of her scheme not to cooperate with her captors, she assumed that if she resisted, one of the gunmen would likely inflict an injury to her that would cause miscarriage. She would have been absolved from the guilt that would undoubtedly follow an abortion, and she would be less likely to damage her relationship with Marty, but still would have stopped the menace growing stronger within her.

She figured the worst-case scenario would be that she might have gotten shot, but was willing to chance that, even with there being a great chance a gunshot wound could kill her. However, as she studied the two robbers throughout their robbery attempt, she noticed that they were not cold-blooded killers, so she figured at best, she would have ended up with a non-fatal gunshot wound. They would have used her injury to set an example in order to garner complete cooperation from the other victims of the hold-up. At any rate, she figured the injury would greatly increase her chance of causing a premature end to the pregnancy.

She flinched as she moved because of the intense pain felt as a consequence of the cracked ribs she received during the brutal kick from the gunman at the diner. When deciding not to cooperate at the diner, she had even quickly considered that an intense blow to her abdomen might also accomplish the outcome she ultimately desired.

It became clear to her that she was going to have to take more drastic steps to be successful at ridding herself of the malicious spirit she was hosting.

As she rested with the engine idling in park and her head down on the steering wheel, she felt something slightly grip her shoulder, "I might be able to help you." The stranger's sudden, unexpected presence startled Annette so much that she reacted by jumping and yelling, "Ahh!" Her voice trailed off, cut short by the pain in her side, "You scared me!" She turned her head, as quickly as her injured ribs would allow, to get a look at the stranger standing outside her vehicle. A glance revealed it was a woman standing behind Annette, still resting a hand on her shoulder.

The woman did not remove her hand. "Are you hurt?" Annette looked down at her bloody hands. Until then, she had been oblivious to the drying blood and matter she was covered in. "No", was her response, unable to think of how to explain her appearance. Annette ventured a guess that the stranger must have approached unnoticed from around the back of the vehicle as she sat there with her head on the steering wheel, sobbing.

Annette sniffled and wiped her eyes with a tissue she had grabbed from the package on the console. "What did you say?" The woman repeated herself, "I might be able to help you with your problem." Having realized there was someone else present, Annette struggled to regain her composure, "Do I know you?" As Annette finished the sentence, she breathed in abruptly as one does when they try to talk after crying, wincing noticeably, favoring her injured side.

The woman removed her hand from Annette's shoulder and reached down, opening the door of the car, "No, you don't know me, and I don't know you, but I have been forewarned you were coming here, and I think I might be able to help you." Annette contorted her face in surprise, "Help me what?" After fully opening the car door, the woman reached for Annette's hand, slowly urging her from the car, taking notice that notice that she was in some degree of pain. As Annette complied with the woman's request, she felt the need to ask, "Who are you?"

After Annette exited the car, the woman reached an arm around her shoulder and began walking slowly, escorting her away from the car. "My name is Lydia, and I would like to help you, Annette." Annette backed away, halting her pace and pulling from the woman's grip, "How do you know my name? The woman who had introduced herself only as Lydia lightly chuckled as she continued, "I'm a clairvoyant, and I recently began having visions foretelling of our meeting." She reached out once again for Annette's hand, "Come inside, where I can try to explain some things better for you."

They approached an older building, covered with chipped paint, that had a large storefront display window and a sign hanging that read, Coming soon, Madam Lydia, supernatural consultant. Lydia led as they opened the front door of the building, and a little bell tinkled slightly, announcing their entrance. She invited Annette to follow her, "Pay no mind to the condition of my waiting room, it's a mess right now, this place won't be ready for weeks yet." "I have a lot of cleaning and painting before I officially open the doors for business." Annette stopped once again, "Lydia, I didn't mean to give you the wrong impression, but I didn't stop by for any supernatural servicing." She continued, "Actually, I did not even realize this was here; I just pulled off the road only to gather myself for a couple of minutes."

Lydia did not release her grasp from Annette's hand and continued persuading her, "This is not about money, Annette. I've known you were going to visit for some time; I did not know the exact day or time you would be coming." She led Annette to a small round table with simple wooden chairs surrounding it, "Please have a seat, I would like to chat with you for a while." "This is where I plan to set up the main area of my shop." Annette felt weary but took a seat at the table, "Ok, but I can't stay long," taking into consideration that she rushed off, leaving Marty unconscious back at the diner.

Lydia raised a single finger into the air, gesturing as she placed it in front of her lips, "Shhh…relax here for a second, let me get you a wet rag to clean up with, while I get you a cup of tea to help calm your nerves so we can talk." She disappeared quickly through the door. A second later, Annette heard the sound of water running in a sink. Lydia reappeared a second later with both a wet and dry towel, "Here, clean up with these", she handed them to Annette, and turned to disappear back through the doorway.

"Wait right there for a second. I have the water on; I will be right back." Annette could hear her clanking and rustling from the other room. Without much thought, she began to wipe the drying blood from her face with the dry towel before noticing and switching to the wet towel. As she cleaned herself, she could hear the recognizable sounds of water being poured from one thing into another. A short time later, Lydia reappeared in the room carrying a tray that contained two cups and a teapot with steam being emitted from the spout, "Here we are, this will help you to relieve your anxiety." She placed a cup of steaming tea in front of Annette and took a seat directly across from her.

"Like I started to tell you outside, ever since coming to this town a few weeks ago, I have been having dream foretelling that I would be meeting you, and encountering the dark one".

Annette had started to sip on the hot tea, but stopped abruptly, choking slightly, "Ooh, that's hot," she replaced the cup atop the table, placing her hand over the painful area on her side. She had become accustomed to Marty insisting on her keeping quiet about the matter around others; it stunned her to hear someone mention it, and she felt the need to continue to pretend, "Excuse me?"

Lydia pushed the tea cup and saucer she had placed in front of Annette aside, "Give me your hands," she said, reaching towards her palms facing up. Curiosity began to override any apprehension Annette was feeling to that point, and she cautiously placed both palms over Lydia's. Lydia clasped her hands around Annette's slightly and rested her head back somewhat, while closing her eyes, "I could feel it from the moment I heard your car pull in." Annette remained silent as she stared unblinking at the woman across the table. Lydia remained with her head in that position, "I sense this child was conceived artificially, and as a result of your ability to outwit nature and alter your course, you have become a vessel for bearing this evil."

Lydia breathed deeply and began to speak again, "I can feel your fear and concern about the child you now carry." "I know it has caused you a great deal of alarm, torment, and suffering." She slumped her head forward, letting it hang loosely between her shoulders, "All that you fear about this child is true." Annette gasped slightly, surprised at the ease with which the woman revealed this, but remained silent, determined not to appear overly concerned.

Lydia repositioned her head to face Annette directly and opened her eyes, revealing no color as they had rolled back. They dropped to focus narrowly on Annette as she exhaled, "Annette, you already know what I say is true. I see that you have been suffering a great deal with the burden of this knowledge, and the dark seed you carry has made quite a stir for you and Martin." Annette remained emotionless, but Lydia continued breathing in again heavily before continuing, "I feel a great deal of distress from the dark one even now as you are in my presence." She continued, "I sense you feel a great deal

of inner turmoil, indecision, and doubt concerning your feelings." "An aura of hesitation persists for you even though you no longer have any misgivings about your conclusion."

Lydia leaned her head back, closing her eyes once again, "I sense there have already been particular events besides your own feelings that would suggest you are aware the one you carry is a very powerful presence capable of inflicting tremendous anguish to those around him." "You know that ability will grow to become increasingly menacing and ruthless with time." "The blood spattered on your face tells a story all its own."

Annette tugged her hands away from Lydia, "How do you know all this?" Lydia righted her head, looking directly once again at Annette, "I've always had a tremendous insight into people's lives, it's a gift really, and I can read the hidden vibes and aura everyone produces." Some are stronger than others, some clear and vivid like a picture, others cloudy, more mysterious, harder to decipher. "Your Aura is strong, the child you carry emits the strongest I've ever encountered, but it's more than just that."

Lydia leaned onto the back of her chair, "There is something different here with you. I dreamt of us meeting. I knew the moment I heard you pull off the road that you were here for a reason. This is no chance encounter." The moment I touched your shoulder, I knew your name and a great deal of your story."

She reached out, grasping Annette's hands once again, "The outlook for you is unclear, very murky, suggesting it hasn't been completely established." "You may still have an opportunity; your indecision clouds the outcome." "It may already be too late," she said, releasing Annette's hands from her grip.

Annette had been listening very intently to what Lydia was saying, at first skeptical, but increasingly believing the more she heard, "You're mistaken. Back at the diner, I decided to put an end to this." Her voice trailed off..."She laid her head on her hands, "You should have to walk a mile in my shoes." Annette looked up, her expression deadly serious, "I don't think you fully comprehend what I have been dealing with. It can manipulate the environment. I don't think it can be stopped."

Lydia knew what Annette said was the truth, "Please forgive me, I misunderstood the vibe I was getting from you, I interpreted it as your own indecision, not something out of your control.

Lydia stood, "Recently, I began to perceive a force that caused an annoying disruption in my day-to-day activity. At first, it was barely noticeable, but grew stronger with each passing day." She began pacing around the room, "I would be doing some chore like painting or tidying, when I would be driven to distraction, something I can't begin to explain would entrance me and propel me to root through the many boxes I have to unpack." "It was as if I had to find something, but I didn't know what," she raised her finger, "Wait there for a second, I'll show you what I am talking about." Lydia headed towards a doorframe covered with strings of beads; they made a tinkling sound as she passed through, and her voice continued from the other room, "My search ended when I came across something I haven't seen, or thought about for years." She reentered through the beads carrying a rather large, aged leather-bound book, "I acquired this from an old mystic woman more than two decades ago when I was very young, touring Europe."

Lydia walked to the table and placed the book in front of Annette, "I was traveling through a village, browsing an open-air market when the old woman approached me." Annette touched the book, marveling at's grand appearance, "This is really nice." "Thank you," Lydia replied, and continued, "The old woman who spoke with a thick accent led me to a dark, damp cottage with an earthen floor and sat across from me on a crudely constructed wooden bench and table." "That elderly woman gave me this book, telling me that she felt that I, too, possess the mystical gift, and I should take this book with me, for I would surely need it someday." Lydia placed her hand on Annette's shoulder, "At first I resisted, but she insisted and I didn't want to offend her, so I accepted, and even offered some money in exchange." Lydia flipped open the cover of the book, "That woman refused any money, but explained to me that I should read the book, and study its contents, because she foresaw in the future I would be needing its understanding."

Lydia continued to flip the pages to reveal elaborate writing and vivid illustrations. "I graciously accepted the old woman's souvenir and left the village shortly thereafter." The book was in marvelous shape for being such an obviously old manuscript. "Throughout the rest of the trip, I did exactly as the old woman had instructed and pored over it, reading it from cover to cover." "It is filled with the earliest notions about existence, the soul, or the very essence of human character, spells and rituals." You see, the author of this book firmly believed in the supernatural and believed everyone is born, predisposed to what they are going to be in life, good, bad, or in between."

Lydia returned to her seat, "After reading the book, I pretty much dismissed the old woman as an eccentric, because there would never be a time that I would be standing by a boiling cauldron bubbling up some potion or ancient concoction." "So I packed the book away, and pretty much forgot about it until a couple of weeks ago when I began getting an overwhelming compulsion that I needed to find something." She paused for a second, "About that time, I began dreaming of meeting a woman with a dark churning eddy shrouding a beast within."

She focused her eyes narrowly on Annette, "I started reviewing this book, and I found that from the dawn of human existence, there has been a belief that souls are predisposed to be what they will inevitably become in life." "Some good, some bad, most a mixture of both, this book even contains a scale by which the reader can associate the differing levels."

Lydia turned pages searching for the illustration she spoke of, and after finding the page spun the book once again for Annette to view, "See most people range somewhere in here within varying degrees," she pointed to the middle of the scale, "but ever so rare a child is conceived with a soul located at either of these ends." She pointed with both hands to the outer edges of the illustration, "Either very righteous, white, and pure, or dark, shadowy, and evil." "This literature suggests that any time a child is born at the darkest of these extremes, it prompts the birth of a child at the purest level to offset the instability caused as a result of the dark presence that has crossed the threshold."

Annette reflected aloud for a second with a glimmer of hope in her tone at what Lydia had just said, "So what this is suggesting is that when a wholly evil child is born, likewise, an equally pure child is born to prevent any devastation from occurring." Lydia, having entertained this very notion, continued, "Don't be misguided, the book simply suggests an honorable soul is brought forth to balance the symbolic scale, but does not make clear if that soul has been specifically put forth to vanquish the treacherous presence."

Lydia refocused her gaze on Annette, staring deeply into her eyes, causing her to shift uncomfortably in her seat. "This book also suggests the parents of the brood whose soul inhabits this outermost edge of the scale." She dragged her finger, pointing it back towards the dismal end, "Will know far in advance whether it is either very good, or very bad, and have a choice to prevent it." Lydia's voice lowered as she tilted slightly further towards Annette, "Those that permit a bad seed to come to pass face eternal damnation."

Both Annette's heart and the presence in her womb jumped simultaneously as they listened to what Lydia said next, "I believe the soul you carry within you dwells here at the most perilous end of this scale, and I am sure you know it too."

Annette offered no response, for she had not been prepared for the current topic of discussion. After a short time, she spoke, "Lydia, when you met me out by the car earlier, you said you might be able to help. What did you mean?" Lydia turned the book to face herself once again and began flipping a few pages, passing richly drawn illustrations of naked men battling ghoulish-looking creatures, "Just yesterday, as I was looking through this book, something caught my eye, and for some reason I was particularly drawn to it."

Once she found the page she was looking for, she turned it once again for Annette to view, revealing an illustration of a pregnant woman heavy with an offspring that resembled something straight from the bowels of hell, complete with horns, a pointy tail, and red eyes.

The moment Annette looked at the page and the illustration, the spawn within her suddenly began thrashing violently, causing her to react with an involuntary jerk in obvious discomfort. Lydia began to explain, "This is an ancient cessation ritual. When I said I might be able to help you earlier, I contemplated the possibility of performing this ritual."

Annette rolled her eyes and shook her head, pursing her lips, "All right then, mmm…Well, I think I have heard about everything now." "No offense, Lydia, but I don't buy into this supernatural mumbo-jumbo."

Lydia did not even bat an eye or lose her composure at all. "None taken." "Indeed, you may not believe, you rank among a good portion of today's society, many have drifted away from any belief in the paranormal, or simply dismissed it as a hoax and hogwash." She leaned in towards Annette, placing both her hands on the book, "But even as skeptical as you are, there is no denying that what I have described, that you are experiencing, is anything but normal." "All this would seem crazy to most, but regardless of what they think or believe, it remains reality for you."

Annette nodded yes, symbolizing her agreement, "I've known since shortly after conception. She paused for a second ", but all the same, you are not seriously suggesting a ritualistic abortion, like bone through your nose, jumping around and chanting stuff." Annette chuckled, half expecting Lydia to roll her eyes and confirm she was kidding.

Lydia sat back again, placing her hands on her lap, "To be honest with you, Annette, I've never done anything like this before, like I said, the book sat unused for years." "But I believe everything happens for some purpose, and if you just examine the basic fact that I was drawn to the book, and you were drawn here should speak volumes." "Furthermore," she continued, "some of the writings and ideas contained in this book date predate ancient Greek and Roman times." "Much of what that old woman translated here is a collection of notions on existence, the soul, good, and evil that do not mirror conventional Western views, and date back to the time when belief in the supernatural was more than just commonplace, for most, it was a way of life." "So it might be in your best interest to try opening your eyes and your mind to the unconventional."

Annette's expression turned somewhat surprised, "You mean I have to actually believe in this for it to work?" Lydia shook her head slightly, "No, I'm not suggesting that, in fact, I am not positive this would even work, I can't confirm the validity of what is written in this book, I've never performed this ritual before." She stabbed a finger harshly Annette's way, and began speaking through her teeth, "Don't you see, everything happens for a reason, you were brought here today for a reason." The pitch of Lydia's voice had risen, an obvious sign of her mounting frustration with not being able to convince Annette to participate, "so far this has all shown to be significant. "Don't you find it uncanny that we are even having this conversation?" Lydia pounded her fists onto the table, "You can't just pretend none of this happened!" Lydia's sudden change in demeanor began to concern Annette, who had jumped slightly in reaction to the sound of her fists pounding hard onto the table. Annette felt a renewed urgency to part ways as quickly as possible with Lydia, for she suddenly felt uncomfortable in her presence. Annette reached for the cup of tea that had spilled a little when Lydia pounded the table, "I should finish my tea and be getting home to my husband."

Lydia sat upright once again, regaining her composure, and placed her hands on her lap, "You don't have to feel obligated or pressured to participate in this ritual. If you feel uncomfortable, you can get up and leave right now." "My mind will be put at ease knowing that I made the offer." "All I can say is this ritual was designed a long time ago to help a woman who suspected she carried a fiendish life-force in her womb to dispose of the evil menace, before it had an opportunity to unleash havoc on the earth."

Lydia stood up from her seat, taking hold of the book and closing it, then started once again through the doorway covered

89

with beads, "Sorry for taking up so much of your time. You can let yourself out."

Annette sat there for a little time contemplating the pros and cons of Lydia's offer. If this ritual were successful, it could be a very simple solution; she could finally be freed of this burden. But then, after about half a minute, she snapped back to reality, "Why the hell am I even giving this any thought?" she whispered, rolling her eyes and shaking her head in disbelief. She even considered slapping herself in the forehead as a punishment.

Annette, with her decision being final, picked up the cup of tea and gulped it down, for it had cooled considerably. After swallowing the contents of the cup, she noticed it was not like the tea she had been used to and did not have a very appealing taste. Her expression became a grimace, and she stuck her tongue out, expressing her displeasure in the flavor, "yuck," she whispered lowly so as not to offend her host.

About the same time she replaced the cup on the saucer, Annette heard what she distinctly recognized as the sound of her car engine revving to life and roaring up the street past the building, "Hey, that's my car!" She yelled, but her effort to jump up and run through the waiting room was cut short by the biting pain in her ribs. Her breath hissed through her teeth as she fought back the pain to stand, "Fuck, this hurts!" Annette made her way through the waiting room towards the entrance of the building, "Stop, that's my car!" She yelled again in some vain hope that the thief would somehow reconsider. She made it to the door and struggled to fling it open, setting the little warning bell to tinkle, but stifled any further attempt at yelling since the pain in her side was now overbearing. Annette watched silently as her car, filled with a bunch of teenage boys, raced out of sight, leaving behind a trail of dust and blue smoke.

Annette stomped her foot in anger and again winced from the pain in her ribcage because, in that instant, she remembered having absent-mindedly left the keys in the ignition: "Those opportunistic bastards!" For a moment, she stood still and reflected, wondering if, when Lydia surprised her, she might have walked away from the car without turning the engine off, "Nah, I couldn't be that stupid," she said aloud as she turned from the door.

As Annette turned, she was startled to find Lydia had unknowingly drawn up behind her and was standing with both hands behind her back. Annette's surprise was quickly overcome by her pain. "Oh," she paused for a second, forcing herself to stand fully erect, her pain became almost paralyzing, causing her to take short, labored breaths and resume the leaned position of favoring her injured ribs. She staggered slightly to the side and put her hand up to her forehead, feeling somewhat lightheaded. A visible bead of sweat had appeared on her upper lip. She ignored the pain and dizziness, "Lydia, do you have a phone here? It seems a group of punk kids just ran off with my car, and I am going to have to call the authorities and my husband."

Annette thought this to be the best time to seize her opportunity to squirm out of participating in the ritual, "So in light of this, I will have to pass on that ritual." Lydia stood still without expression. "I kind of expected that." Annette felt it necessary to be honest, "But even without having the car stolen, I would not have felt at ease with going through a superstitious, waste of time." Annette reached in Lydia's direction, "I hope

You understand, it's nothing personal, but like I said earlier, I've never really bought into any mystical practices, and I would feel really foolish even trying."

Lydia moved to the side, removing one hand from behind her back to point back through the doorway Annette had just passed through when making her way to witness her car vanish, "It's in the other room." Annette retreated at a lackluster pace towards the direction Lydia had pointed, "I can't believe this shit," she said, passing Lydia, "Excuse the language, but I am really pissed right now, and I dread having to explain all this to my husband." As she entered the room where they had been previously sitting,

Annette looked around, unable to locate the phone. She turned back towards the direction where she had just passed Lydia, "There's no ph…" stopping mid-sentence as she turned, noticing Lydia had scampered her way to the front door and was in the process of drawing the shade down. Annette immediately became suspicious of Lydia's action, "Why are you pulling down that shade?" Lydia, having been distracted by Annette's question, slowed, drawing the shade, "I don't want anyone passing by to think I am open for business," as she completed the task.

Annette's sneaking wariness of her host became more intense as Lydia turned, placing her back to the door, fully revealing she was concealing a black club about a foot in length. Once again, Annette's head began to swirl, making it increasingly difficult for her to focus and causing her to stagger forward a step. Lydia moved a few steps away from the door in Annette's direction, "I can't let you just walk out of here." Annette's body swayed in a circular motion, making it more obvious she was having difficulty keeping her balance. "Of course, I'm not going to just walk right out of here, I have to use the phone first," she chuckled, trying to make an artificial attempt at humor. Lydia continued quickening her pace in Annette's direction, "I can't leave it to chance that you are going to unleash that beast to exact mayhem on innocent and unsuspecting."

By now, Annette's temple had begun throbbing, and her vision blurred, but she recognized the gravity of the current situation and turned, attempting to escape Lydia's advance. As she turned to take her shaky first step, Lydia closed in, raising the club above her head, landing a harsh blow across the base of Annette's skull, knocking her unconscious and sending her body crashing forward through the door covered with beads, ripping the nails out, causing them to shower down all around her. Annette's limp body skidded to a halt; she lay on her side, halfway through the doorway, her lower body and legs remaining in the room where they had been seated. Her upper body and one arm stretched inside the kitchen, her right arm positioned flat against her side.

Lydia waited for a little while to make sure the blow she had dealt to Annette was sufficient to keep her down, ready to strike the fallen woman again and again if necessary, until she would offer no resistance. But Annette remained in the position she had fallen, motionless with the exception of her stomach, which was shifting and jerking from the movement of the baby inside. Lydia stood over Annette, breathing heavily, and after a few moments had passed with no stirring, she shoved Annette with her foot, rolling her from the position in which she had collapsed onto the flat of her back. Annette's left arm remained outstretched above her head, reaching into the kitchen.

Lydia reached the club towards Annette's face, shoving it into her cheek, "I tried to convince you to cooperate with me and get this over with the easy way, but you had to make things more difficult." She reached for the strung beads that had fallen and tangled around Annette's legs and body, struggling to pull them free. Some strings lingered entwined around her limbs, held strongly in place under Annette's weight, and as Lydia pulled harder, a strand snapped under the pressure, scattering the beads it contained across the wooden floor, causing Lydia to stumble a couple of steps backwards. Clearly frustrated, she threw the strings that had broken free off to her side and hastily stepped over and began her way past Annette's still motionless body, into the kitchen.

Once in the kitchen, Lydia anxiously dashed to the cupboards and pulled open a cabinet drawer, searching hastily through its contents, not taking the time to shut it before moving on to the next. Then she hurried onto the next drawer, pulling it open much too hard and dropping it onto the floor and spilling the contents, "Shit!" She yelled, her voice attained a frenzied pitch, her heart pounded so vigorously that she could feel it in her throat, "Where is it?" Lydia continued her search frantically pulling out the next drawer, also dumping its contents on the floor, she moved onto the boxes that lay on the floor waiting to be unpacked, dumping their contents as well, she became increasingly agitated with every fruitless hunt.

She had worked her way through most of the drawers and boxes, kicking their contents out of her way as she searched, "It's not in here; the movers must have put that box in another room." She headed towards the kitchen door once again, making her way past Annette's limp frame, making her way towards the door across the room leading to the basement. She fumbled with the doorknob, turning it several times without popping the door. "I hate this damn doorknob; it takes too much effort to open it." All at once, the doorknob caught the internal mechanism and popped open the basement door, which creaked loudly as she pulled it open. Lydia reached in and pulled the string to an overhead light, which illuminated the wooden staircase leading to the basement, and started for the stairs. As she began descending the stairs, she stopped at about the third step from the top and thought the box was probably in another room, and not in the basement. With that thought, she changed her mind and retreated through the basement door, noticing once again the prominent squeak of the hinge as she swung it shut. As she closed the basement door, she realized that she had forgotten to pull the chain to turn off the light, "Oh fuck it, I don't have time to screw with the damn doorknob again." And turned, leaving the room, scurrying through the waiting room, and shoving a few times with her shoulder against the heavy, stuck door leading to another room that was empty except for the stacks of boxes that lined the wall. She wasted no time racing to the stack of boxes and grabbed one, dumping its contents onto the floor. She felt hurried, and thought aloud as she fumbled through the debris she had scattered, "Think, Annette, where did you put the knife the old woman gave you, along with the book? She said it was important, and that in the future I would face great peril and be confronted with a dark menace."

Once again, Lydia could not find the object for which she searched; the natural light in the house had become dim since the two ladies first entered, as the sun loomed ominously low over the horizon. She rushed to flip on the overhead light, shuddering slightly as her eyes adjusted to the light, darting about the room searching for the box she could feel was close. She walked to the center of the room and closed her eyes, halting briefly to clear her mind and concentrate on the location of the dagger, "Reveal to me your location."

Immediately, a stack of boxes began swaying back and forth and toppled, bursting open and dispersing their contents in a random pattern about the room. As if on cue, the dagger Lydia had been searching for slid handle-first towards her, stopping as it reached her foot. Lydia opened her eyes but was not startled to see the target of her search spinning on the floor before her, "Ah, yet another sign, this is meant to be." She bent, picking the dagger from the floor, "It has been foretold."

As she turned to exit the room, her mind drifted back to the time of her chance encounter with the old woman who passed the book and dagger on, "What was her name?" she wondered aloud, snapping her fingers as she tried to remember. Lydia drifted back as she replayed the event in her mind's eye, recalling how she felt slightly confused as she followed behind the old woman, not understanding why she felt compelled to continue.

Neither Lydia nor the old woman uttered a word as they walked along the winding path towards the cottage. She remembered the earthen smell that greeted them as they entered the cottage, and the harsh feel of the wood against the skin on her legs as she sat on the bench where the old woman had instructed. Just then, the old woman's name came rushing back, "Magda, that's the name she said when she grabbed my arm at the market, that's right," Lydia said to herself, feeling pleased that she had been able to remember.

Lydia struggled to recall the events of that day so many years before. The old woman named Magda walked out of the room, but returned quickly to reveal she had retrieved the book and the dagger Lydia had just searched for, placing both on the table. After recovering her seat, Magda began flipping through the heavy pages for the then much younger Lydia to view as she explained, "I have translated a group of ancient writings into this manuscript. I believe it bears great relevance and will offer you guidance. She explained all that Lydia had told Annette earlier, as it concerned the predisposition of souls to be good or evil and how each soul has a position somewhere on the scale. But Magda went on to explain something Lydia had omitted in her earlier explanation to Annette, "You will need to know this book's writings to be successful at your task."

The old woman surprised her guest as she unexpectedly reached across the table, grabbing tightly hold of Lydia's wrist and motioning for her to move closer with her other hand. Lydia did not offer any resistance, and she drew so close that she could smell the old woman's warm, foul breath rushing against her cheek. Magda seized her other wrist in a tight grip, "Child, pay attention to this warning, you will be faced with a grave situation in the future, you must begin preparing now, for someday a grim presence will cross your path."

Magda continued breathing heavily as she spoke, her breath wreaked a pungent aroma, and her words caused Lydia's hair to move with every word she spoke, "You must be brave for you will be faced with a perilous struggle, and have the chance to terminate the ascension of darkness to supremacy, or depart this life…" Magda paused and left loose of her grip from Lydia's wrists, wincing and sliding backwards until she sat level on her crude bench seat once again, her hands remained twisted in almost the same position they had been in as they gripped tightly around Lydia's wrists. Her eyes remained fixed on Lydia, and began to take on a glazed over appearance as she came to rest. Suddenly, she threw her head back in an obvious display of pain and began coughing a sickening, "Gaaak, gaaak," sound as she clutched at her chest.

The old woman's chest heaved slightly as she labored for breath. "I've waited a long time for this encounter, but the spirits enlightened me many years ago that I would have to pass on the knowledge." Her weathered body appeared to weaken and sway as she spoke, "Not long ago, I pleaded for your arrival, for I have grown weary with age." She continued after emitting another round of hacking coughs, "I have the obligation to protect the innocent by passing on to you the tools and knowledge you will need to triumph over the evil seed."

Lydia had stood quickly, realizing that the woman was in distress, and rushed to her side, catching her as she began to slump backwards, helping to ease her descent. Before the old woman lost her stature, she had firmly held the book and dagger. Lydia's heart went out to the woman she had just met within the hour. "Don't talk, I can get help," she said, looking around the area for a phone. Lydia returned her gaze to the old woman, "Magda, do you have a telephone?" Shaking her head no, the old woman wheezed in another labored breath, "You will need to vanquish the evil before it has the chance to get a foothold." She hacked again, this time causing both herself and Lydia to jerk by the violent motion, "Take these two instruments of knowledge, this book contains what you need to know, look here for what I speak of," she began, raising her hand to turn the page.

Magda righted her head and looked again at Lydia, "My time at this moment is quickly drawing to a close, things are growing dim, but I must warn you that the grizzly seed destined to evolve is the consequence of a poisonous tree that must be smitten at the root." Magda's breath whispered a final time before she began slipping away. A faint voice billowed out with her last words, "Take heed…" Her hand slowly went limp as the dagger came to rest, pointing to the illustration of the woman pregnant with the demonic spawn. The old woman's form grew limp as death encompassed her. As she lay in Lydia's arms, she breathed no more; her eyes remained locked unblinking in position as she embraced eternal sleep.

Chapter 7: The Plight of Mediocrity

Lydia's memory of the encounter she had so many years before began to disappear gradually as she remembered repositioning Magda's lifeless body to rest comfortably on the bench, then sliding her fingers gently over those lifeless eyes, setting them to rest forever. Lydia was abruptly thrust from reminiscing by the sound of the heavy wooden door she had flung open when entering the room, slamming closed with tremendous force, as if a sudden strong gust of wind had taken hold of it. As she turned, startled by the loud bang that echoed through the empty room, the overhead light shut off, giving Lydia the creeping suspicion that something was very wrong.

She moved carefully to the door, putting her foot against it for leverage in the event it were to fly open; she didn't want it to hit her in the face. Lydia then placed her ear close to the door, listening to see if anything was amiss on the other side. She listened carefully, only hearing silence. Slowly, she reached for the doorknob, purposely turning it little by little to make barely any noise. She kept her foot wedged at the edge of the door while opening it just a crack to ensure some level of control if someone tried to force entry into the room. She peered out, looking to the left and right, but did not see anything unusual, then she placed her ear to the crack to listen for any sign of activity around the door. She heard nothing, just silence, so she scanned once again through the crack, being able to clearly see through the waiting room that the shade and front door had not been disturbed.

Lydia thought it should be safe to open the door further, so she attempted to move her foot, causing the door to move slightly and close the crack she had just created to peer out. She opened the door to discover a far different sight, the walls she had just looked upon now appeared charred black, a distinct smell of burnt wood and flesh filled her nostrils. Lydia felt surreal as she stepped into the hallway and looked all around her to hear the muffled, echoing sound of crackling fire filling the air, but could not distinguish the light or heat from the flames. She could make out the indistinguishable, far-off-sounding voices, swirling all around her, and her mind became awash with muddled thoughts. Lydia then heard the sound of Magda's voice emanating from the room where Annette had been knocked unconscious, "Child, you must be brave, for you will be faced with a perilous struggle. Someday, a grim presence will cross your path." Lydia turned to fully face the direction of the room. Fiery shadows danced on the walls of the hallway surrounding the doorframe. Lydia's instincts screamed for her to run away to safety, flee the building, but at the same time, she felt strangely drawn to the room at the end of the hall.

She hesitated, lingering by the door of the room she had just come from, the indecipherable voices continued registering in her ears, but still sounded far off, disconnected. Lydia began moving forward slowly, heading in the direction of the room where Annette was last seen. Just as she moved from that spot, a burning piece of material crashed down behind her, causing her to jump around and scream.

Lydia reconsidered her option of flight, as she lingered again, watching the flames behind her spread up the wall and into the room she had just stepped out of. If she jumped

Through the flames, there was still a chance she could make it to the front door safely. But the flames spread quickly, racing up the wall into the stairs leading to the second floor, and into the waiting room. Now her fate was sealed; she had no choice but to go down the hall and face what lay just out of sight through the doorway that loomed just feet in front of her. Lydia tightened her grip on the dagger and proceeded forward, stepping slowly towards the room, getting closer, and still closer, beginning the expose what lay just beyond the doorframe. As Lydia reached just to the outside of the door, she became unable to control her breathing rate, sweat began dripping down her face, her heart raced, for she was terrified to face what may be waiting just out of her sight beyond the threshold of the door. Panic engulfed her emotions; she could not bear to push on. Something was terribly wrong. A mixture of alarm and dread overwhelmed her. A blast of searing heat erupted around her, stinging her flesh and singeing away her eyebrows, inducing her to conclude her only option was to face her inevitable fate. Lydia gradually peered into the room and could make out the form of Annette still lying in the position she had been forced into, looking the same as before Lydia had left the room; blood-soaked and unconscious.

Seeing Annette undisturbed eased Lydia's tension somewhat, as she warily slinked into the room, never taking her gaze from Annette, gripping the dagger tightly, ready to contend with her would-be aggressor if need be. The sound of the roaring flames still present around her made her realize that she would need a plan if she were going to complete the ritual. Lydia headed towards the table where she had placed the book, still not looking away from Annette's motionless body, for she feared that at any second the woman might spring up and attack.

As Lydia reached the location of the table, she placed her hand on the edge and immediately noticed a difference in the recognizable texture and feel of the piece; it felt foreign to her touch but yet vaguely familiar, rough. Lydia's heart remained in overdrive as she took her eyes from Annette, gazing down to find herself touching the crude wooden bench and table that she had occupied years before at the cottage. Her eyes grew wide as she took notice that on the bench before her lay the corpse of the old woman, looking as she had when she died in Lydia's arms, eyes open and glazed over in an ominous stare.

Lydia stood frozen, paralyzed by shock as the manifestation of Magda bolted straight up from the position where she lay on the bench, pointing in her direction. Her mouth remained wide open as it produced her ill-omened gurgling tone, "Child, pay attention to this warning, you must begin preparing now, for someday a grim presence will cross your path."

Lydia's response rang of remorse, for she knew all was not right, "But I did as you instructed, I read the book cover to cover, and I have maintained possession of both the dagger and book ever since you passed them on." She backed up, becoming horrified as she witnessed the sight of the old woman rotting before her, as the skin melted to bone. Another foreboding revelation was uttered forth, **"Mediocrity, escorts demise."** With that, Magda's bones began to crumple to dust. As the final bits fell into a pile, Lydia's attention shifted to where the book lay on the table. As she looked closer, she could make out a dark, almost shadowy silhouette crouched on the table top, staring down at the pages, flipping page after page, fingering over the words they contained before moving to the next page. As it reached the page that contained the ghoulish illustration of the mother burdened with the evil imp, it paused for a second and slowly raised its head, staring at Lydia with eyes glowing red as coal hot embers. Lydia shuddered at the weight of its stare; she could feel as if the creature were burning a presence directly into her soul. The shadowy figure returned its gaze towards the book and, without hesitation, ripped the page containing the illustration from the text, and again fixed its cold, burning stare upon Lydia, causing her heart to pound so hard she could feel it throb in her temples. The beast then flashed her a wicked smile, revealing a set of pointed white, slimy teeth, before proceeding to shove the torn page into its mouth. It closed its mouth around the old woman's interpretation but did not chew, simply swallowed, emitting an audible swallowing sound while simultaneously rubbing its belly. The shadowy figure again looked down in the direction of the book for a second before rearing its head once again, but this time its face had taken on the appearance of the illustration it had just swallowed. It had become an animated version of the picture in the text, complete with red eyes and pointed horns.

Lydia's horror and fear began to change to unbridled rage, for she knew this was the grim presence Magda had warned her about. She tightened her grip on the dagger and, without wavering, attempted to charge the fiend with the intent of plunging the dagger into its chest. As Lydia took her first step in its direction, the beast's appearance resumed its original shadowy form with ember eyes, and it raised a hand, pointing a single finger up towards the sky, stopping Lydia's attack as if she had been tethered by a chain to the wall. She became suspended about six inches from the floor. It cocked its head slightly as it began waiving that upraised finger, waiving it from side to side while simultaneously shaking its head no.

Lydia remained suspended in place as the insidious being flicked its upraised finger once again. Lydia closed her eyes and screamed in agony, for it felt as if something inside her was being ripped from her. She gnashed her teeth in response to the intense pain, but remained suspended there, writhing and convulsing wildly as the creature looked on, smirking, as it enjoyed her suffering. Lydia opened her eyes the instant her head snapped violently backwards, not unlike one who has suddenly released the rope during a tug of war match. Once she focused, she was aghast to see a transparent version of her own head and neck jutting away from her physical body. She panicked, thrashing even more wildly since she realized the creature was tearing out her very soul. Her struggle was futile for the beast held her firmly under control. All she could do was watch helplessly in horror and agony as her soul tore further and further from her flailing body.

Once the last portion of her soul had been detached completely free from her, the beast again rotated its raised finger, which immediately set Lydia's soul to rotate around and hover face to face with her. As she looked at the mirror image of herself, she could vaguely see her entire history to date playing out within the interior walls of the transparent form. She saw little images drifting about, ranging from her earliest childhood with her mother feeding and playing with her. The image of her dad teaching her to ride a bicycle caught her attention. One after the other, long-forgotten memories became apparent before her eyes. Like watching videos of her life enclosed in little glowing blobs, in a short time, she was able to relive getting her beloved first puppy, Rosebud, and how her heart broke and she sobbed for days when he died. A tear welled up in her eye and rolled down her cheek as some of the images brought back very stirring emotions.

Lydia could make out the time she encountered Magda the European Mystic, she witnessed in awe, as recent events, including meeting and bludgeoning Annette unconscious, only a short time before, were all visible. The last thing she noticed was the moment she entered the room in search of the missing dagger.

The shadowy figure stood from the position it had been crouching, and lowered its upraised hand, causing Lydia's body to abruptly drift back and rest on the floor. As soon as her feet touched, she again attempted an attack, but once again, she was stopped short as if tethered to the wall. The beast turned its gaze towards the direction where Magda's bones had disintegrated to dust; miraculously, the old woman's corpse began to regenerate, literally the same as it departed. The dust re-formed bones and the skull, organs re-emerged inside the cavernous bone structure. Eyeballs refilled the empty sockets, cartilage and ligaments reattached to the bones, and before long, skin and hair were slinking back over the old woman's skull and bones.

Magda's eyes flicked open and darted around; she appeared slightly dazed. She sat up on the bench and surveyed her surroundings, shaking her head slightly to clear the cobwebs from her brain. Once the old woman gained her composure, she looked up at the beast, becoming wide-eyed and shuddering slightly. Then she looked, discovering Lydia standing close, with her soul still suspended slightly above and in front of her. Suddenly, everything that was occurring became clear to Magda: "Child, try to be defiant in the face of impending doom." A pained expression of sorrow and support became apparent on Magda's face: "Glory be with righteousness, do not falter in the face of the wicked, for it will assuredly reward your suffering." Magda raised her arms in Lydia's direction, "Resist; sacrifice your shell to save your soul."

No sooner had Magda spoken those words than the shadowy figure gracefully vaulted its body with the ease of a professional gymnast from atop the table, landing directly alongside where the old woman sat on the bench, quickly grabbing her with both hands around her throat and shaking her unmercifully. Her weary old frame offered no resistance as she flailed weakly in its grasp, her head snapping back and forth in a violent, painful manner. Eventually, the creature halted its vile reaction to Magda's dissent, and a trickle of blood ran from her nose; it appeared as though she were about to black out. Unable to lift her head any longer, Magda made a valiant final effort of resistance to offer a few faint words of wisdom and encouragement to Lydia, "Abandoning your purpose will oblige you, minion, to serve the onslaught of evil."

In a display of disdain for Magda, the dark one violently thrust her limp body into its embrace, causing a rush of breath to be forced from her lungs. Suddenly, Magda's body burst into flames as the creature continued its forced embrace on her flaming body. The beast opened its mouth, exposing those pointed white teeth, and ferociously bit onto her throat, clamping its jaw hard, tearing through her flesh. Magda's tortured cry had been cut short by the jagged teeth as they pierced her esophagus. Blood coursed from the wound as it was being inflicted. The old woman's eyes rolled back in her head, and she began to convulse involuntarily, as the creature continued to bite yet harder, causing audible crunching and sickening ripping sounds. Lydia was overwhelmed at the sight playing out before her, in a combination of sorrow and revulsion overtook her as the smell of Magda's burning flesh filled her nostrils. Lydia's emotions spilled over as she was forced to witness the extreme level of Magda's suffering. Lydia could not bear to be witness to the horrifying sight as she cried out, pleading, "No, stop, please!" Lydia's heart wrenched, and she sobbed as she felt helpless, unable to assist the old woman being viciously ripped apart and burned simultaneously. Because even though she had not known the old woman for very long, she felt an unusual bond for the short time they had spent together.

The brute concluded its ruthless attack, as it forcefully shoved Magda's flaming body back away from its powerful embrace while continuing to keep a tight grasp, with jaws clenched around her throat, ripping the flesh and internal organs free as it pushed. As the remainder of Magda's flesh gave way to the biting and ripping motion, she lay flat once again across the bench, convulsing slightly, blood coursed from the wound, and gurgled audibly in her mouth. The old woman's chest heaved up, trying in vain to gasp in a last breath as the life ebbed once again from her form. The beast turned its murderous red gaze towards Lydia, purposely to catch her attention while callously spitting the old woman's still flaming flesh onto the floor, before flipping once again gracefully through the air, reclaiming its perch on the table top.

The shadowy demonic figure stepped forward, then crouched and sat with its legs and feet dangling from the edge of the table, swinging towards the floor. Lydia could feel the piercing power of its menacing stare as it looked up towards her, raising a hand that had been placed flat on the table top. A small glowing dot appeared above the creature's upraised palm and began growing in size and brightness. The dot grew to the size of a marble, then the size of a grape, and then to the size of an egg. Something was becoming increasingly visible, swirling within the interior of the now snow globe-sized orb. As Lydia looked closer, straining her eyes somewhat to focus on the glowing ball, she began to recognize her own image being displayed. The image playing out within the globe remained cloudy, barely able to be recognized, but she could see herself looking happy, being accompanied by an unidentifiable male; she wore a white dress and donned a beautifully flowered veil in her hair. The image she could discern gave her the impression that she may be witnessing her own future wedding; a warm feeling of happiness and security overtook her as she looked on.

The glowing orb she had been looking upon drew further back from her view as another glowing dot appeared in its spot. Once again, the dot started small in size and began increasing, growing steadily larger, and larger until it too revealed a small, blurry scene swirling about within. The scene remained unclear, but small, barely audible, faraway sounds emanated from within the glowing orb. Lydia began to recognize her own voice, sounding somewhat pained and distressed, then followed by words of encouragement, "Push, you're almost there, I can see the head," immediately followed by the sound of a newborn scream. Shortly, that orb also drifted back to rest by the other that was still hovering in the background.

Yet another glowing orb began forming, growing faster than the previous two. Within just a short time, the globe had grown, revealing another blurry scene of Lydia looking happy and running, the sound of little kids laughing quickly poured out to greet her before the globe disappeared once again, as the others had before. No sooner had that orb moved when two more glowing dots formed and grew much more quickly than the others. Quickly, they had inflated to full size before inaudible sounds of her laughter, and voices were detectable. This continued for a while, new dots began appearing, growing and crowding back in rows of three and then rows of four, each time growing more quickly until there seemed to be many glowing spheres hovering above the beast's hand.

The sound surrounding Lydia was becoming maddening as the creature motioned, sending the swirling spheres floating in a line around the head and body of Lydia's still suspended soul. Lydia closed her eyes and covered her ears, and accidentally dropped the dagger in an attempt to block the churning sights and sounds that whipped quickly past her. The spheres whipped by her for just a short time before she felt them stop suddenly, and remain frozen in place before she opened her eyes to see what was going on. As she opened her eyes, her hands remained cupping her ears to block the sounds that remained, and she saw the line of glowing orbs being sucked back towards the dark creature still seated on the table. Quickly, one at a time, the line raced back, being sucked into the grim figure's outstretched palm one at a time, until they had all disappeared from view.

Lydia looked on as the sinister creature stood fully on the floor and began to advance towards her; she panicked and attempted to reach down for the dagger. As the creature approached where

Lydia's soul remained suspended in the air, it pressed on, undaunted as it passed its head and shoulder directly through her soul's feet and lower legs. An electrical sound came forth as the creature's dark presence passed through the boundaries of her soul. Lydia shuddered from the contact as the dark one passed through her soul, for she could feel its cold presence coursing through her entire body, like an evil current. In the mere fraction of time it took the beast to pass through her soul, Lydia became fully aware of the intensity of its power. She reached frantically, trying to pick up the dagger as the dark one drew closer toward her. Lydia felt the dagger by her feet and grabbed, standing just in time to be met with the approaching beasts' piercing red eyes, staring face to face with her.

The faceless, shadowy creature stood before Lydia, staring into her eyes. It smirked for it delighted in her fear as her heart pounded visibly pulsating her jugular veins. Lydia's eyes quivered back and for as she struggled to focus on any particular visible features of the creature's face, she noticed the glint of its pointed white teeth as it smirked, an obvious sign of its enjoyment of her discomfort. She struggled to search for any other facial features, but it's eyes, she did not want to look directly into those eyes. Nothing became immediately apparent as the creature drew closer; its face had the appearance of smoke captured in a bubble, dark, murky, and swirling, lacking any form or visible attributes. The beast drew its head closer, forcing Lydia to look into its amber eyes.

Gaze's eyes bore into the core of her being, as they flickered with murderous intent. Lydia remained still, for she was paralyzed with fear, trembling slightly as the shadowy figure drew within inches of her. She turned her head, unable to bear to look upon it for another second. The unearthly form drew even closer until it almost touched its face against hers.

Suddenly, without thinking, Lydia thrust the dagger upwards, striking the beast just below where she thought its chin should be, causing the weapon to jolt, slipping slightly in her grasp. The creature jumped, emitting an ear drum piercing shriek as the blow seemed to have taken it by surprise, and again, after readjusting her grip, she thrust upward with all her might, hoping to witness the pointed end of the blade come bursting out the top of the shadowy head.

Lydia could feel something cold coursing from the wound she had inflicted over her fists, as she continued to keep them grasped firmly onto the handle of the dagger, where it remained lodged deeply within the beast. The substance did not feel like blood, or even liquid, but more of a thick, cold, gassy substance that did not leave her skin feeling wet as it passed, dropping to the floor and disappearing. She continued struggling to force the blade into the creature, hoping it would pierce completely through, when suddenly she became alarmed to hear Magda's familiar accent all around her, "Child, pay attention to this warning, you will be faced with a grave situation in the future, you must begin preparing now…" Lydia noticed Magda's voice had trailed on the last word, making a noticeable emphasis on it.

Lydia looked around to see if she could catch a glimpse of Magda's apparition, but was distracted by the jerky movements of the creature hooked by the blade of the dagger she held firmly in her grasp. As she looked back towards the creature she noticed it's head resting just on top of the point of the dagger, it's mouth opened slightly and it began to speak in Magda's voice, "Mediocrity escorts demise," her voice hissed forth, it's moved perfectly in time as it pronounced the syllables in her distinct accent, laughing in a demonic, witchey voice that continued to sound like Magda's mixed with someone else's.

No sooner had those words surprised Lydia into turning her eyes back to face the beast, when the creature raised its head, jamming it back onto the blade of the dagger hard enough to puncture straight through the top as Lydia had hoped would happen for her. Lydia's eyes widened at the sight, and she let go of the dagger handle, partly due to the astonishment of the creature thrashing about, but more as a result of shock that the creature would throw itself onto the blade in such a violent manner.

As Lydia let go of the blade, the beast once again flashed its white teeth as it smirked at her. It grabbed the handle of the dagger with both hands and slowly began inching the blade that had lodged firmly in its head. As the tip of the blade exited the wound, where it had been thrust, a small amount of murky swirling substance dripped from the wound onto the blade. A glint of smugness seemed to be evident in its eyes, for otherwise the creature's face did not show any other discernible expressions. The creature raised the blade face level, as a long, snaking, forked tongue slinked quickly from its mouth, wrapping around the blade of the dagger, becoming coated in the murky substance that had leaked onto the blade as it was yanked free from the gaping self-inflicted wound. After collecting every drop of substance from the blade, the creature reeled its vile tongue back up into the black hollow from where it had produced.

Without a word, the creature again raised its hand, pointing a single finger into the air, and began waving it from side to side while shaking its head back and forth. Swiftly, her fiendish foe flipped backwards through the air, passing completely through the boundaries of Lydia's soul once again, causing a shockwave of current to jolt her body. The creature's mouth formed a snarling appearance, exposing its pointed teeth as it flipped gracefully back atop the table. Lydia was overwhelmed by terror because she knew her dissent to the malicious figure's presence would surely lead to her demise. She watched in horror as the creature pointed to her still suspended soul, causing it to visibly jar as the dark one regained its invisible grip. Suddenly, Lydia's soul rotated harshly, stopping abruptly to face the dark beast's terrible fury.

Lydia became dismayed, for she sensed the beast would be merciless in its vengeance for her dissension. The dark creature raised its hand, pointing towards Lydia's soul, causing it to quiver rapidly. The vile figure whipped its upraised hand in a swooping motion to the right, causing her soul to simultaneously soar through the air and slam forcefully backwards, directly into the oil lamps Lydia had lit before meeting Annette. The impact of the lamps caused oil and flames to gush forth and engulf her soul. Lydia writhed about as she could feel the searing agony of the heat within her body, as the flames quickly began to spread and incinerate her very essence. The creature hunched down on all fours before leaping over to her blazing life force, and without hesitation began biting and slashing into the fiery mass, ripping bits and shreds of flaming material and consuming them ravenously.

In the distance, Lydia could more distinctly make out the sound of voices she had heard when leaving the room in search of the dagger. The very distinct sound of roaring flames and breaking glass filled the air around her. The dark one stood aside, Lydia's still flaming soul, its shadowy silhouette began fading from view, before it disappeared, it pointed in her direction and uttered a low growled warning, "Do not interfere." Suddenly, firefighters burst into the blazing room, spraying water from a hose. Lydia could make out their voices muffled by the protective breathing equipment they wore: "Over there, it looks like a body on fire, pull the hose this way."

Chapter 8: Fight or Flight

Lydia continued to hear the activities of the firefighters as she ascended from her dreamlike trans. The sounds began to trail off, but she could still hear them shouting to douse the burning corpse. Suddenly, she snapped into reality and realized that she had been standing in the same position where the dagger had slid from its hiding place in the box towards her feet, and she had subsequently retrieved it from there. She stood there still holding the dagger, taking heaving breaths and perspiring a great deal, for she could still feel the last of the intense heat and burning sensation just beginning to subside as she reminisced about her soul becoming consumed by the flames, and torn apart by the dark menace.

Thinking of it made her weak, and she wobbled, slightly unsteady, dropping the dagger so that it stuck blade-first into the hardwood floor, swaying side to side. As she wiped the streams of sweat from her forehead, face, and neck, Lydia began to feel weak in the knees, causing her to slump down to her knees on the floor. She would remain there until able to regain her composure. She remained there with her hands in front of her knees, bracing her upper body as it slumped forward with her head hanging, as droplets of sweat continued to trickle from her forehead and the end of her nose, each droplet falling as if in slow motion, echoing like an explosion in her ears as it spattered on the floor.

She remained in that position until she regained her breath, again wiping the accumulating sweat from her brow. Lydia looked down at her body to reveal that all of her clothing had become drenched with sweat, resulting from her encounter with the agent of evil. After a few minutes in that position, she had regained her composure enough to venture a look around the room, noticing it looked exactly as it had before, door open, boxes scattered, and the overhead light still on. Much to her surprise, as she gazed about the room and out the window, it became apparent that she had been caught up in the hallucination for only a short time, even though it seemed as if it had been far longer, hours even. She discovered the sun still hung low over the horizon, only a little lower than when she first entered the room in search of the dagger.

Lydia stood from her kneeling position, pulled the handle of the dagger, and wiggled back and forth until it came loose from where it had stuck in the floor. As she stood in place motionless, Lydia began to second-guess her prior convictions about her duty to rid the world of this evil menace. Her brain became awash with many doubts and reservations, for she was shaken to the core when she considered the consequences as revealed to her in the dark figure's vision. "After all," she thought aloud, "Magda didn't give me much instruction before she shoved off; she just simply instructed me to take the book and read it cover to cover, for someday I would need the knowledge it contained." Lydia raised her fist, shaking it angrily in the air, "Well, I did that, dammit, but it's not good enough!" She shouted in frustration, "How could I have known that I should have memorized it word for word?"

Lydia slumped back to the floor sobbing gently, for she knew that facing the dark one most assuredly meant her demise, "Why should I risk my life in vain?" Her voice choked off as she buried her head once again into her folded arms. She sat there in silence except for the sound of her sobs, half expecting that she would experience some supernatural intervention from Magda directing her away from peril, offering her more detailed instructions as to defeat the dark force, but alas, she heard nothing.

Suddenly, the door she had left open upon entering the room slammed shut with a tremendous bang, causing Lydia to jump and clutch her chest. A second later, the overhead light she had turned on before searching for the dagger shut off, adding to her already heightened state of anxiety. Lydia's heart once again began racing, "Fuck, this can't be happening." She couldn't accept that this could be the end for her, after all she had tried to be a good person, there was no reason why her life should have to be snuffed so short, "Let someone else take the risk, someone who's prepared to sacrifice themselves."

Lydia stood to her feet and began trying to convince herself that this was the proper course of action, "Yeah, certainly it won't make any difference if I try and fail only to pass the burden on to someone else anyway." She began pacing back and forth, "It doesn't make sense to sacrifice myself only to lose out in the end anyway, who would blame me?" She had just about made up her mind, "Yeah, I can just leave and act like nothing happened, or help rouse Annette and send her on her way, maybe she won't remember me hitting her with the club, then I could just convince her that she fainted and hit her head during the fall." Lydia's thoughts of cowardice became of great solace to her, "Yeah, I could just put this all behind me, pack up and start over again in another town far from this place."

Lydia had herself convinced that this was going to be her plan of action, but as she reached the doorknob of the room, she began to rethink the situation: "What if the dark one had conjured up those visions in an attempt to scare me off?" She stopped for a second to consider the situation from that perspective, "Kind of like bluffing, by trying to put a good scare in me even though it knows I really have the upper hand in this situation." Lydia's mind raced as she weighed each of the possibilities. She felt compelled to recall something that Magda had said during her encounter with the dark figure: "Magda said something like Glory be with righteousness, do not falter in the face of the wicked, for it will assuredly reward your suffering."

Lydia's mood lightened somewhat after recalling Magda's words, "Ahh, that shrewd old woman, she was subtly trying to tell me that although encountering this peril would not be easy, if I stand strong, I will prevail over the unborn menace." Lydia was starting to swing her decision towards taking action instead of fleeing from the situation. "Magda gave me the tools I need to be successful at snuffing out the menace when it is at its most vulnerable." Lydia leaned her shoulder against the door, "Magda had said something about smiting the evil seed at the root, mmm…," her voice trailed off, for she began to contemplate what that may have meant. She turned to see that the sun had sunk even further on the horizon, time was passing, and she needed to act quickly. "Does that mean I am supposed to do away with Annette as well, I wonder?"

Lydia decided she could waste no more time contemplating, "I wish I had paid more attention to Madga's guidance years ago; I would be so much more prepared for this now." With that, she placed her foot against the door for leverage, just as she had done in her vision of confronting the dark one, and placed her ear close by the door to see if she could hear anything stirring or breathing on the other side. After listening intently for a time and hearing nothing, she slowly turned the knob, being careful not to make any noise. She kept her foot wedged at the edge of the door, while opening it just a crack, to ensure some level of control if someone, or something, tried to force entry into the room.

Lydia pulled the door open just a crack of about two inches and peeked out to the left and right, to scope out what danger could be lurking on the other side of the only barrier that could separate her from hazard. Again, nothing unusual appeared; she could see the front door remained closed with the shade drawn just as she had left it. She then put her ear to the crack to listen for any sign of activity around the door. She heard nothing, just silence. She ventured a guess that it might be safe for her to open the door further, and as she shifted her weight to remove her foot from its wedged position against the open door, her hand slipped from the knob, causing the door to shut completely. "Oh shit", she recoiled because that is exactly what had happened during the earlier hallucination, she imagined opening the door to the smell of burning wood and black walls.

Lydia prepared herself for anything as she pulled the door open slightly and looked out again. Everything appeared normal, so she poked her head through the opening to peer out, turning to survey the situation to the left and right. She could see clearly down the hallway leading to the room where the two women had been sitting and saw that Annette remained in the position she had fallen. Lydia gasped a sigh of relief and chuckled a little, "If the walls had been black, I probably would have jumped out through the glass of the window to safety."

She gathered her courage and stepped from the room. The moment she entered the hallway leading from the waiting room, where Annette still lay unconscious, she immediately became uneasy, and her skin crawled, giving her the distinct impression that something was amiss. Lydia warily looked up above the doorway she had just walked through; it was shrouded in shadow, and nothing seemed abnormal at first glance. But Lydia abruptly bounded backwards, smashing full force into the hall wall behind her, as she saw a pair of ember red eyes appear in the darkness above the doorframe. Suddenly, she noticed an outline of the grim figure which had been hidden in the shadows perched on the wall above the doorframe, exacting its ember red glare directly at her. She screamed for in the split second that she noticed its presence, the vile beast began reaching towards her.

Lydia lost her nerve and simply shut her eyes and began screaming in response as she covered her head with her arms, hoping to shield herself from its advance. She stood there in that position, cringing and screaming repeatedly for a short time, but was somewhat surprised when she was not swooped off her feet to some wickedly cruel demise. She opened her eyes and lowered her arms from her line of vision. There was nothing around her. Lydia did not let her guard down and continued scanning the area in the halls, and rushed to flip on the light switch, illuminating every corner of the hallway, her heart still flailing. She looked back up to the wall over the door frame to see nothing more than a lone spider scurrying from the light; she had just imagined seeing the shadowy figure clinging to the wall in the darkness.

Lydia felt ridiculous for overreacting, and she scolded herself aloud, "Way to keep your head under pressure, Lydia." She slapped her forehead as a sign of visible disgust and continued to head in Annette's direction, but left the light on in the hallway for security. She carefully approached the door leading to the room and leaned on the wall, a little hesitant to look around the corner, for she did not want to be surprised to see the shadowy figure perched on top of the table. Lydia could still clearly see Annette's unconscious blood blood-spattered form lying in the same position she had last seen her in (although it felt like hours), only minutes before. She gathered her courage and slowly pushed her head into the room, looking towards the direction of the table, and was relieved to find nothing there. She then reached her hand across the wall and flipped on the overhead light, and turned her head to look above the door, ensuring she was not going to be surprised by any more figments of her imagination perched on the wall above the doorframe. She breathed a sigh of relief, for there was no agent of evil lying in wait to seize the opportunity to pounce on her.

Lydia, having checked all around to ensure it was safe, entered the room and immediately went over to where Annette was located, and made note that she had not even moved from the position Lydia had pushed her into. She then retrieved the book and began flipping through the pages in search of the section she wanted. As soon as Lydia picked up the book, she noticed Annette's belly began heaving and expanding, "Ah, you know something is going on out here." Lydia stopped flipping when she reached the illustration of the mother pregnant with the evil spawn. She flipped to the next page and noticed a picture of the same pregnant woman lying out across a table with her hands and feet bound, a man dressed in a black robe stood over her with the dagger in hand. Lydia began to read aloud what was written, "The evil soul must enter the earth, being born of a woman with whom it will share little or no maternal bond after delivery." She continued reading, glancing from the text over to Annette to watch for her to stir, "Annette should be out for a good couple of hours because of the sedative I added to her tea."

She continued reading, "The evil soul singles out its host, the chosen mother is most likely unable to sustain life within her frail womb, and has conceived an empty soulless shell that would normally be expelled, incapable of survival." "The foul essence fills the empty vessel and begins to strengthen its negative energy." Lydia turned the page and looked at the next illustration, which depicted the evil-looking imp alongside an angelic-looking baby; the drawing of the pure soul even included a halo. "The introduction of the evil seed will prompt another empty vessel to be filled with a virtuous presence, to offset the negative impact."

Lydia was becoming increasingly impatient to get the ritual underway, so she skimmed the text and flipped the next page, which contained another illustration depicting a woman with her hands and feet bound. Two men stood by the bound woman, one held her down at the shoulders, while the other was reading from the book. This illustration prompted Lydia to read more carefully, "An assistant should be present during the ceremony to help subdue the recipient should she become uncooperative, and the assistant's task also includes acting as guardian to the circle. Lydia rolled her eyes in disgust, for she was alone. After mulling over that she did not have anyone to help her, she decided to push on with the ritual, "I probably won't need any help since Annette has been heavily sedated."

She came across the ingredients essential to conducting the ritual: "I need to surround the altar with four lighted candles placed at foot level just outside each point of the square." Reading aloud, she continued, "Lamp oil must be heated in preparation to rub on the stomach of the host; this will overcome the perception of the dark spirit from within the womb, and aid in extracting and driving the ghastly presence from its haven." As Lydia read those words, Annette's arms and legs began to twitch in a jerky manner, her stomach heaved more noticeably, for just a few seconds, before seizing all movement and becoming perfectly still. Lydia glanced over, barely taking notice of the temporary increase in Annette's activity, but did not pay it any mind, for it was short-lived. Lydia turned her attention back to the reading and became more deeply immersed in preparing the sacred space for the ritual. She read on, "Incense must be lit and left to smolder as it is placed around the head and feet of the host."

Lydia stopped reading and hurriedly dashed past Annette, for some of the ingredients she needed were located in the kitchen. She shuffled carefully, so as not to trip over the debris that remained strewn about the floor, as she passed through the dimly lit room. She headed towards the cabinet where she knew the bottles of lamp oil had been stored, flinging the door open with a bang. Lydia struggled in the dark to see inside the cabinet and diverted her attention, for a moment, to push in the power button, causing the light located in the stove hood to flicker on. Once some light helped illuminate her search, she reached once again into the cupboard, feeling around for a full bottle of lamp oil. Her first grab produced a half-empty bottle, but her second reach yielded a full, unopened bottle. She quickly unscrewed the top and emptied the contents into a pot, and placed it onto the stove burner, setting the range on simmer. After placing the lamp oil to heat up, she squatted on her hands and knees and began sifting through the debris that had been emptied earlier from the drawers during her frantic search for the dagger. Lydia swiped through the debris, causing it to scatter further yet in all directions, eventually producing one, two, then a third and fourth black candle from the rubble. She stood and began making her way back past Annette to where she had left the book on the table, placing the four black candles onto the table before turning to retrieve a dozen incense holders and a pack of incense from the drawer inside the table.

Lydia inserted the incense into the holders and rested them on the table next to the candles. She began searching for the place in the book where she had last finished reading. As she found where she had left off, she continued reading, "The burning incense must be placed upon the altar, surrounding the head, and tightly bound hands and feet of the host to the evil spirit." The illustration on the next page depicts the naked woman with her feet bound to a board to keep them apart. Restraints secured her arms so that they rested behind her neck, and the rope appeared to wrap around her throat as well. "The smoldering incense will fill the circle and aid in clouding the vision of the dark one, offering a degree of protection to those inhabiting the inner sanctum, from the enraged menace as it is expelled from its host." "The heated oil must be rubbed on the stomach of the host to create an unsavory environment for the dark spirit to remain, helping to smooth the goal of the extraction."

Lydia quickened her pace, reading on again, scanning the writing for any directions as to how the ritual should be conducted. After a little while, her eyes locked onto what she considered could be a significant step and began reading the instructions aloud, "The goal of the cleansing ritual is to purge the vile spirit while it is most vulnerable, in the womb." "For any offspring inhabited by an acutely negative spirit will be destined to rise and make a very harmful impact during its existence." "It is essential to create a sacred space which is to contains an altar of wood or stone. The sacred space is to be enclosed by a circle of power that can be constructed of wax, chalk, sand, or stone, within which the energy of darkness will be contained."

Lydia immediately thought the wooden table she and Annette had been sitting at would serve as an altar. She stood from the bench she had been kneeling on while reading the book and removed the teacup Annette had left behind, placing it on the floor before trying to grab the edge of the table and drag it to rest in the middle of the room. She tried several times unsuccessfully to get a sufficient grip on the edge of the heavy wooden table, but struggled in vain. Finally, after several tries, she became frustrated, and at about the time, she lost her footing and flopped hard backward on the floor onto her rear.

Lydia sat in that position for a second before realizing that she could clench the dagger in between her teeth, freeing up her hands to allow a better grip on the table. She grabbed onto the edge of the table and planted her feet in such a way that she figured would give her the best leverage, and heaved backwards with all her might. The heavy wooden table remained stuck for another second before beginning to give way, making a cracking sound as it moved about six inches from the place it had settled, sending Lydia once again flopping painfully onto her backside. She immediately got up and headed to where the table had initially rested by the wall, and placed her foot against the wall, heaving once again until she had moved the table even further out from the wall. Lydia was determined that she was going to move the table into the middle of the room and moved it in between the table and the wall, placing her back against the wall and shoving with the force of her legs to move the table another two feet. She stood and shoved with the bottom of her feet planted against the wall, pushing until her arms stretched out fully. Lydia then approached the table and heaved with the force of her rump until she was finally able to force the bulky table into the center of the room.

Lydia was nearly exhausted by the time she dragged the bench over to where she had struggled to move the table, and continued to use it to kneel on as she read, "The sacred space must be prepared to receive the unholy spirit and effectively contain it to be permanently and forever cast out of its host." She continued reading, "Create a half circle around the altar with the chosen material, and begin reciting the incantation to summon forth the spirits of purity and the guardians of banishment and exile, before placing the subject of the ritual, lying face up, onto the altar."

Lydia opened the drawer in the table and pulled out a large piece of chalk, and placed the dagger on top of the table as she picked up the book to read the incantation. She began to draw the half circle on the floor as instructed, leaving a path wide enough that a person could easily walk around the entire area of the table while performing the ritual. As she began drawing, she also read the incantation, "I invoke the presence and the power of all the spirits of purity." "Raise up and come forth, oh divine forces of fertility." She continued drawing the circle, reading as she did, "I appeal to the spirits of banishment, and the guardians of exile, come forth and manifest your presence within this circle." "Lend your influence and guidance in this struggle to purge the vile presence forth from the body of this woman." "Oh, keepers of symmetry and stability, the scales have been tilted in favor of all that is foul. Come forth now to inhibit the ascension of wickedness." "I call upon you now to intervene before the dark spirit has a chance to exact its destructive force upon us."

Lydia finished drawing the half circle about the same time she completed the required incantation, "I implore you to demonstrate a revelation of your presence without delay." Lydia stood erect, grasping the book with both hands, and held her breath, looking around the room and listening intently for an indication that she had accomplished anything. After a short pause, she could make out the sound of rumbling, similar to a faraway thunderstorm off in the distance. The sound started faint and far off, but began growing louder as if it were a storm quickly approaching. As the sound drew closer, Lydia took notice of a faint tremble under her feet that intensified with each passing second, so much, that the smaller contents of the house began to audibly vibrate. The vibration and thunderous sound quickly became increasingly intense as it approached and roared over and around the house. The sky outside turned black as night, blocking the sunset, and the reddish-gold skyline completely vanished from view. Lydia's jaw dropped and her eyes widened in astonishment at the sight she witnessed; the wind whipped hard outside the window, it blasted powerfully enough against the house to start the overhead light above the table swaying and flickering. The thunderous sound and force of the air became so intense that Lydia noticed the hair on her head beginning to drift up into the air as it created a vacuum inside the structure. A bolt of lightning struck a tree visible from the window where she stood, sending a branch crashing to the ground. Just as the storm outside seemed to be reaching gale force strength, it simply vanished, the wind died away, and the rolling sound of thunder simply ceased, revealing once again the sun setting on the horizon.

Lydia stood in place for a moment, pausing because she was completely awe-struck, and it took a moment for her to collect herself before continuing. She returned her gaze to the book and began reading once again, "It is necessary to bind her feet at a distance from each other, remaining separated by the span of a wooden block, to ensure uninterrupted exposure to the portal separating the wicked seed from its hiding place within her body." "Her hands must be bound together at the wrists and secured behind the neck, with the bindings being additionally secured by being knotted around the throat." Lydia felt a little disconcerted by the harsh nature of the bindings, but continued reading, "The hands and wrists must be bound in this way before beginning the ritual, to ensure the safety of the participants of the inner circle, for she may become combative and is capable of attack, but will not be accountable for her actions."

Lydia paused for a moment to ponder where she could find the materials needed next, and snapped her fingers as the idea came to her, "There is scrap wood piled behind the storage shed in the back yard, and I saw a coil of rope hanging from a nail inside the shed." As she had the thought, she took hold of the book and headed towards the back door, making note of Annette's stillness as she made her way past. Again, she was careful to shuffle her way through the debris scattered on the floor. As she reached the back door and turned the lock, which produced an audible click, she looked back a final time at Annette, who remained unmoving in the same position.

Lydia opened the back door, taking notice that the hinges on this door creaked, too. "I've really got to do something with all these creaky, broken, and stuck doors in this house." She remained focused on the door as she started to take her first step through, when she suddenly felt something wrapped around her feet hindering her ability to walk properly, knocking her off balance. She tripped forward, taking small shuffling steps as she tried to regain her composure, stumbling onto the wooden porch, unable to regain her steadiness, for whatever had wrapped around her feet remained. She lost her grasp on the book, and it flew from her hands as it tumbled down the steps. She reached for the banister in an attempt to stop herself. Lydia reached out for the banister to steady herself, and about the same time, she began to plummet headfirst down eight or ten wooden stairs leading to the grassy backyard. She felt searing pain as her nails and fingers bent back from the force of her hand striking the banister as she fell, and her knees and wrists thudded across every step as gravity and inertia drug her body down towards the yard. She came to rest with one hand in the grass, another had whacked hard onto the post that secured the banister at the bottom of the steps.

She stayed in that position for a second, reeling from the pain, before readjusting her arm and crawling on her hands and aching knees from the steps until she rested safely on the grass. Once there, the searing pain from her busted knees prompted her to quickly flip into a sitting position to assess her injuries. After sitting, she looked at her knees to see that both of them had been scraped open and were oozing blood from the wounds. She gritted her teeth and her breath hissed past them as she inhaled, as a result of the pain. Then she noticed that she had broken several nails on her hand as she tried to grab the banister in a failed attempt to stop herself from falling down the steps.

Lydia soon discovered, it was the towel she had given Annette to wipe the blood from her face, which had caused her to trip unexpectedly. Unbeknownst to her, it had become tangled around her feet as she dragged them through the debris on the kitchen floor. She did not want to waste a lot of time despairing over her wounds, so she unwrapped the towel from around her feet and simply searched for a clean spot on the already blood-stained towel and applied pressure to her injured knees, wincing from the pain as she did.

The blood from her wounded knees did not take long before it slowed enough for her to stand, and she carried the towel with her as she limped over and bent to retrieve the book, which had slid about four feet from the base of the stairs. She flipped it open and searched for the illustration of the bound woman to use as an example for finding the perfect piece of wood, and then began limping across the yard toward the shed. Lydia opened the door to the shed and retrieved the coiled rope from the nail, and then limped over to the woodpile in search piece of wood she could use to bind Annette's legs apart for the ritual. She picked up the first piece and immediately discarded it to the side, and she continued sorting through piece after piece, but none of them she had picked up seemed right. She continued picking up scraps and boards of wood, quickening her pace as she rejected one piece after another. As she began to thin out the pile, a piece she had thrown shifted some tall weeds and grass, revealing something shiny that caught Lydia's attention. She limped over and parted the grass even further, and peered in, but could not quite make out what had caught her attention, lying shrouded in the overgrowth. Still unable to figure out what it was, she reached in and pulled out a small log about three feet long, with two railroad spikes driven so they poked straight up on both ends. A nail from one of the boards she had discarded must have put a shiny nick in one of the railroad spikes that caught a ray from the descending sun.

Lydia studied the log for a few moments, for it seemed to be the perfect size for binding Annette's legs, "This may be exactly what I was looking for." She picked it up by the spikes that protruded upwards, "Oh, it's heavier than I expected," and replaced it on the ground before she could stand erect. She placed a foot in the middle of the log to brace it still and tugged vigorously with both hands on each of the spikes to test their sturdiness. Neither spike budged slightly, for they were firmly embedded in the log. Lydia noticed visible, round impressions located in various places all around the area of the spikes. "This is probably the handiwork of a pre-teen boy who experimented with his dad's hammer, testing himself to see just how far he could drive the spikes in."

That was all the convincing she needed. She placed the coil of rope around her neck, poking her arm through to allow it to rest comfortably at her side, for she did not want to make another trip down the yard to carry something back. She then grabbed the log in the middle, careful to balance it with one hand as she retrieved the book from the ground with the other. Lydia noticed the towel she had been using to wipe the blood from her gashed knees had fallen to the ground, but decided she had too much stuff, awkward stuff to carry with the book, rope, and the log that weighed over thirty pounds, "I will get that some other time."

As she made her way back towards the house, she began to formulate a plan as to how she had to proceed with the ritual. She thought aloud as she walked, "First thing, I will bind her feet, because if the sedative begins to wear off before I get her onto the altar, those feet will be entirely too hard to control if she is kicking and fighting." "Next, I will bind her wrists, and I have to remember to keep enough of a length so I can secure it around her throat." As Lydia approached the stairs she had plunged just minutes before, she considered the difficulty involved in dragging Annette across the room and hoisting her onto the altar, "Now that will probably be very tough since Annette is unconscious, she is bound to be completely limp and dead weight." As she contemplated the struggle of dragging Annette to the altar, so too did she believe there lay glory that would far reward her...

Although she had scanned the book just a few days earlier, Lydia remembered back to when she had read it years before. Her mind drifted back to the time when she originally flipped through the pages as she traveled on the bus tour through Europe. She envisioned herself studying the illustrations of scenes that portrayed a man participating within the inner sanctum, fending off the woman who had apparently broken free from her bindings and had the chain, with which she was originally bound, wrapped tightly around his throat. She recalled another image on the following page that revealed the same woman restrained to the altar with her head thrown back in obvious pain, one of the men, dagger in hand, held the body of the infant, which had been purged from the woman's body. Lydia then called to mind the image on the next page, which, at the time, and even days before meeting Annette, meant little to her, but now became the essence of her terror. The image revealed the man who was holding the child's body had pierced the pointed blade into its skull through the nostril, releasing the dark soul it harbored, which appeared in preparation to pounce upon the man holding the dagger. The words she had read from the pages so many years before rang ominously out of her mouth, "Be vigilant, for once the vile spirit has been released from its earthly domain, it will seek vengeance on those responsible for its discharge." Lydia could plainly see the illustration on the next page, which revealed the man who had gouged the blade into the skull of the newborn, lying in a puddle of his own blood, all of his limbs and head had been severed and lay strewn about his torso. The dark spirit hovered above the circle and was engaged in a heated struggle with several other specters as they battled to subdue the vile soul.

Lydia began thinking about the near future as she envisioned herself binding Annette's hands and feet as the book instructed. She visualized dragging Annette's body and struggling to hoist her limp frame to rest on top of the altar. The mental image Lydia was conjuring up was very distinct as she saw herself securing Annette to the altar, and even pounding nails into the tabletop to keep the woman firmly in place in the event she began to struggle. Lydia could see herself performing the ritual, shouting over Annette's howls and screams of protest and appeal. She imagined Annette thrashing wildly, for she would surely try to free herself from the bindings, when her pleading went unanswered. Lydia pictured Annette struggling to the point that she might even pull out the nails that had been pounded into the table top, meant to secure the ropes around her wrists and throat. It could be possible if she struggled vigorously, Annette might even rub the skin from her neck and wrists raw enough to bleed, for the rope she carried was very coarse.

While none of this seemed very pleasant to Lydia, she figured it was probably an inevitable reaction that she would have to ignore. The mere notion that she could have to defend herself from the wrath of unadulterated evil suddenly became the basis for her rekindled reservations. As she reached the first step leading up to the back door, her apprehension closed in on her;

126

she felt a grave foreboding sense. Her intuition was giving her a distinct alert of impending trouble. Her skin crawled, and she tensed up as she placed her foot on the first step. Suddenly, her limbs felt very heavy, and she began to experience tunnel vision, which made the back door seem very far away. She became lightheaded and swayed slightly, having to lean against the banister for support. It was clear to her, at that moment, that she was experiencing a premonition forewarning of jeopardy. She had only experienced this sort of eerie feeling twice before, and both times she altered her plans and avoided the mishaps.

Once during high school, at the last minute, she backed out of plans to hitch a ride with four girlfriends to a party. She just knew not to get into the car with them. Lydia remembered how those girls goaded her to get in the back seat, opening the driver's side door, revealing a bottle of liquor resting on the lap of the driver, who leaned the seat of the two-door convertible forward, "Come on, Lydia, climb in the back seat. Mickey Post's party started a half hour ago." Lydia shook her head no as a gesture of refusal, and approached the car and took hold of the driver's hand pushing the seat back again, as she began to plead with them, "Girls, please skip the party tonight, I have a bad feeling, stay here with me we can order a pizza and listen to records, my treat." The occupants of the car exchanged astonished glances before they collectively refused, and one of them said, "Let's get out of here, it's her loss, Lydia, you're a fucking weirdo."

Lydia's mother had been standing out of sight by the door listening to what the teens were saying to each other, and stepped forward, as the carload of friends roared away and barreled down the road disappearing from view, "Lydia dear, why didn't you go with your friends?" Lydia turned around to face her mother, as tears welled in her eyes and rolled down her cheeks, "Mom, I have a really bad feeling something awful was going to happen with my friends in that car." Lydia dashed up the porch stairs, being careful to avoid her mother's embrace, and raced up the stairs and closed her bedroom door as she jumped onto her bed, burying her face deep into the pillow. She lay there for some time imagining her friends driving along, laughing and passing the liquor bottle around, the wind whipping through their hair as they whizzed along. Lydia drifted into a state that lay somewhere between sleep and wake, and her body began to jolt as she envisioned a passenger in the back seat quickly point forward and scream, "Look out!" All eyes in the car faced forward to see the cow in the process of emerging from the woods and stepping onto the road directly into the path of the oncoming car. Lydia jerked again, her expression a pained grimace as she imagined the driver whipping the wheel to try to avoid the animal, causing the car to swerve and strike an embankment, which hurled the convertible upside down as it flew through the air, ejecting the driver and passenger directly behind her from their seats. Lydia could hear the terrified screams of her classmates and breaking glass and crunching metal as the airborne wreck impacted upside down and skidded to a grinding halt. Lydia sat on the edge of her bed and, covering her face with her hands, "Oh, please don't let it be true." She needed to drown out the terrible vision she was having, and grabbed her headphones, placing them over her ears and turning the volume up all the way.

Later that evening, her mother frantically burst into Lydia's room. Lydia remained lying motionless as she removed the earphones. She spoke in an eerie, droll tone, "They're all dead, aren't they?" Her mother hurriedly approached the side of the bed and sat, hugging Lydia as tears began streaming down her own face, "Lydia honey, I just saw on the news that there was an accident on Old Hollow Road." "The four female occupants in the car were dead on the scene. They didn't identify anyone, but I recognized the wreckage. I swear it was the car I saw your friends leaving here in." Her mother lingered on her bed for some time that night, hugging and rocking her daughter, thanking merciful God for intervening. The following morning, the newspaper confirmed her mother's suspicion; from then on, her parents never again dismissed Lydia as eccentric.

Another time, Lydia recalled having a foreboding premonition was the time she and her friend Terri had decided to take an unplanned shopping trip to New York City for the day. As she drove on the return trip, Lydia had that spontaneous, inexplicable urge to exit the Interstate at a town more than fifty miles from their destination of home. They were traveling in the left lane of a four-lane divided highway when Lydia, without warning, decided to exit the highway, changing lanes without signaling, and prompting a hail of horn blowing, arm waving, and obscene finger gestures. Lydia actually had to drive over the median on the exit in order to make it onto the ramp. The suddenness of the turn caused Terri to clutch the dashboard so tight that her knuckles turned white as the vehicle squealed quickly from one lane to the next. Terri was helpless to do anything other than stare out the windshield wide-eyed. She blurted out, her voice reached a fevered pitch, "What the hell are you doing, Lydia?!" "Are you trying to get us killed?"

Terri sat back and placed her hand up on her chest, "My heart is racing, I think you're trying to give me a heart attack." Lydia slowed at the bottom of the exit ramp, as she neared a fork, which gave her the option to go either north or south, "This route follows in the same direction as the highway; in fact, they run almost parallel with each other from here all the way back home." Terri rolled her eyes as she was somewhat annoyed by Lydia's sudden change from interstate travel to the rural route, "Lydia, this way will take longer, the speed limit is only fifty at best, but we can fly home at sixty, or sixty-five on the interstate."

Lydia merged onto the rural route and accelerated quickly to the speed limit, for she could sense her friend's annoyance with her driving, "Terri, just humor me, I had an overpowering impulse to get off the highway right then, without delay, before it was too late." "It's hard to explain, but I have learned to follow my instincts, for they rarely mislead me." "And besides," Lydia continued, reaching for Terri's hand, "We can hop back onto the interstate at the next town if you would like, just consider this is the scenic route."

Terri's expression softened as she took hold of Lydia's hand, for the sincerity in Lydia's tone and presentation dissuaded her from being angry, "Ok, Lydia, you win, I guess I don't mind the scenic route, just no more crazy driving, please." Terri continued, "Just keep an eye out for a gas station, as long as we are off the highway, I might as well make a pit stop." Lydia diverted her eyes from the road to look at her friend, "That sounds like a great idea."

The two ladies continued on the rural route running parallel to the highway to their left; the vehicles traveling up there were just barely visible from where they rode below. Lydia suddenly jolted forward as she drove, for she envisioned a tractor-trailer driver dozing at the wheel as his rig continued traveling along, heading down the opposite side of the highway that Lydia and Terri had just been driving. Her body jerked once again as she saw the tanker hauling highly explosive chemicals drift over the berm of the road and plunge the slight embankment heading straight for oncoming travelers on the opposite side of the highway. Terri noticed that Lydia had convulsed forward the first time and put her hand on Lydia's shoulder, "Lydia, are you ok?" As Lydia convulsed for the second time, Terri too began to experience Lydia's vision, and they both jerked simultaneously, as the vision revealed the truck leveling out at the bottom of the embankment, gaining momentum as it traveled, for the sleeping driver's foot remained depressing the accelerator pedal. The shift from the impact of the tractor-trailer reaching the bottom of the embankment jarred him awake, and he reacted by slamming with all his might onto the air brakes, causing the tires to bite into the soft grass and swerve the entire rig, skidding sideways towards the oncoming traffic. Lydia slammed on the car brakes, causing the vehicle to skid to a halt. Blue smoke rose from the pavement as the two women and all the contents of the car were thrust forward. A second later, the women saw a huge explosion from the highway above them and felt a shockwave and a heat burst over them through the car's open windows. A couple of seconds passed, followed by burning shrapnel and flaming liquid as it rained down all around the car. Both women screamed and reacted by quickly rolling up the windows as a flaming chunk of metal crashed onto the hood.

Lydia and Terri sat quietly awe struck for a short time before Terri spoke, "Holy shit, what the hell happened up there?" Although she had shared in Lydia's horrific premonition, she could not bring herself to believe it was actually possible. Lydia's voice came forth in that melancholy tone, "There's been a horrible accident, with many people involved." She turned towards Terri, whose expression mirrored how startled she felt, "The stink of death is all around us, you feel it too; don't you?" Terri did not utter a word and remained unblinking as she nodded her head in confirmation. Lydia eased her foot from the brake and began slowly maneuvering around the burning debris that lay strewn all around the street. She drove about a quarter mile down the road to get closer to the thick black plume of smoke that rose from the highway above them, pulled off the side, and shifted the transmission into park. Both women exited the car and struggled as they climbed up the steep embankment. As they reached the top, a scene of massive chaos and grisly carnage came into view. An assortment of twisted burning vehicles surrounded the burning hull of the tractor-trailer and the flaming cargo it had towed only minutes before. The agonized screams of people pleading for help filled the air, which was heavy with the stench of burning rubber and flesh. The women choked, and their eyes watered, for the thick smoke that filled the air was too harsh to breathe. They did not move from the spot they had originally climbed, for the fire was still raging on the wreckage, generating intense heat that was still noticeable even from the distance they were at. They could only stand there, unable to help anyone, trying to comprehend the scene before them as police and rescue personnel began arriving. Terri turned to Lydia, "If you had not turned off the highway when you did, we would probably have been involved in this crash." Terri's voice sounded almost gleeful as she continued, "It's truly a miracle that you knew how to turn off like that; if you didn't, we both could be dead right now."

Lydia suddenly snapped back to reality and realized that she had stood in place on the first step leading up to the back entrance for several minutes while she thought back on those earlier premonitions. She felt certain that once again, this was her fundamental instinct warning her of imminent danger, leaving her with the recurring gut reaction to avoid her current course of action.

She continued limping slightly up the steps, shaking her head in disagreement as she spoke aloud, "This is my destiny, the dark spirit has been delivered to me for a reason." "I have been chosen to confront this shadowy soul, and expel it from our presence, forcing it to exist, once again in exile until it can inhabit another soulless shell." As Lydia's foot landed on the step that marked the halfway point between the ground below and the porch, Annette's still slumbering form came into view. It still lay sprawled out in the middle of the kitchen door. Lydia climbed the remainder of the stairs and entered through the still-open back door. She had to stop and put down the log and the book, for they were quite awkward, making it impossible for her to hold them while engaging the lock on the back door. After she closed the back door, she turned the lock, making sure to listen for the clicking sound, for she wanted to slow down Annette's escape if she suddenly awoke and bolted for the door. She turned and picked up the awkward book and heavy log; the rope remained easy to carry since it remained looped around her neck and under her arm like one carries a handbag. She made her way straight past Annette and headed towards the altar, setting the book and log to rest on it.

Lydia opened the cover and began flipping through the pages, looking for the place she had last read just minutes before. She stopped when she recognized where she had last read, and continued reading aloud, "The nurturer of the iniquitous brood must be disrobed and placed upon the altar once having her hands bound tightly by the wrists and her feet bound to the wooden plank." " A lot of blood must be harvested from each of the participants within the inner circle, and the bearer of the vile soul. All of the blood must be collected from an incision made on the wrist with the blade of the dagger. "All the blood must be collected in a silver goblet and mixed with the heated oil, followed by reciting the ceremonial cleansing chant, to purify the mixture. This will help bolster the great effort it will take to coerce the wicked soul from its earthly shell." "This mixture is to be spread over the stomach of the woman within which the wicked seed has taken root, while repeating the incantation compelling it to withdraw from the earthly vessel and relinquish its mortal existence."

Lydia stopped reading and made her way past Annette as she headed straight to a cupboard from which she produced a large silver cup being stored there with the rest of her fine silver. She thought aloud as she headed past Annette once again, "So I have to drag you up on top of the Altar, strip you down, and bind you up, but not before slitting both of our wrists with this dagger and mixing our blood with the hot oil in this finely crafted, genuine silver goblet." Lydia made sure to grab the lamp oil as she passed, which was still simmering on the stove burner. "I see why it advises about having several participants within the sacred space of the inner circle; there's a whole lot of material to prepare for this ritual."

She returned to the altar and placed the pot containing the simmering oil down. While holding the handle of the dagger with one hand, she positioned the sharp, pointed blade toward her wrist. Lydia gritted her teeth as she prepared to prick the blade into her skin. She pressed hard enough so that the pointed edge of the blade caused a visible indentation in her flesh. Then, with one swift bang of the blade on the table, the tip of the blade pierced the thin skin on her wrist, causing a narrow stream of blood to flow down over the blade, and the handle over her hand that she used to keep the handle steady. Lydia's breath hissed through her teeth as she inhaled, for the puncture wound she had inflicted on her wrist was more painful than she had anticipated.

Lydia felt woozy as she positioned her bleeding hand over the goblet, allowing it to drip forth from her fingers and collect within the cup. She felt ever so weak in the knees and knelt slightly, becoming overwhelmed with nausea, for she could never stand the sight of her own blood. Lydia turned her head so she would not have the witness-sickening sight of her blood as it coursed from the wound into the collecting cup; her stomach churned, and her temples pulsated as she felt the wound on her wrist throbbing as it hemorrhaged. Her head spun and her mouth watered as she tried to think of anything other than the pain and the crimson liquid flowing from her wrist. It was all too much for her to bear; she had become seized in the moment and could think of nothing else as she craned her neck and began heaving violently, vomiting on the floor.

Once she had emptied the contents of her stomach onto the floor, Lydia struggled to regain her composure and ventured a peek at the cup to find out if enough blood had been collected. Much to her surprise, the cup had overflowed with blood, for she had expected to see her fingers crusted with dried blood. "That's enough blood from me, now to find something to wrap around this," she thought for a moment and figured out what she needed. She opened a drawer of the table and retrieved an old printed handkerchief that she would occasionally use to tie around her head when she felt like looking especially gypsy like. She tied it tightly around her wrist using her teeth and her free hand to pull the knot tight and apply pressure to the puncture wound.

Lydia figured it was time to get Annette onto the altar, so after she secured the handkerchief to her wrist, she walked over to where the unconscious woman remained sprawled on the floor. She knelt by Annette's fallen body, "Well, you little monster, it's time to get this underway," and she reached out, grabbing hold of Annette's ankles, preparing to heave her limp frame by the legs over to the altar. Lydia grasped Annette's one ankle and secured it in her grip, then she started reaching for the other ankle when, without any indication, Annette sprang up from the position she had remained in on the floor, striking Lydia directly across the side of her face and neck with a forceful blow delivered hard enough to catch Lydia completely off guard.

Annette clobbered her so hard that the blow shifted her jaw painfully to the side and blurred her vision, and knocked her slightly off balance so that she had to release Annette's ankle to catch herself from falling completely over.

Annette's eyes shone with total blackness as her pupils were completely dilated, covering the whites of her eyes. Annette's pupils mutated into a swirling, murky eddy as she once again lunged toward Lydia, mercilessly gouging her fingernails across the side of her throat and cheek. Her nails slashed into Lydia's flesh, laying open four prominent gashes that stretched from the side of her throat in a line that halted by her lips. Lydia reacted to the searing pain inflicted by the wound by pulling away from her attacker, and recoiling for when she touched her face, she could feel the raw flesh that had been exposed.

Lydia realized that Annette couldn't be in control of her movements, for she should still be heavily sedated from the tea she had consumed earlier. And because the dark one had gained control of the situation, Lydia recognized that she was in grave danger and immediately began shuffling her hands and feet, trying to beat a hasty retreat backwards away from her aggressor. Annette lunged once again at her and took hold of the rope that remained coiled around her neck and under her arm, just as Lydia had flipped her body onto her hands and knees to crawl. Although her knees throbbed from the pain of the injuries she had received as she fell down the steps, she struggled through the pain to crawl over towards the altar, and reached one hand, grabbing hold of the dagger. Just as Lydia retrieved the dagger, Annette had gotten to her feet, and heaved with extraordinary strength on the rope still wrapped around Lydia, causing it to constrict around her throat and wrench her body violently backwards, and send her tumbling to the floor. As Lydia was jerked off balance, she lost the feeble grip she had just gotten on the dagger, and it slid just inches from where her hand could reach. Lydia thrust herself towards where the dagger had fallen with her free hand, but before she had the opportunity to readjust her position enough to reach it, Annette pulled the rope, dragging

135

Lydia's flailing body closer. As she struggled, Lydia's one leg came upon the dagger, and she bore down hard so as not to lose it as Annette dragged her even closer yet to where she stood.

The tension on the rope lessened for a moment, allowing Lydia enough of an opportunity to fumble for the dagger under the back of her calf. She reached and grabbed it about the same time she heard an unearthly growling sound and looked to see Annette charging toward her with a meat mallet in her hand raised above her head. Annette had stopped pulling Lydia towards her so she could bend and retrieve the heavy wooden mallet from the floor, for it was amongst the items that had been scattered during Lydia's frantic search for the dagger. Lydia had not noticed Annette retrieving the mallet since she was concentrating on being inconspicuous while she retrieved the dagger from under her leg. Lydia had very little reaction time, for Annette was unrelenting as she charged and swung the meat mallet with a great deal of force, landing the first blow right in the middle of her forehead. The intensity of the blow created a distinct square impression in the shape of the mallet in the flesh of Lydia's forehead. Little red dots appeared where the notched wooden bumps contacted her skull, and a small amount of blood formed and oozed tiny droplets from the crush wound she had sustained.

During the momentary lapse of time that Annette had paused to study the injury inflicted by the mallet, Lydia concluded she could detect an eerie look of satisfaction in Annette's expression. Lydia looked into Annette's coal black, swirling eyes, for they glimmered with an appearance of gratification at the effect the mallet strike had left on Lydia's forehead. Annette only paused for a moment before quickly raising the mallet once again to inflict another vicious blow. Lydia remained slightly dazed from the first walloping blow she had gotten from Annette, as she attempted to move her just moments before from the position where she rested on the floor. Lydia screamed and raised her forearms in front of her in a reactionary attempt to defend her face from the second blow about to be unleashed on her. When she raised her arms, the dagger, which remained in her hand, deflected the intensity of the strike, emitting an audible clanking sound as the wooden head of the mallet made contact with the blade. The force of the mallet as it glanced off the dagger blade forced the weapon from Lydia's grip, causing it to skid about three feet from where she lay. Lydia rolled back onto her knees and started crawling towards where the dagger had stopped. Annette grabbed her by the back of her shirt and pulled her away from the blade, and unleashed another whack, and then another brutal whack onto the back of Lydia's skull. The first whack had not made much of a difference, but as the second whack impacted, Lydia fell forward and grabbed the back of her head, "Ahh...", at first starting as a scream of pain, her voice trailed off as she rolled back onto her back to face Annette.

Lydia had only just rolled onto her back when her foe slammed the mallet down hard on her nose, causing blood to flow forth in an extremely heavy flow. She immediately threw her hands and legs in front of herself for defense of her face and skull, when the dark menace controlling Annette unfurled another vicious cluster of whacks with the mallet randomly about her forearms, knees, and shins. Lydia wailed in pain as the beast landed blow after blow with the mallet. She felt certain that she was about to black out from the intense pain, so she began to plead for her life, "Stop!" "Stop!" Please stop!" The blood from her nose streamed into her mouth, and her voice gurgled out as she pleaded with the dark one, "Please, please be merciful!"

Lydia had hardly noticed that a pause in the strikes that were being unleashed upon her with the mallet had occurred, as she remained crouched in the fetal position for a few seconds after the whacks ceased, still reeling in agony. She opened her eyes to notice Annette had walked over to where the dagger had slid and had retrieved it and was heading back in her direction. A shear wave of panic overtook Lydia, and she reacted by breaking from her defensive fetal position so that she could flee from the menace that was closing in on her. It was too late, for as she broke from that cowering position, Annette was merely a few steps away from her, and only had to quicken her pace a little to be in a position to overpower Lydia. She hardly had the chance to put her hands and feet to the floor to try to scurry before Annette was close enough to pounce upon her.

Annette held onto the dagger as she closed in on Lydia, who began backing up in a vain attempt to escape her encroaching advance. Annette reached down and grabbed Lydia by the throat, and hoisted her up until her feet dangled just inches from the floor. Annette maintained her grip on Lydia's throat, cutting off her ability to breathe and forcing her to look deep into the total swirling, stormy blackness of the dark one's eyes. Lydia attempted to speak, for she felt the urgency to plead once again for mercy, but her words remained choked off by the grip Annette maintained on her throat. Annette raised the dagger and forced Lydia's head to turn towards the direction she had raised it to. Annette raised the pointer finger on her hand, exposing shards of bloody skin under her nails from where she had gouged Lydia's face, and shook her head no while simultaneously waving her pointer finger from side to side. Lydia seized the opportunity to lash out her arms and knock the dagger from Annette's grasp. The dagger twirled slightly through the air as it struck the floor and bounced a few feet away from where Annette stood. Lydia was suspended by her throat.

Lydia's final act of aggression seemed to infuriate the sinister inhabitant of Annette's body, for the moment after being distracted and looking away as the dagger hit the floor, as she turned her gaze from Lydia, her eyes had become ablaze with ferocity. She released her grip slightly on Lydia's throat, setting her back on the floor just long enough for her to gasp in some precious air, and turned, looking in the direction in which the dagger had flown. It seemed obvious to Lydia that the vile soul was contemplating retrieving the blade again. After Lydia had taken in a couple of breaths, she began to plead once again, "Please don't kill me, I beg you," her voice choked off as she began to weep. Annette suddenly turned on Lydia with all the ferociousness and intensity of a rabid wild tiger, grabbing her around the throat once again, but this time with both hands, and lifted her body straight into the air. Lydia did her best to loosen Annette's grip by grabbing hold of her wrists and thrashing her feet wildly, kicking her into the air, striking Annette in the stomach several times, and hitting the altar, spilling the silver goblet of her blood and the pot of lamp oil all over the table top and onto the floor by their feet. The beast was undeterred and shook Lydia violently, causing her head to snap back and forth several times. As Lydia righted her head, in between each of Annette's unrelenting shakes, she could plainly see a vision of the shadowy figure outlining Annette's frame, its arms extended along with Annette's, forming the death grip it maintained on her throat. It became clear to her that she was being attacked by the soul of the beast shrouded within Annette's frame.

Lydia began to lose consciousness as her legs stopped kicking, her body became limp, and her eyes rolled back. As Lydia became less responsive, the grim soul withdrew its attack, no longer shaking her as it placed her feet once again onto the floor, releasing some of the pressure from her throat so she could breathe. Annette cupped her hands around Lydia's head and forced her to gaze in her direction. The grim one was still visible to her as it outlined the features of Annette's face and body. It smiled, flashing its pointed white teeth, and Lydia understood that she was helpless to resist any longer. She gave in and submitted herself completely to the grim figure's command, nodding her head weakly in affirmation that the beast's message had been clearly understood.

The vile presence grinned for it took pleasure in the ability to overcome, subdue, and ultimately crush her spirit; she had totally succumbed to its power, to the degree that it no longer mattered that she resist and stand in defiance. Instead, she simply accepted its domination and was willing to relinquish her own physical well-being to have this battle end in her swift defeat. After the beast finished reveling in its victory, it once again picked Lydia from the floor by her throat and moved while thrusting her toward the wall containing the stand with the candles and lamps that Lydia had lit before Annette's arrival.

Lydia remained unflinching as she flashed back to her earlier vision, for she realized it was then that she had been warned that this would be the consequence of her defiance.

As the unmerciful soul slammed her hard enough against the wall to knock some of the lamps and candles crashing to the floor, catching ablaze the lamp oil which had spilled from the altar, spreading flames throughout the room. The beast held her by the throat with one hand, pinning her to the wall as it ripped off the glass flame guard of an oil lamp, smashing it off the floor, and retrieved the lit lamp from the shelf with the other. She drew the lamp's flame close enough so that the flickering flame could be seen reflecting in Annette's stormy black eyes. It drew the flame towards Lydia's upper arm and placed the heat of the flame directly onto the fabric, causing the polyester-blend robe to sizzle and emit a foul-smelling black smoke. Lydia struggled once again in a great effort to free herself from Annette's unrelenting grip, the words, "Let go," choked short as Annette squeezed even more tightly on her throat. The melting liquid from the robe mixed with the fabric from her shirt and adhered to her skin as it continued to crackle and hiss, burning deeply into the flesh on her upper arm. Lydia screamed from the agony she felt as her clothing began to become more engulfed.

The flames that had started by the falling lamps began spreading all around them, swallowing up the walls, and casting familiar flickering, dancing shadows all around. The blaze quickly spread down the hall and into the kitchen, blasting intense heat on Lydia and Annette. The pain from the blazing clothing on her arm became unbearable as she screamed and writhed in pain for a short time before going completely limp as she lost consciousness. The vile spirit continued to hold her in place for a time as it watched the flames on her clothing spread further up, consuming her shoulder and singeing her hair. Then the dark menace growled as a sign of contempt for its foe, and simply tossed Lydia's limp, flaming body aside with such force that she skidded partway over the altar. The force of Lydia's body hitting the table caused the legs to collapse, and both crashed violently to the floor, surrounded by flames. Lydia lay where she had been thrown; her body did not flinch to move from the position she had fallen, the stoic symbol of a conquered warrior.

Chapter 9: A Brush with Death

The sound from the blaring sirens was low at first, then gradually increasing in intensity, filtered in to stir Marty from unconsciousness. He did not open his eyes immediately, for the moment after he recognized the sound of the sirens, he winced with a pained expression from the excruciating pain in his head. At that moment, he heard voices by him, and someone pried his eyelid open and shone a light in his eyes. His reaction was to resist, for the light intensified the pain in his head. The man who pried his eyelid open left it closed as he asked, "How long has this man been unconscious?" Then he continued, prying Marty's other eyelid apart and again shining a light in, another male voice responded, "He's been out probably about thirty minutes now." Marty opened his eyes slightly and again flinched from the pain in his head, "I've got a fierce headache," he said as he started to place his hand on his forehead.

The man standing over him stopped his hand midway, "You don't want to touch your head right, you're sporting a pretty good-sized gash on your forehead." Marty didn't resist the man as he replaced his hand by his side, his vision was blurred, and it hurt to move his eyes, but he wanted to look around. "Where am I?" The same man who said how long he had been unconscious answered, "You're at the Silver Tracks diner, don't you remember?" The memory of the armed bandits suddenly overwhelmed him, and he started sitting up, "Where's Annette? Is she ok?" The man who pried his eyelid open again prevented him from sitting up: "Just stay put for now, you're pretty banged up, and I don't think you're in any shape to be sitting up." Marty lay back down and opened his eyes, blinking a few times, trying to clear his vision as they darted around uncontrollably. After a little while, he was able to focus somewhat on his surroundings, and he noticed that he was lying in the booth he and Annette had been dining in earlier, for he could see the silverware still jutting from the ceiling above the table.

Marty was able to recall all the events up to and including quietly pleading with Annette to cooperate, but that was all. Annette's adamant refusal to cooperate and his being attacked and hit on the head by the gunman had been wiped from his memory. He became agitated when no one answered his question, "Can anyone tell me where my wife is?" A woman's voice replied, "The woman you were dining with ran out of here after the guy with the guns was dead." Another voice that sounded like a young guy straight from the California coast chimed in, "Yeah, dude, it was like totally bizarre, the one robber shot the other robber from behind while he was fighting with your chick; man, she was giving that dude a hard time." The tanned blonde guy who was talking stepped into Marty's view. He started swinging his hands to make like he was air boxing, "And then like the ugly dude with the gross teeth, way shot himself right in the face, it was totally fucked up."

The paramedic who had been checking Marty over turned to the people who had surrounded them, and motioned with his hands, "Ok, everyone, let's back up and give the guy some air." Then he talked into a radio transmitter, "We are about to transport a Caucasian, mid twenties to early thirties, that has suffered blunt force trauma to the forehead, and has a laceration that more than likely needed suturing, also a possible concussion."

Within a couple of minutes, another paramedic had entered into view, pulling a stretcher. The two of them began stabilizing his neck, placed a board under his back, and strapped him to that, further immobilizing him and restricting his ability to move freely. As they placed him on the stretcher, Marty was able to observe a few police detectives and a guy wearing a jacket that had coroner written in bold yellow letters on the back snapping photos of the dead gunman, both of their corpses surrounded by massive pools of their own blood. Marty fought against the head and neck restraints, trying to get a better look as he noticed a police detective exit through the swinging doors leading to the kitchen. Before the detective released the door from his grasp, Marty was able to make out another coroner with a camera in the kitchen, snapping pictures of the dead dishwasher. It was then that Marty was able to recall fully the details of the bloody, horrid event of that afternoon. He felt sorrow for the young man lying dead in the kitchen, having been so brutally snuffed out at the very earliest stage of living, "How tragic."

The pain in Marty's head intensified as he was jostled on the stretcher while being wheeled through the diner and over the pavement of the parking lot. In no time flat, he had been whisked off into the back of an ambulance, and with sirens blaring, he could feel the ambulance pulling out and barreling down the road. He felt everything jump as the vehicle raced over the railroad tracks he and Annette had crossed on their way to the diner. He knew from the direction they were headed that he soon would be admitted to the same hospital he and Annette had visited earlier for testing.

As the ambulance swayed and dipped with the contours of the road, Marty felt as if his brain were bouncing around inside his skull, and he began to fade out of consciousness, descending into a hazy, dreamlike state. He could not see anything but the misty fog that surrounded him as he opened his eyes; his body no longer felt restrained, and the pain in his head felt dull and distant as he sat up, trying to distinguish where he was. In the distance, he could hear a hollow, echoing sound that he immediately recognized as Annette sobbing. He called out to her, "Annette." He listened intently, hoping to get an idea of where the sound was coming from, but it seemed to be generated from all around him, surrounding him, but somehow distant, as if it was echoing into a valley from afar. All of his perceptions felt askew, and he remained hesitant to venture from where he stood because of the thick mist that surrounded him. He carefully reached out with both hands, feeling and turning slowly around for anything that might be right by him, but still he felt nothing. Once again, distant sound echoed around him. As he listened closely, he could make out the sound of an engine idling, and voices echoed to him. This time, he heard a woman's voice that was not Annette's, "I might be able to help you." Then Annette's voice once again, "No offense, Lydia, but I don't buy into this supernatural mumbo-jumbo."

The sounds began to fade and grow even more distant, and his ability to see, hear, and even comprehend anything around him diminished; it felt as if he were spinning and about to be sick. Suddenly, he drifted closer to reality and was able to open his eyes enough to be able to recognize his stretcher being wheeled through a set of swinging doors with a plaque reading emergency room mounted on each. Marty fought to keep his eyes open as he was wheeled and placed alongside another bed. The paramedic who had been riding in the back of the ambulance with him spoke with the doctor, "His name is Martin Sooner; he was wounded struggling with the gunmen during a botched robbery attempt out at the old Silver Tracks diner." The paramedic looked up from his chart at the doctor, "Some of the other diners told me he took a pretty hard whack on the forehead from the butt of a pump-action sawed-off shotgun, causing a visible laceration and possible brain trauma, and he has been in and out of consciousness since we left the scene."

The other doctors and nurses in the emergency room, on the count of three, transferred Marty from one stretcher to the other and began cutting his clothes off and examining him for evidence of further injuries. The idea of being stripped naked and lying there exposed in front of a room full of people made Marty feel very uncomfortable, but the throbbing in his head and the restrictive nature of the collar around his neck prevented him from voicing any protest, and his head began to spin at the slightest attempt. As his clothes were being cut off, he jumped in reaction to feeling a sharp stabbing pain in his hand, as a nurse had unbeknownst to him begun to pierce an intravenous needle into a vein on the back of his hand, he felt a cold sensation running up his arms as the fluid spilled into his veins. Another nurse placed a blood pressure cuff and heart monitor on his other arm, and Marty could feel the pressure from the cuff as it periodically inflated and gradually deflated to measure his blood pressure and heart rate.

The doctor who had been talking to the paramedic approached the stretcher and carefully removed the neck brace and positioned his hands by Marty's neck and began pressing his fingers into the skin at the base of his skull. Suddenly, the room began to spin, and Marty closed his eyes with the hope that the spinning sensation would stop. The doctor leaned in close, "Martin, do you have any pain or numbness where I am touching?" Marty opened his eyes and tried to focus on the doctor, as everything around him continued to spin. "No," was the only response he could muster. His eyes rolled and closed as he began slipping out of consciousness once again. "Martin, open your eyes, I need you to try to stay awake," the doctor said as he roused Marty slightly by pressing and rolling his knuckle uncomfortably hard into his sternum. Marty squirmed in discomfort as the doctor did that, but was quickly becoming less responsive to what was happening to him, and soon began slipping back into a state of unconsciousness. The spinning sensation increased, and Marty felt himself gagging, "Turn him on his side, he's going to vomit," the lead doctor ordered. Marty could feel himself heaving involuntarily, before they reacted to turn him on his side, and remained completely limp and weak, unable to take action to avoid throwing up on himself; he could distinguish the combination of liquid and solid matter gurgling up from his stomach and into his throat. He had become violently ill and could feel pressure building in his face as he struggled between rounds of heaving to catch his breath. Marty suddenly began choking fiercely and tried desperately to get some air into his lungs; his arms and legs started trembling uncontrollably. The lead doctor yelled out as a response, "He is seizing, get a bite stick into his mouth!" He could sense people scurrying about all around him, but remained unable to open his eyes and look around. He was able to distinguish a feverish-sounding female voice: "All of his vital signs are extremely elevated, and he is going into shock." The last clear thing Marty could understand before he began to descend back into a state of unconsciousness was the lead doctor's voice, "Make sure his airway is clean in the event he has to be intubated."

Marty began to fade from consciousness again, right as he could hear a man's voice growing increasingly faint and trailing off as he spoke, "Let's get him cleaned up and stabilized." "Nurse Rowley, notify x-ray and MRI that he is being sent for emergency imaging, so we can get a better look at the extent of his head wound and any possible neck injury."

As he was being tended to, the voices of the doctor and nurses that were providing his medical attention began to grow fainter, and his perception of light became restricted to a circle that began to shrink as if he were traveling backwards into a hole of darkness. The light grew increasingly distant until it was no bigger than a pinpoint, and then it was gone, and Marty was surrounded by nothing but grim obscurity since he could not recognize a single shape. He remained lying still, surrounded by darkness, only for a short time when a bright light flooded from overhead, illuminating his body, lying still, covered by a thin white sheet.

He remained there lying still with his eyes closed, listening as he could still hear the barely audible voices of the doctors and nurses as they continued to tend to him. In the distance, he could detect a faint crackling sound that was quickly growing louder. The sound increased to the point that it was almost deafening and drowned out the voices of those around him. It sounded like he could be in a room that was surrounded by a raging inferno, but he could only hear the flames. Suddenly, the sound of the fire mixed with the tortured wailing of an unfamiliar female voice desperately pleading for mercy, and the sound of that same woman locked in an intensely heated struggle. He could make out the distinct sounds of feet and hands scratching and scuffling as if fighting to escape her attacker's offensive, and her blood-curdling scream, suggesting she was being subjected to utter torture, followed by some more vigorous struggling, and then a period of silence. The silence was drowned out by the steadily increasing roar of growing flames. After a few moments, he heard an unearthly growl, followed by what he believed to be the sound a body makes if thrust with a great deal of force, for he could make out the sound of skin and clothing skidding, followed by cracking wood and an abrupt crash.

Marty listened intently for a few moments, struggling to discern any noise over the intense noise generated by the spreading flames. He then heard a sound that resembled someone being dragged, immediately followed by slight ripping noises, as if the person was being dragged by their clothing, and the material was faltering slightly with each new movement. Next, he was able to make out what a sound that resembled a doorknob being fumbled with, and then being fumbled with again, and again, followed by a low, frustrated-sounding snarl. The doorknob sounded to Marty as if it could not be opened with ease, and the person trying to open it was becoming increasingly frustrated as they continued turning the handle more violently. Suddenly, there was a click sound and further jostling of the knob, giving him the impression that the person turning the knob had not immediately realized the door had popped open, followed by the conspicuous audible creaking noise of a hinge in serious need of lubrication. Marty could distinguish the dragging and ripping sounds once again, for just a short time, immediately followed by the conspicuous commotion that is caused when a person plummets down a flight of steps.

Marty recoiled as he heard that sound, for he imagined it could possibly be Annette being attacked and knocked down a flight of steps.

Just then, he visualized a blood-spattered Annette surrounded by roaring flames, holding out extended arms towards him. Marty bolted straight up from the position he was lying in and reached out, trying to touch the apparition in front of him, feeling a great deal of angst having seen the image of his wife in danger. He felt a great urgency to yell out to her, "Oh Annette, honey, please, please, tell me where you are, if you give me an idea, maybe I can help you!" He hoped that if she could hear him, maybe she would give him a signal or a sign, any clue to where she could be. Instead, his effort went unheard, and Marty watched on in horror-filled tension as the flames grew in intensity and surrounded his wife until she disappeared from view. A short time later, Marty breathed a sigh of relief as he was able to see Annette. She appeared through the wall of flames, walking slowly out through a burning doorway and beginning to descend some steps towards safety, the burning building a contrast to the dusk sky behind her as the scene faded from his sight.

Marty rested back and closed his eyes, feeling comforted by the knowledge that Annette was safe. A sensation of complete serenity swept over him, soothing and relaxing away the tension that had recently dictated his world, and lingered like a black storm cloud over a golden horizon. He began to slip into a passive state of relaxation and euphoria that alleviated his despair, a place of no worry or concern, somewhere to dwell without the burden that had weighted him down, and for some peculiar reason, he liked the feeling. All of a sudden, an electric shock pulsated through his body, causing him to jolt involuntarily as his head and legs arced, raising his back and shoulders slightly from the mattress. Marty resisted renouncing his newfound claim on tranquility, for he recognized that the journey that lay ahead of him filled his heart with dread, and he preferred not to cope with it.

The stern and familiar voice of his dead father caused Marty's eyes to fly open wide, "Martin Sooner, what the hell do you think you are doing?" Marty lay there awestruck at the sight of his beloved dad standing at his side, and he wanted to jump up and hug him and tell him how very much he missed him, but alas, he could not budge. Marty was overjoyed, for it had been too many years since he had laid eyes on his dad, looking vibrant and healthy, but he could not utter a word or move a muscle, giving him the overwhelming impression that he was being forced to listen. Almost as if they were working behind the scenes, Marty could make out the outline of medical personnel scampering about, working feverishly around him. The sounds of their voices faintly echoed in a garbled manner into his perception, but he did discern the lead doctor announce, "He still has not established a clearly normal heart rhythm, continue chest compressions."

Marty's dad spoke again, "Your time has not yet come; you must not linger here much longer, or it will not be possible to return." "The sentinel chosen to exile the grim spirit has failed, and yielded to its influence." "Do not let your unease mislead you; the dark spirit prefers your absence, for it remains uncertain if your devotion to your wife will dissolve your ability and willingness to influence her judgment in its benefit." Marty's dad began to fade as he spoke on, "Go quickly, and be on guard as you will be enticed by your ethics and the dark ones' sinister manipulation of your senses; it may even make you question your sanity." The doctor's voice filtered in once again as his father completely disappeared from view; "He's still in fibrillation, stop compressions, powering up, clear." With that, another electric current passed through Marty's body, compelling him back into an absolute state of existence. He immediately became conscious and sat straight up on the stretcher, much to the surprise of every medical professional present, and suddenly gasped in a loud, rushing, deep breath. Every eye in the emergency room fell upon him, and they stopped and stared in silent amazement as Marty sat there panting heavily. After a moment, he became aware that he was the center of attention, "Well, I feel pretty popular right about now." They all exchanged surprised glances, but did not speak a word.

No sooner had he spoken when the vivid reminder of the pain in his head came pounding back full force. He winced from the pain and started to raise his hand to his forehead, when the doctor stopped him, "No, no; there now, Martin, just lie back here and relax for a little while, we still have some work to do yet."

Marty did not need a lot of convincing as he complied with the doctor's request, for his head still actively throbbed, and he began feeling dizzy once again. The nurses continued to clean the remaining vomit from Marty, and they covered his shivering body with a blanket. The doctor began to place a temporary dressing on his still open head wound, "That will do just fine for now." The doctor turned to an older nurse by his side, who had a large birthmark on her left cheek, "Now that he has been stabilized, transport him to imaging, and page me on my beeper when we have the results." With that, he turned and began removing his facemask as he exited the room.

As the doctor instructed, the nurses with the birthmark immediately raised the side rails while another younger blonde nurse ensured his intravenous line was not tangled around anything as they released the brake and whisked the stretcher from the emergency room toward an elevator. Marty felt very tired and began slipping in and out of a hazy state of semi-consciousness as he was being transported to the imaging wing of the hospital, causing the journey to be very choppy, similar to being wheeled in total darkness only to have his surroundings revealed to him by the bright flash of a strobe light. The ding of the elevator as it stopped at their floor resonated through Marty's senses, causing him to open his eyes. Everything around him seemed unusual as the blonde nurse stepped onto the elevator and pulled the switch to keep the doors open while the nurse with the birthmark wheeled him on. The rattling of the stretcher wheels as it entered the elevator jarred Marty slightly, and he noticed that everything sounded like it echoed in his ears as the two nurses finished pushing the stretcher through the door. A tall, heavy-set black man dressed in janitor's garb with a bucket and mop had already been riding the elevator, and moved to the side and smiled and nodded slightly at Marty, the nurse with the birth mark stepped on and the doors slid shut, Marty returned the gesture with a pained expression as he slightly nodded his head. The overhead light of the elevator got really intensely bright, and then flickered off for a second, and Marty thought it strange, but it seemed to go unnoticed by the other occupants, so he figured he would just close his eyes and ignore it too. The light flickered once again, and Marty prepared to joke with the janitor about taking care of that right away, when he opened his eyes, the janitor's face was directly in his field of vision, only inches from his face, staring with coal black eyes directly into his eyes. Marty

151

jumped at the unexpected sight startled him. The janitor's hot breath whooshed over his face as he exhaled, and he heard the air draw into his flared nostrils as he inhaled. His voice echoed deeply as he spoke, "Your infidelity and betrayal will not be tolerated." In that instant, the elevator's motion began to conspicuously slow as it drew closer to the proper floor. As the elevator came to a halt, the bell sounded, distracting Marty for an instant, and he diverted his vision towards the lighted floor indicator. Marty had only glanced at the floor indicator above the entrance of the elevator for a fraction of a second, and when he looked back a moment later, the janitor was right back in the position where he had been before, standing to the side, leaning ever so slightly on the wall.

The blonde nurse moved towards the feet of the stretcher, while the nurse with the birthmark on her face remained guiding by his head. The nurses guided the stretcher from the elevator and began pushing it down the hall. The janitor waved goodbye to Marty before he exited the elevator, and as they made their way down the hall, he could hear the doors slide shut and the elevator begin moving to its next destination. Marty once again began to feel like everything around him was surreal. He had a creeping suspicion that something was amiss as they guided his stretcher around a corner, heading in the same direction as a sign on the wall pointed towards the maternity ward. As they rounded the corner and started down the narrow corridor, Marty blinked. They had only just begun the long corridor when he closed his eyes, and in the split second it took him to open his eyes, they had traveled the entire length of the hall, and the stretcher began pushing through the doors with signs reading Maternity Ward.

As the stretcher entered the doors, everything going on around him seemed to be moving in slow motion. The sound of the stretcher passing through the doors clanged and echoed ominously in his ears. His apprehension grew at the sight of a woman, standing, seemingly unaffected by the raging fire that consumed the right sleeve of her shirt, from her elbow to her shoulder. Around her neck, she bore a thick thorn-covered collar tethered from the back by a heavy chain that was held in the hand of an individual wearing a long black hooded cloak that completely covered their appearance. The collar appeared to be so tight that streams of blood were evident from the spots that thorns had pierced into the flesh of her neck. The same nurse with the prominent birthmark on her cheek was standing directly in front of the woman, handing her an infant bundled in a blanket so that only its face was shown, "You must be so proud, your baby is simply beautiful." Marty turned and looked for the same nurse who was still pushing at the head of his stretcher. He could not endure the thought of what he was about to witness and yelled out, "No, stop, the baby will be burned!" The nurses continued to push his stretcher past the flaming woman and nurse, unaffected by his plea. The flaming woman and the nurse with the birthmark were positioned in front of a large well well-lit glass glass-enclosed room full of baby incubators and empty bassinets. Marty could see there were two bassinets lined up side by side right in front of the window. He became distraught as he noticed that each bassinet had a sign reading sooner pinned to the hood. One bassinet was empty, but Marty was aghast to see the other contained the corpse of a decomposed infant. While Marty was horrified at the sight, the nurses guiding his stretcher seemed oblivious to the spectacle as they relentlessly guided his stretcher along.

Marty leaned over on his side so he could get a better look as the stretcher began to pass. The flaming woman took hold of the baby being handed her way and, after cradling the infant in her arms, began walking and leading her darkly clad master towards the exit of the maternity ward. Marty could not bear it any longer and started freaking out, "No, stop that woman, she is stealing my baby!" But the nurses pushing his stretcher just continued without even acknowledging him, so Marty concluded he had to take action himself, and prepared to get off the stretcher by raising his body from the bed and balancing on his outstretched arms. As he sat in that position for a second, his head throbbed and he became incredibly dizzy, but he had to ignore those symptoms to stop the abduction. Marty fumbled to find the release for the upraised bed rails and became distracted by the familiar sound of Annette's sobs. As he turned his attention towards the direction of the sobbing, he was met by the unexpected presence of Doctor Sohon sitting, legs crossed, and looking at him from the foot of the stretcher. Her eyes also had the same completely black as coal appearance. "You won't be taking home any bundle of joy; you will learn it is not wise to ignore the consequences of betrayal." The doctor stretched out her arm and pointed a finger in his direction, causing him to look down at his sheet-covered frame. At that moment, he noticed a crimson spot soaking into the sheet. Marty clutched a hand over the spot; his expression contorted into a grimace in response to the piercing pain that accompanied the blood. As he moved the sheet away from his skin, he discovered a wound had appeared from which the blood was actively oozing. He placed a hand over the wound to apply pressure, and the blood squeezed from between his fingers. He returned his gaze towards the exit of the Maternity ward to see the flaming woman exiting the door, followed closely behind by her shady cohort. Marty looked up from his wound, about to plead with Doctor Sohon for help, but she had vanished from her spot at the foot of his stretcher, so instead he turned to the nurse with the birthmark, "Please get help, I am bleeding," but she continued pushing the stretcher along, completely oblivious to what was going on. He then yelled towards the blonde nurse at the guiding the foot of the stretcher, "Nurse, I need your help." his words went unacknowledged by her as well.

The scenery surrounding Marty continued to play out in slow motion as he lay backwards and tried once again to find a release lever that would allow him to lower the sides of the stretcher. He could hear his heart beating in his ears, and his breath becoming more shallow and labored. He turned his head to the left as they began to pass some patient rooms with open doors, and noticed Annette lying slightly elevated in a bed with blankets positioned at waist level. Her belly was no longer round and distended. Doctor Sohon was in the room, and Marty could hear Annette cry out, "He just can't be gone!" "I need to see my husband.

154

Please take me to him." As he was wheeled past the room, he could see his distraught-looking wife struggling in obvious pain to get herself out of the bed, and Doctor Sohon rushing to her side, "Annette, now is not the best time. Stay here and collect yourself, and you will be able to see your husband in a little while." As they passed the room and retreated further away, Marty could hear Annette's crying fade away, and his heart ached as he longed to be able to be there to offer her some comfort.

Marty once again rolled onto his back, but he no longer felt his heart pounding in his ears and was not so aware of the sounds of his own breathing. Suddenly, the nurse with the birthmark that had been pushing the stretcher looked at him from above, and her voice rang out in a surprised expression as she covered her mouth, "Oh no, I didn't notice that the sheet was not covering his face!" The blonde nurse turned slightly and looked at both of them, "Do you think it has been down this whole time we were moving him?" Marty just lay there, disgusted because these two goofy nurses remained completely unaware that any of what he just experienced had happened, and now they were suddenly so concerned that the sheet was disturbed. He was just about to give them a piece of his mind when, to his surprise, he could not move to speak, and he couldn't even move his eyes or any other part of his body; he was frozen in place, completely paralyzed. The blonde nurse also stood with her hand on her mouth for a moment. "Do you think we should close his eyes?" The nurse with the birthmark looked down more closely at Marty, "No, when they come in DOA like this, we are not allowed to touch them at all, they have to remain in the condition they arrived until after the coroner has started the autopsy." As she was speaking, she reached over, grabbed the blood-soaked sheet, and quickly pulled it up over Marty's face, blocking everything from his view. Marty felt confused by what she had just said, "Dead on arrival, autopsy." he tried to speak the words out loud, with the hope of scaring the wits out of them, but once again, he remained unable to move a muscle to speak or respond.

Marty listened as the nurse who had pulled the sheet over his head continued, "I am not sure, but I think it has something to do with corrupting the evidence. That is the reason why when we handle the body, we have to wear these latex gloves, so we don't leave behind any fingerprints. As he felt the stretcher begin to roll again, Marty's mind became awash with a myriad of thoughts. He wondered if it was true that he was indeed dead, or maybe someone had made a terrible mistake and he was in a coma instead, but no one was aware of it. The stretcher banged hard against something, and Marty could vaguely make out through the thin veil of the sheet that they had just pushed through another set of doors. A few moments later and the stretcher had stopped moving, and he heard the creak of the foot brake on the stretcher being set. Marty could make out the outline of the woman through the sheet as they stood close by the stretcher. The nurses wandered around him for a couple of minutes before he recognized the voice of the blonde nurse. "So what do you think happened to him?" Her voice sounded very apathetic, as if she were hardened to this sort of sight. The voice of the nurse with the birthmark followed immediately in response, "Well, this guy is one of four victims of a knife-wielding psycho at a clinic across town." "The paramedic that brought this one in told me they transported two victims here, this guy was DOA, and his wife was also suffering from several stab wounds to her abdomen, which resulted in a still birth." "The two others from the attack were also critically injured, and they were transported to the state hospital trauma unit."

The blonde nurse came up and removed the sheet once again from covering Marty's face. "The past two days have gone pretty crazy in this quiet little town, starting yesterday with those guys robbing the Silver Tracks diner, and the fire out on Deer Run Road that injured those two firemen, and now this, it's pretty sad." The nurse with the birthmark looked down at Marty, "Yeah, well, here is the weirdest twist in this whole story; I heard this guy and his upstairs wife were also at the diner when it was robbed, and he was in the hospital just yesterday for medical care as a result of the injuries he received." The nurse with the birthmark leaned slightly over the stretcher, whispering to her coworker, "He was

just released this morning after being held overnight for medical observation." She pointed, motioning with her thumb over her shoulder, "And get this, the bodies of the robbers and the worker who was killed at the diner are all here in this morgue as we speak."

The blonde nurse looked around the room, "Now that gives me the creeps, so what are we waiting around here for anyway?" The nurse with the birthmark replaced the sheet over Marty's face as she replied, "I always wait around until the examining coroner is here, just to make sure there is not something else that might need to be done. As she was talking, Marty could hear that she was walking across the room, "But I don't think we will have to wait around now, it seems the coroner has stepped out to lunch, and won't be back for another thirty-five minutes." The sounds of the nurse sifting through objects at the desk could be detected. "I will just leave him a note to page me overhead if he needs me for anything, so you and I could go outside and sneak an unscheduled smoke break." Within a few moments, the ladies were opening the door and turning off the lights in the morgue as they exited. He could hear the blonde nurse's voice fading as they headed away from the morgue, "It's really not wise to disregard the significance of a warning." Marty could barely make out the voice of the nurse with the birthmark before they completely moved out of his range of hearing, "The message was given, his choice made clear…"

Marty could do nothing but lie there in the dimly lit room, paralyzed, feeling trapped inside the cold hollow casing of a body that once housed a living and vibrant person. His heart did not beat, his eyes stared blankly forward, he could not blink or even focus, his vision had been reduced to a blurry peripheral of what was in immediate range of him, and only the blood-stained sheet covered his face. He remained there for some time, not really thinking about anything, for his mind had gone completely blank and numb. He was honestly too terrified to even consider anything, not the future, nor the past, for then he would have to face the regrets of things he should have done differently, and how those choices would, could have, or even might have affected his future. However, thinking like that would not serve any purpose for him now, and he was not the type to wallow in self-pity, so he chose not to think about it for the time being. Instead, he wanted to concentrate on overcoming his present inability to do anything. However, no matter how he tried, there was nothing he could do to gain control of his physical being; in fact, his vision continued to blur more. As more time passed, the horror of the situation began to make an enormous impact on his psyche, for he felt as if the cold chill of death had truly descended its grip upon him. He began to feel physical symptoms he had never experienced before that moment; his bones and joints began to ache and tighten painfully, worse than any cramp he had ever experienced. As they did, he could detect minute crackling sounds. And as he lay there, he imagined he could feel his eyes and organs settling and sagging towards the floor from within his body, as they succumbed to gravity, and the life force that had once inhabited him and pumped them full of blood was no longer present. His hearing became muffled, reminding him of the way he heard when he was at work wearing earplugs, but gone were the familiar sounds of his heartbeat and air filling his lungs as he inhaled and exhaled; instead, those sounds had been replaced with the low, eerie hum of silence.

Marty lay trapped there in maddening silence for what felt like a very long time, trapped within the silent confines of his own cold corpse, unable to do anything more than brood over how utterly powerless he was, when suddenly a very faint sound filtered in through the deafening silence, and his own mind reeled in silent but screaming thoughts. As quickly as he had noticed the sound, it had vanished, leaving him wondering what it could have been. A moment later, he heard it again, this time it was more of a distinguishable buzzing sound, before it stopped. Once again, the buzzing sound came within the range of his hearing, but this time he realized what was producing the noise as the outline of an insect landed within his vision on the sheet covering him.

Right then, only a single thought came to him, "Oh fuck I am starting to draw flies!" Marty watched on in silent revulsion as the grotesque fly wasted no time in making its way up the sheet towards his forehead, before buzzing once again into the air. In life, he hated the idea of being buried, for he always feared the thought of being trapped inside his body and being slowly consumed by insects, the whole time feeling them crawl and slither around inside him while they slowly but eagerly consume him from the inside out.

Marty's memory traveled back to the time of his childhood, when he was about four years of age. As he dug playfully in the dirt, he could see himself as he dug and played with his toy trucks; he remembered how he would find beetles and worms, or ants, and how he loved to play with them. Sometimes keeping them as pets, and other times covering them with little fists full of dirt to see if they could dig their way out. Sometimes, he would be merciless as he ran them over with his truck or crushed them beneath his sneaker, listening to them crunch and pop underneath the pressure. He could clearly see himself one sunny afternoon digging gleefully in the dirt with some gardening tools his mother had left out, and how the tools began to carve a hole into the soil. He continued to dig the hole deeper and deeper until the little gardening spade he was using hit something solid. At first, when he reached in to pull the object out, it was stuck and required him to dig around it further before it began to dislodge. Eventually, he was able to dig free enough soil to get a grip on the object and pull it free from the earth. He heaved it up and placed it alongside him on the mound of soil he had removed from the hole, discovering he had unearthed a small wooden box. He imagined it to be the buried treasure left behind by pirates long before. He relived the elation he felt as he anticipated how happy his mother would be as she wore the elaborate jewelry and how they would dance and celebrate his wondrous discovery. But his delight quickly turned to horror as he popped open the lid on the box to have the sickening aroma of rotting flesh waft up and fill his nostrils and make his eyes water, for the box contained a rotting cat carcass squirming with maggots and other disgusting larvae. As he watched the squirming mass of white sacks, he had not noticed that beetles were swarming out of the box and began running up his pant legs. He sat there gazing in awe at the box, when suddenly he felt the scratching and crawling underneath his pants legs, causing him to jump to his feet, screaming in sheer panic as he struggled to strip off his pants. His mother flew from inside the house, prompted by her young son's terrified screams, and rushed down the length of their backyard with the intention of rescuing him from whatever terrible situation he had found his way into. She rushed upon him to discover him writhing on the ground and struggling to remove his pants, "What's wrong, Martin?" He frantically pointed to the box that was still crawling with insects, "Maamaa, they're biting me!" He wailed in pain, and his mother became panic-stricken as she rushed to her child and began to rip his clothing off, putting aside her own lifelong abhorrence of creepy-crawly insects. As she struggled to remove his pants, some of the insects made their way onto her hands and began entering the sleeve of her housecoat. After what seemed to be an extended struggle that really only took a few seconds, young Martin's pants had been removed, and he and his mother worked feverishly to swat the remainder of the insects from his skin. Martin quickly got to his feet and exclaimed, "Mamma, they are crawling up your arms!" At that moment, his mother felt a scratchy, crawling sensation under the sleeve of her housecoat and blurted out a dismayed, "Ewwh!" As she quickly removed her housecoat and swiped the few insects that had remained from her skin, and grabbed Marty into her arms and beat a hasty retreat back to the house. His mother rushed him into the bathroom, placed him in the tub, and removed the remainder of his clothing while she inspected his body for any insects that may possibly have remained, and showered him. Later on, after all the commotion had settled, his mother started a fire in the barrel they used to burn old newspaper and yard waste. She carefully used a rake to place both his pants and her housecoat into the flames, and then she scooped the box onto the end of a shovel and dumped that into the flames as well. It was at that moment, so early in life, as he watched the squirming insects succumb to the flames, that Marty made the decision not to be buried in the ground, because it's not only where the bugs live, but it's also where, and what they eat.

Within a short time, the buzzing sound had returned as the fly once again landed on the sheet covering Marty. He could sense that the creepy little insect was becoming increasingly bold, as it got no negative response to its presence. This little vile messenger of death served as a stark reminder to Marty that there would be no escape; death had him firmly within its relentless grip. The fly scurried over to the bloodstain on the sheet and rested there for a moment, sipping the sample of the feast that lay just beneath. As the fly lingered on the stain, Marty could make out yet another buzzing sound approaching, and another fly landed directly where his nose extended the sheet. The fly that had settled on the bloodstain rushed the trespasser, and they swirled around in frenzy a few inches above him, and disappeared. A few seconds later, the two flies buzzed back and landed almost simultaneously. One rushed towards the bloodstain, while the other made its way towards the top of his head and slipped underneath the sheet. Marty's dread turned to utter disgust as the fly squirmed between the weight of the sheet and his flesh, emerging first with darting black legs, and then forcing its round black head into his vision. The fly halted for a second as it flicked its head around surveying the surroundings and proceeded to free the rest of its body from between the sheet and his forehead, coming to rest positioned between his eyelid and brow. Marty watched as the fly lingered for a moment to rub its back legs over its wings and body, and then its front legs swept over its head and eyes several times. He was powerless to react as the fly suddenly made its way directly onto his eyeball, and his thoughts raged with complete revulsion as the insect dropped its mouth onto his cornea and emitted a foul seepage that completely distorted the already blurred vision in that eye, as it slurped fervently on the mixture it produced. These little soldiers of death were there on a single mission: to start the process of returning his ruined remains to the earth.

Suddenly, Marty could make out the sound of a male voice talking and becoming louder as they drew closer, followed by the sound of a door opening, and the click of a switch as the overhead light flickered on. The fly that had perched on the bloodstain flew away as soon as the light illuminated the room, but the one under the sheet remained sucking feverishly on Marty's eyeball. The men approached the stretcher and pulled at his toe tag, "While we were out to lunch, we got a new arrival, one Mister Martin Sooner." Marty could barely make out the outline of the man who had spoken through the distraction of the fly dancing about and feeding on his eyeball, but he could make out the outline of one of the men walking towards the desk where the nurses had left the note. The man who had read the toe tag began moving and reaching for the sheet that covered his face, "Let's see what we have here," as he pulled the sheet down to reveal Marty's face. The fly lingered for a mere moment more before taking flight from his eye. The man closest to Marty shook his head, with a somewhat disgusted expression, "It does not take long for the insects to close in; we have got to remind the nurses to place the cadavers directly into the refrigeration unit if there is no one here to receive them." The man at the desk was holding the note left by the nurse, "It seems Mister sooner was delivered by Nurse Gortham." The man standing by Marty turned his head to face him. "Who?" The man at the desk responded, "You know the older one with the birthmark," as he positioned a hand to his cheek for effect. The man, still leaning over Marty, nodded his head, "Oh yeah, ok, I know who that is."

The sound of a phone echoed through the room, and the man at the desk picked it up, "Post-mortem examination, Jay Pintah speaking." The sound of inaudible speaking could be heard coming from the phone receiver, followed by Jay, "Could you hold please," and he clicked a button while holding his hand over the mouth piece, "Hey Dave, apparently this guys wife is demanding to see his body, they are giving us a heads up that she is on her way down." Dave rolled his eyes, "We haven't had the chance to tend to him at all, and she will have a stroke if she sees him all covered in blood and full of holes like this." He turned and looked Marty over once more before turning back to Jay, "Ask them how long we have." Jay clicked the phone from hold. "How long would you estimate we have before she gets here?" After a couple of seconds, he graciously thanked the caller for the warning and hung up the phone, "They said his wife had just boarded the elevator a few seconds before we got this call." Dave shook his head, "Shit, that doesn't even give us enough time to get him into a body bag," he paused for a second, Let's get another sheet over him, and pull it over his head, hopefully, the blood will not soak through before we can get her out of here."

Jay jumped up from the seat as Dave ran to a supply room and emerged with a fresh white sheet. They both worked together to cover Marty, once again pulling the cover directly over his face. He could hear Dave's voice, "When she comes in, we have to try to keep her away from him, because if we pull the blanket much further past his chin, she is going to freak at the sight of these injuries." The fresh covering flowed down over Marty once again, shrouding his vision in a veil of white. He could make out the outline of the men checking to ensure there were no obvious signs of his traumatic injuries visible. They no more than had the fresh covering in place when Jay stopped, "I think I might have heard the elevator door, but I can't be sure." He had no sooner gotten those words out when the nurse escorting Annette in a wheelchair pushed her way backwards through the door, as she spoke loud enough for the men in the room to be on the ready for their entrance, "Ok, Mrs. Sooner, now remember we are not going to be allowed to stay here very long."

There was a moment of awkward silence as the nurse finished pulling the handles of Annette's wheelchair as they entered and turned her to face the two men standing by Marty's body. The nurse cleared her throat before continuing, "Good afternoon, doctor Pintah and doctor Pacci, this is Mrs. Annette Sooner. She has requested to take this opportunity to identify her husband. Dave stepped forward and kneeled in front of Annette, "Mrs. Sooner, please accept my deepest sympathy, but your husband was carrying his driver's license when he arrived, so we have already established an identification; there is no pressing need to subject yourself to this right now."

Annette's voice quivered as she began to speak, "Doctor, I appreciate your concern, but I have to see for myself that my husband is…" Her voice trailed off for a moment as she hung her head and shut her eyes, sobbing quietly and twitching slightly for a few seconds as she struggled to regain her composure. Then, after a little while, she cleared her throat and repositioned her head while she dabbed a tear that had welled up and run from her eye, "I'm sorry, but I have to see with my own eyes if it is really true." "I have to know firsthand if Marty is truly gone," she looked at Dave with pleading, puffy red eyes, as she sniffled, "And I can't wait any longer to see him." Her voice ended abruptly as she held back another sob, "You don't understand, I just have to see him now."

The apparent anguish and sadness in Annette's voice laid Marty's emotions bare, for he could never bear it when his wife cried and became distraught. He hated it because, most of all, he was completely helpless to change how things were while The thought of himself being dead bothered him immensely; it paled in comparison to the misery it brought him to witness Annette hurting like this.

Dave stood to his feet and looked back at Jay, the hospital examiner, for some signal or backup that he, too, disagreed with Annette identifying Marty at that moment. Jay at first shrugged his shoulders and widened his eyes as if to suggest he was not sure how he wanted to signal. Annette caught on to the silent communication between the hospital examiner and the coroner, and interrupted, "You two should have to put yourself in my place, imagine if you were told that your wife, or child had died; wouldn't you want to be able to see them even if just to verify that it was true or not?" The pitch of her voice rose and trembled as she continued, "Both of you know you would want to see for sure with your own two eyes that what they have told you is true." "You would hold out some glimmer of hope that someone, somehow, has made a mistake, and the person you love most dearly in the world is not lost forever." Annette's eyes filled with tears that quickly began streaming down both sides of her cheeks, "If you put yourself in my place for even a second, you know you would do the same thing."

Hearing the tone of Annette's voice made Marty hope that the coroner would stand firm and turn her away before she could see him like this. He figured there would surely be a few days until the viewing, and he remained hopeful, by that time, the process of death would have had enough time to complete its cycle. By the time of the viewing, his soul

would have passed totally from this state of consciousness, into the next stage of existence, leaving his body behind to be a truly vacant shell, unable to detect any of his beloved wife's grief. This was something his family believed for years and passed on to him. He remembered back to his childhood, back to when he was eight years old, just a short time after his grandfather had died, having battled a lengthy illness and a stay in the hospital. He remembered his mother dressing his younger sister and himself in their winter coats and hats, and kneeling down with a very sad look in her eyes, "We are going to the hospital to help comfort grandmother in her time of need. I need both of you to be as quiet as church mice while we are there." No one spoke a single word as his aunt drove his mother in the front seat and them in the back seat. As Marty's mother led him down the familiar hallways of the hospital towards his grandfather's room, Marty felt very sad that his grandpa would not be around anymore, and he began to cry silently, for he had many fond memories of time spent with the kind-hearted old man. Marty's mother heard her son's sadness and knelt down in front of him. As she did, Marty burst into the sincerest sobs of open grief, "Momma, I don't want grandpa to be dead, I still want him to finish teaching me to play cards with him and listen while he reads me stories." "I love him, Momma, I don't want him to go away," Marty remembered feeling as if his heart would break as he stood there sobbing heartfelt tears that rolled down the shoulders of his mother's coat as she held and comforted him in her arms. His mother continued to hug Marty as she spoke, choking back her own tears, "I know you love your grandpa very much, dear, and so do I, and we will all miss him terribly." Young Marty picked his head up from his mother's shoulder and looked into her eyes, "But Momma, grandpa is such a good man, he shouldn't have died now," he said as he sniffed and wiped his nose on the sleeve of his coat. He continued crying, and growing increasingly frustrated at the thought of suffering the loss of the grandpa that he loved so much, "But Momma, he shouldn't die since he is so good, and we all love him so much, and don't want him to go, we should tell him not to go, and maybe he will come back."

Marty had barely noticed his grandmother had approached them while he was being consoled by his mother. She placed a hand on his mother's shoulder, as she took him by the hand, "Let me talk with my grandson for a while, you go see your father, I will bring Martin in a little while." As Marty's mom stood, she wiped the tears from his eyes and kissed him on the forehead, "Now you listen carefully to what your grandma is going to tell you." Then she turned and hugged her mother, as she began to sob quietly, "Momma, are you all right?" Marty's grandmother let go of his hand and hugged her daughter, "Grieve lightly now, dear, for we must spend as much time as possible with your father now, remembering all the fun and wonderful times he has shared with all of us, so he will feel a sense of comfort as he passes." His grandmother hugged her for a moment longer and then placed her hands on her shoulders and pulled her a little distance away, "Come, let me see how you look." She wiped her fingers under his mother's eyes to remove the tears. His grandmother kissed his mother on the top of the forehead, "Just remember its ok to let him know you will miss him, but be sure to let him know how much you love him for the great and loving, and fun father he was." His grandmother reached down, took his younger sister's hand, and placed it in his mother's, "You take his granddaughter in to visit for a while, and I will bring young Martin in after a short walk."

Marty's grandmother took him by the hand, and they walked in the opposite direction that his mother and sister headed for a short while before she spoke, "Martin, I know you love your grandpa a great deal, and your heart hurts so much right now because you are sad and hurt, and angry that he will no longer be around." Tears welled up in Marty's eyes and rolled down his cheeks, and he had a huge lump in his throat that so choked him up he could not even speak, so he nodded his head in agreement. His grandmother turned to face him, "My darling grandson, I understand exactly how you feel. Your grandfather was a wonderful man; he was a wonderful husband and father, and the best grandpa a kid could ever want." She pulled a hanky from her coat pocket to wipe the tears from his rosy cheeks, "And because you love him and he loves you so very much that you must be a brave little man when you go in to see him." "For even though your heart may be aching, you should tell him how much you love him and remember all the fun and love the two of you shared." His grandmother cupped his head in between her hands and rubbed his temples, "You see, Martin, your grandpa's body has just departed this life, but his soul is still present, and his brain is still able to understand what is being said and done around him." "We want him to feel at peace and dearly loved and appreciated for the times he shared with us, so we don't want to say anything that may upset or trouble him, so that his soul can pass peacefully to the other side, and not linger worrying about those he is leaving behind." Marty's grandmother ran her hands through his hair and rubbed his shoulder slightly, "It is ok for you to let your grandpa know that you love him and you will miss him." "Tell him how thankful you are for all the wonderful times the two of you shared. Share with him a few happy memories, try to laugh as you remember. This will help him to be content in the very special love the two of you shared, and he will be at peace in his final moments with us."

Marty was grateful for the words of wisdom his grandmother had shared as he opened his arms and gave her a tight squeeze, "I love you, Grandma." His grandmother sighed and returned his love, "I love you too." For as young as he was, Marty knew what his grandmother said was true, and though his heart ached, he held out his hand, and his grandmother stood and placed hers gently over his. "Let's not waste another minute." Together, they prepared to do what neither really wanted to: say their final goodbye. Marty spent the rest of his time hugging his grandpa, laughing as he remembered out loud some of the fun times they shared. He cried a few unavoidable tears as he said how much he loved and would miss him, and before he left, he squeezed his grandpa a final time; "I promise I will finish learning how to play cards with grandma."

Marty had only briefly shared that experience with Annette, and at the time she hugged him, saying how sweet she thought he was, which made him feel like a big sap, and defeated the purpose of sending the departed away with content feelings. There was never a reason to broach the subject after that, for even when his dad had died, he was not able to make it to the hospital within the hours following his passing.

There was an awkward pause, for no one in the room really wanted to confront the emotions that would inevitably happen with either a yes or no answer. The coroner pondered for a moment and reluctantly agreed that Annette had a valid point, but felt the need to hold out, hoping she would change her mind if discouraged. "Mrs. Sooner, at times like these, when an identification has been established, it's usually best when the survivors of the deceased see their loved ones at the viewing." Try as he might, Annette was having no part of Dave's argument, "Doctor, you don't understand, I simply have to see him now....please," her tone was that of complete vulnerability and pleading. The coroner had a pretty good idea that there was probably no changing Annette's mind on the subject: "All right, Mrs. Sooner, I will remove the cover from Mr. Sooner's face so that you can make the identification." After having said that, Dave very carefully began to gently slide the sheet down over Marty's face, stopping at the base of his chin so as not to expose any of his injuries to her, and stepped out of Annette's line of vision.

The moment Dave had stepped out of the way, Annette set her eyes upon the person she had been praying would not be there; she placed a trembling hand over her open mouth, as she broke into a silent jerking cry. The nurse who had escorted her for the trip placed a hand on her shoulder as a gesture of comfort, "Come now, Mrs. Sooner, I will take you back to your room." The nurse began trying to move Annette in her wheelchair towards the exit, but she resisted by holding one of the wheels, preventing further movement. "Give me a second, wheel me over to my husband." As Annette spoke those words, Dave and Jay both started moving at the same time, but Dave spoke as he replaced the sheet over Marty's face, "Mrs. Sooner, you are not going to be able to touch your husband at this time." Annette simply could not imagine what was wrong if she wanted to touch Marty, "Why can't I touch my husband?" Dave approached her and kneeled down, "You can't touch your husband at this time because Dr. Pintah and I have not completed our examination yet." Like a bolt of lightning striking from out of the blue, Annette suddenly understood what the coroner was implying, "You mean an autopsy? I did not permit that." Dave immediately regretted having slipped up by letting on about an impending autopsy, and recoiled silently in his mind as Annette made the connection.

The sound of the word 'autopsy' coming from Annette's mouth echoed over and over again in Marty's mind, filling him with dread and making him wish he could jump up and scream for them to end the madness of that moment. As upset as Annette was until that point, it became clear to the coroner that she was becoming increasingly more upset. Dave was going to try to keep the situation from boiling over: "Mrs. Sooner, in every case of suspected homicide, the law requires an autopsy to be performed to establish the exact cause of death." He placed his hand over hers, with the hope of offering her some degree of comfort as he continued to explain, "I know it is hard to deal with, but the results of the autopsy will be critical to the criminal case when the person responsible for your husband's death is tried in court."

Annette looked past the coroner towards the direction where Marty's body lay completely hidden under the sheet, and renewed tears began to flow, "I think that sweet man has suffered far too much already, and you want to cut him even more." The coroner's next sentence shrieked through Marty's mind like an electric shock, "Let me reassure you that your husband will not know, or feel anything during the process." He stood purposely to block her view of her husband lying just a few feet away, concealed beneath the white sheet, "Try not to think of this as a bad thing, especially how it relates to helping convict the person that attacked you and your husband." While Annette knew what the coroner said was true, she did not think her heart could bear the thought of her beloved husband being made to suffer through any further misery; "But doctor Pacci, he has been through so much already, I hate the thought of him having to suffer even for one more minute, please don't go through with this." Dave could not compromise on the issue, but his tone remained gentle and subdued as he spoke, "Mrs. Sooner, even if I and Dr. Pintah refused to conduct this examination, the district attorney's office would secure a coroner and medical examiner from another county and another hospital." Jay, who had remained silent since Annette had arrived, spoke up, "Everything doctor Pacci is saying is the truth, and if we did refuse based on your request, we would lose our jobs."

Jay walked over and stood alongside Dave, "I think now is a good time to have Nurse Williams escort you back to your room so you can get some rest." As he spoke, Jay made a circular motion with his fingers and looked intently at Nurse Williams, hoping to make his point with her. The nurse did take the hint and began to rotate Annette's wheelchair to face the door to exit where they had entered. Annette immediately began to try to plead with them, "Please, wait, hold on for a minute," as she removed her feet from the footrests and dug them into the floor in an attempt to impede the nurse from moving her any further. Dave reached out his arm and tapped Jay slightly on the shoulder as he turned and whispered, "Get ready to make a call for help." He then walked over, turned, and knelt by Annette, talking in a calm, firm tone, "Mrs. Sooner, please listen to me. I know how difficult this must be for you, but right now, I need you to be cooperative and go with Nurse Williams." Annette glared directly into his eyes, her expression became a mixture of animosity and disbelief, "Do you really know how difficult this must be for me?" The angry expression quickly turned to one of overwhelmed grief, "Because, doctor, if you did, you would understand that the last thing I could possibly want to do right now is leave the man I love alone, to be dissected and inspected by a couple of insensitive strangers." She stared at Dave through tear-filled eyes, hoping to find some glimmer of compassion, "I didn't even get to say goodbye, or tell him how much I love him, and how very much I will miss his companionship." Marty felt besieged with despair as he could sense his wife's mounting sadness. From the moment he had fallen in love with Annette, the thought that filled him with the most dread was whether one of them was to die, leaving the other behind to deal with the loss.

Dave realized there was going to be no compromising with Annette and, without a word, looked at Jay, prompting him to call for backup. "Mrs. Sooner, I assure you that your husband will be treated with the utmost dignity and respect, but I have to insist you cooperate with Nurse Williams and return to your room now." He gently placed both hands on her ankle, "Just lift your feet back onto the footrests, and we can get you safely back to your room." Annette complied without fully realizing at the moment that he was physically prompting her, but as he guided her foot and gently placed his hands over her other ankle, she held firmly back and then replaced her other foot on the floor. Just after he made that request, Doctor Sohon, another nurse, and a security guard stepped into view behind him, and he stood and motioned a hand in their direction, "Doctor Sohon has come to help ease your worries, and I implore you to let her help you through this trying time." Doctor Sohon stepped up to Annette and placed a hand on her shoulder, "Annette, it is best you come with me." Annette slumped her head onto the opposite shoulder as tears streamed down her cheeks and down the sleeve of her hospital gown, "I would rather be dead than continue without him; he is my soul mate." Doctor Sohon rubbed Annette's shoulder, trying her best to be a comforting presence, "You must not be thinking like that, I am sure Martin knows you love him." "You are going to have to try to be strong over the next few days for both of you, and we have staff members here at the hospital that can help you cope with the transition." She bent at the waist to bring herself closer to Annette, "But first we have to get you away from your source of pain, so that the healing process can begin." Annette glared right into Dr. Sohon's eyes, "I don't want to leave the source of my pain, I want to stay right here with my husband." As soon as she finished saying that, she unexpectedly thrust her bodyweight sideways and at the same time pushed her feet with all her strength on the floor, knocking the wheelchair off balance. The sudden movement caught everyone surrounding her off guard as they all scrambled unsuccessfully to try and catch her from falling to the floor. As she strained to push the wheelchair off balance, the stab wounds in her abdomen began to painfully stretch, causing the sutures to pop open and ooze blood from the wounds. Annette screamed in agony, "Marty, I can't leave you alone like this!" Annette struggled with the hospital staff despite the pain, as she tried crawling out of the chair in his direction, "You can't cut him up anymore, I won't let you." The blood from her stab wounds began to seep through the thin material of the hospital gown and drip onto the floor. Doctor Sohon and the coroner rushed to help pick Annette from the floor, while the nurse picked the wheelchair back up. Jay walked around to confront Annette as she continued to crawl towards Marty, "Doctor Sohon, help me get her back into the chair." As they helped Annette to her feet doctor, the coroner held her in place and addressed her eye to eye, "Annette, are you sure this is the way you want to continue to act?" It was obvious to her that he had become quite annoyed, "Because if it is, I will be forced to have you restrained and removed from here until you calm down." Annette looked up towards the ceiling, for the pain from her wounds had become very intense, and she was quickly realizing this struggle was not doing her any good, "No, doctor Pacci, you are right, please just help me to the wheelchair and I promise not to give you any more hassles." Marty was consumed by feelings of dismay as he had no choice but to lie there and listen to the commotion taking place across the room. It ripped at his emotions that he was so immobilized, powerless to comfort his wife. He wished that he could leap from the table, rush to her side, and reassure her that everything would be all right. Doctors Sohon and Pacci gently eased Annette to her feet, and she winced slightly from the pain as she moved.

After a few moments of carefully placed steps, Annette was again sitting safely in the wheelchair. The tears gushed from her eyes as Dr. Sohon replaced her feet on the footrests. "Doctor Pacci, can I have a pair of latex gloves?" Without a word, Dr. Pacci retrieved the gloves as she requested, and she slipped her hands in, snapping each at the wrist like an audible note that they fit properly. "Annette, lift your gown so that I can have a look at your injuries." Annette continued to weep, sniveling slightly as she carefully lifted her gown over her knees to expose the dressed wounds. Doctor Sohon gently pulled back the white tape surrounding the blood-soaked sterile cloth to reveal the still lightly bleeding wounds. "It looks like you have ripped a few of your sutures," she looked at the nurse, "Let's get her back to her room, I may be able to take care of this without having to re-stitch them closed." Doctor Sohon turned to the security guard who had accompanied her, "Thank you for your time, but I don't think we will need you from here on out." The security guard tipped his hat, "Ok then, everyone has a nice night," and he turned and exited their presence.

Doctor Sohon lowered Annette's gown and replaced it over her legs. "It does not appear as if you have done too much damage, but let's get you back to your room so I can get a better look." She looked at Nurse Williams, who instantly moved the wheelchair slightly forward. Annette interjected suddenly, "Wait," and she turned toward the coroner, grabbing hold of his hand, "Doctor Pacci, I am truly sorry for causing such an uproar. Please forgive me," her voice cut short as she sniveled another time. He bent over closer to her, "Mrs. Sooner, don't even give it a second thought, you will be in my prayers." Doctor Sohon started down the hall, with nurse Williams pushing Annette following closely behind. Marty listened intently as the sound of his wife's delicate sobs became paler as they moved further away.

Doctors Pintah and Pacci stood silently and watched as the trio entered the elevator, and they both waited there watching until the doors slid closed, eliminating the women from view. They both breathed a heavy sigh of relief and turned to face one another. Doctor Pacci raised a hand, wiping a figurative bead of sweat from his brow, "Whew, thank God that's over. Having to be a witness to the grief and despair is by far the worst part of this job for me." Doctor Pintah nodded his head in agreement, "It really sucks having to put on a brave facade when dealing with those who have lost a loved one, when in reality you just want to cry right along with them." Both doctors walked up alongside Marty, and Doctor Pacci pulled the sheet covering him down, exposing his head and upper chest. "I've gotta tell you, she genuinely seems to love this poor bastard." Although Marty's vision was blurred, he was still able to see the two doctors hovering over him. Doctor Pacci reached with two latex glove-covered hands and used his fingers to spread apart a rather large, elongated puncture wound located on the side of his throat about three inches below his left ear, "Now whoever is responsible for this felt somewhat different about Mr. Sooner." Doctor Pintah turned slightly and faced his colleague, "What do you say we put this guy on ice, and go grab a cup of Joe, my treat." Doctor Pacci nodded in agreement, "Ah, Jay, that sounds great. After all that drama, I could really use a break, and since you're buying, that makes it an even sweeter deal." He walked over and popped open a large silver door that led into a refrigeration unit, and then began helping Jay guide the portable table containing Marty's body into the refrigeration unit. Dave continued, "Once we get done with the coffee break, we are going to have to push ourselves into overdrive to catch up, because we still have to conduct the autopsies on the two John Does killed at that diner yesterday, plus the body that was pulled from that psychic store fire yesterday." After they slid him into the appropriate spot, Jay depressed the foot brake to lock the wheels. "On the bright side, at least we were able to get the autopsy finished on that dishwasher and the husband and wife that were killed during the diner robbery before you were called out to investigate the scene of that fire." Dave produced a sly smirk, "Jay, I can always count on you to point out the silver lining in every cloud." Dave gave Jay a slight tap on the shoulder, "Get a load of this coincidence, Mr. Martin Sooner here was at that diner yesterday when the hold up went down." Jay stopped dead in his tracks, "Get the hell out of here, you are kidding me, right?" Dave put his left hand over his heart and raised his right hand, "Right hand to God, I swear it's the truth. I was the coroner who investigated the crime scene, and I remember him being taken out in an ambulance." The two men turned to look at Marty once again, as Dave continued, "In fact, I believe he was treated at this hospital for that bump you see right there on his forehead, that is where he took a pretty mean whack from the barrel of a sawed-off shotgun." Jay had an expression of obvious surprise, "Now that is too weird, bad luck seems to have had it out for this guy, it's pretty sad to say."

The two men started exiting the cooler and shutting the door. Jay chuckled a little, "Well, I guess there is no need to introduce them." Dave shoved him playfully, "Get outta here, you clown, you are just full of humor today." Marty could hear their voices become silenced as the cooler door swung shut; the noise from the latch echoed ominously in his brain. He lay there for some time, trying not to think of anything as he watched the strip of yellow plastic tied to the grate covering the blower fan flap. The sound of the fan in the cooler seemed the perfect distraction to help him escape from his concerns. After a short time, he began to sense that his body temperature was dropping, and he became overwhelmed by a feeling of being utterly cold and isolated. At that moment, he became distraught when he recognized that he was so very alone; never again would he enjoy a loving embrace with Annette. His sadness intensified as he thought of his dreams of sharing a long and happy marriage had been stripped from him; he would never know the joy of raising a family and growing old with his beloved wife. He felt upset at the notion that he would never even be able to tell Annette how very much he loves her and how much joy she had brought into his life.

As Marty lay there becoming consumed with self-pity, he had not noticed that a short distance away from him, a slight squirming movement began under the dark material of a zipped body bag. The movement continued unnoticed by him until the cooler motor shut off, allowing the room to become silent except for the sound of whatever was moving in that bag. At first, he was perplexed by the noise, wondering what it could be, and since his eyes were locked in position, it took a few moments until the movement became evident to his peripheral vision. But once he knew something was awry within that bag, his mind snapped into a state of unbridled terror as he just imagined what kind of ghoulish force could be lurking just a short distance away. The movement had started slowly, but was growing more spastic and frenzied with every ticking second, as he could make out the clear, distinct clawing, struggling movements against the fabric. The body bag began to shift and roll, causing the table it was set upon to bang against the wall of the cooler, and suddenly, whatever had become animated within its confines bolted straight up into a sitting position, drawing the material tight, exposing a clear outline of the person's head and body. The body bag remained sitting unmoving in that upright position for a few moments, but then Marty noticed the movement of arms reaching towards where the zipper was located in the front of the bag, towards the top of its head. A single finger poked out, creating a small hole where the zipper ended, and then disappeared for a split second before two fingers snaked out, then four, and within seconds, two hands were visible pulling and widening the hole as the zipper gave way to the pressure.

Within seconds, a vaguely familiar face appeared through the hole. Marty recognized the face as familiar at first, but it took a second to sink in who it belonged to. Then he quickly realized the face he saw in his peripheral vision belonged to the vicious gunman, Fitzy, from the diner robbery. The last time he had seen Fitzy, he was lying next to his cohort, surrounded by a pool of blood. His mask had been removed by the coroner and was placed on his chest, as photographs of the crime scene were being taken. Marty had grown a sense of fear of this man, and rightfully so, since he had witnessed him gun down the dishwasher in cold blood, and had he himself been on the receiving end, his physical brutality would have been the recipient of the strike from the gun that knocked his skull wide open. Fitzy sat still for a short time without moving at all, but then turned his head slowly, looking in Marty's direction. Marty wished he could scream just then because he knew what was happening for some insane reason designed to torture him. Fitzy turned and swung his feet still encased in the body bag so they dangled above the floor, and with a pushing motion, he thudded onto the floor and began walking towards Marty. As he stepped on the material, the body bag began slipping down past his shoulders and then to his waist, causing the black mask he had used to conceal his identity at the diner to fall to the floor. Eventually, the body bag came completely off, discarded behind him as he continued. His movements were jerky, and he had a zombie-like appearance as he closed the distance, walking towards Marty, stopping as he banged into the table Marty was placed upon. Fitzy's eyes were completely coal black as he moved his head closer towards Marty's face. Dried blood surrounded the bullet wound under his chin, left behind by the self-inflicted shot that ended his life, and the sight of torn flesh and exposed bone was enough to make Marty feel sick as Fitzy stood looking ominously down upon him. A thick discharge of brown ooze began to seep from the wound and dripped on Marty as he lay frozen in position. The ghastly sight before him became worse as Fitzy opened his mouth, revealing his rotted teeth and a tongue that had been shredded by the force of the bullet. His voice resounded with a gurgling, grating sound, "You will be spared retribution for your simple allegiance." Fitzy cupped Marty's face in his hands, "Do not disrupt what has been set into motion, or you will endure immense torment."

Chapter 10: The Detectives Are On the Case

Everything surrounding Marty began to fade from his sight and became shrouded by darkness. Suddenly, his ability to move returned, and Marty scrambled backwards, desperately wanting to escape the grip of the grotesque messenger. He was panting heavily and shouted, "Stay away from me!" Gradually, his sight began to return, and he looked around to discover that he was no longer in the cooler being pawed by the corpse of Fitzy, but instead, he was crouched at the head of a regular hospital bed, with his back pushed firmly against the wall. A nurse who heard his shouts came rushing into the room, "Shhh, it's ok, Mr. Sooner, you are fine, just try to relax." The nurse straightened the blankets he had messed in his struggle, and Marty looked around him, initially confused, "Where am I?" The nurse urged him back into a lying position, "Let's get you back under the blankets, you are at the hospital, and once we get you settled down, I will page the doctor to talk with you." Marty complied with her request and scooted under the covers. He looked through the window in his room to discover that it was dark outside. "Do you know what time it is?" The nurse looked at her watch, "It is about eleven fifty at night." Marty looked at her with a perplexed expression, "But what day is it?" She chuckled a little, "It's Saturday right now, but in ten minutes it will be Sunday." Since he had awakened at the diner, he had lost all sense of time, and it felt like days had passed, when indeed it was only hours since he and Annette had been at that very same hospital for tests.

The nurse finished straightening his blankets, "Now you rest, the doctor will be by to talk to you during his next set of rounds." She pointed to a call button on the bedrail to his side, "If you need something, just buzz the nurses' station using that button." She turned and walked over and opened a door, and flipped on a light, "Here is the bathroom, just buzz the nurses station in case you need it, and somebody will come by with a bedpan or assist you, but do not get out of bed without someone being here," and then she turned and walked out of the room. Marty lay back into the pillow and breathed deeply. He placed a hand on his forehead, which immediately gave him a painful reminder of the wound he was sporting, "Ouch, that hurts." As he crossed his fingers on his chest, he became consumed with concerned thoughts for Annette. He wondered why she had left him behind at the diner, and why she even left the diner in the first place, especially since she had no idea if he was badly hurt, or even killed, but the thought that burdened him the most was wondering if she was ok. He recalled how the patrons at the diner recounted her struggle with the armed bandit and worried that she might have been injured in the process. He got a chill thinking that she could be lying God knows where, slumped across the steering wheel, injured, with no one nearby to help her. He could not shake the eerie feeling that when he heard her voice while he was unconscious, maybe it was her trying to communicate to him that something was terribly wrong with her.

Having thought that something could be wrong with Annette compelled Marty to try to find her, and he decided not to waste any more time and sat up and fumbled with the different buttons on the upraised side rail, before finding the release button and lowering it. He began pulling off the chest pads that connected him to the heart monitor, causing the audible beeping sounds to cease and become one long flat tone. He placed his feet onto the cold floor and stood from the bed, his head thumped fiercely, and he felt somewhat dizzy and nauseated, but he felt he had to continue, and started taking small steps towards the door of the room. He was stopped suddenly by a burning tugging sensation in his hand, and realized after he looked down that he had not removed the intravenous line from his vein, and it had wrapped around the bed rail he had lowered, and was pulling his skin up because of the tape being used to secure it in place.

Marty was in the process of reaching to pull the intravenous from his vein when he was distracted by a hurried-sounding female voice entering his room, "Mr. Sooner, what are you doing out of bed?" When he removed the heart monitor pads from his chest, he sent off an alarm at the nurses' station, which prompted them to race to his room, No, Mr. Sooner, it is not a good idea for you to be up in your condition without supervision." Marty complied as the two nurses who had entered his room gently guided him back into a sitting position on the side of the bed. "Does anyone know anything about my wife, Annette?" The one nurse gently urged him to lay back in the bed while the other took hold of his legs, placing back onto the mattress, "No Mr. Sooner, I have not heard anything about your wife, or seen her since coming onto my shift at eight p.m., but visiting hours end at nine, so she probably will not be around until tomorrow morning." Marty was becoming frustrated that they did not seem to know what he was talking about: "My wife was at the diner with me when it was robbed. Is she a patient at this hospital?" The nurses looked at each other, and then both shook their heads slightly, "We can check the patient log, but to our memory, you are the only person with the last name Sooner that we recall seeing." The nurse who had helped pick up Marty's feet spoke, "I have been here since around two o'clock this afternoon, and I seriously do not remember any other person with the last name Sooner being admitted as a patient here." Marty noticed the nurse who first entered the room wore a name tag containing the name Burna. "Nurse Burna, would you please do me that favor and check your log, and buzz me back and let me know?" Nurse Burna nodded her head in agreement, "But first, promise you will stay put in bed, the doctor has been paged and should be up to see you very shortly." Marty nodded slightly, "Ok, I will stay put until the doctor gets here."

As if on cue man in a white coat walked through the door and approached him with an outstretched hand, "Hello Martin, my name is Doctor Blake, I was on duty when you first were admitted through the emergency room." Marty reached out and shook the doctor's hand, "Hey doc, I was wondering if you know whether my wife Annette was also brought here as a patient today." Doctor Blake scratched his head and rolled his eyes towards the ceiling, "No, I don't recall working on two traumas with the last name Sooner today." Marty had not noticed that as the doctor entered the room, both nurses slipped into the background and then left the room as he began to speak. Marty looked around the room, " I need a phone so I can call the other hospital to see if she has been admitted there instead." Doctor Blake put up two hands. "Whoa, hold on a second, you should probably take it easy for a little while, you have suffered a pretty good blow to your head." Marty touched his bandaged head wound, "Yeah, you don't have to tell me about it, my head has been pounding like hell ever since I woke up." Doctor Blake continued, "The injury you suffered was pretty severe; you are very lucky to be alive right now." Marty's expression became a mixture of shock, followed immediately by a wince caused by the pain in his head, "Go on, doc." Doctor Blake reached over and placed his hand on Marty's shoulder, "You ended up with a fractured skull from the force of the blow, and your brain swelled as a result. You have been under close observation in the intensive care unit for a couple of hours until you stabilize." Doctor Blake removed his hand and flipped through some papers on a clipboard at the side of his bed. He reached into his coat pocket, "Look straight ahead while I shine this light into your eyes." Marty felt a little sensitivity to the light the doctor shone in his eyes, but tried to remain still without a complaint. Doctor Blake clicked off the light and replaced it in his pocket, and jotted something on the clipboard, "I think you have come along nicely over the past hour. I will downgrade your condition to severe concussion, so we are going to move you down to a regular room, where you will be able to make your phone call." He motioned backwards with his head towards the door, "On my way out, I will let the nurses know they can move you."

The doctor turned to exit the room and then looked as if he just remembered something and snapped his fingers as he turned back around, "Oh, that's right, two police detectives were here earlier wanting to ask you a few questions, but I had to turn them away because you were unresponsive at the time." Marty looked anxiously at him, "Did they tell you what they wanted to talk to me about?" The doctor shook his head, "Not really, they just

181

said they had a few routine questions to ask you and your wife in connection with the investigation of the diner robbery you witnessed." He looked down at his watch, "I can call the station to let them know you have come around, but I would suspect they won't send anyone out to chat with you until the morning." The doctor headed towards the door, dimming the light, "In the meantime, try to get some rest. Someone will be in to transport you to another room soon. I will see you in the morning before you are discharged."

The last thing Marty could think about was sleep, for wondering where his wife could possibly be, and worrying if she was safe, consumed his mind. Part of him wanted to get up and search for her, but the constant throb in his head convinced him to keep still, because any slight movement he made caused the pain to become more intense. Even though he tried to resist sleep eventually, he drifted off into a peaceful slumber, dreamless and restful, only interrupted temporarily when two nurses came to gently transfer him to another room. After being relocated, Marty slept soundly; he hardly noticed that several times throughout the night, he was awakened purposely by hospital staff, ensuring he remained responsive.

The morning sun shining through the window was the culprit that caused Marty to slowly come out of his slumber as his one eye flicked open; the other eyelid remained stubbornly closed, glued shut by annoying eye boogers. He only had the patience to struggle with his stuck eyelid for a second before reaching up and forcing it open with his fingers. He lay there for a moment, mentally preparing for the throbbing pain in his brain to come rushing in, but much to his delight, it did not, and after waiting for a little while, he sat up feeling a sense of extraordinary joy to be alive. He stretched and yawned before feeling a slight pain from the wound on his forehead, which he paid little attention to other than to acknowledge its presence. All of a sudden, he felt incredibly guilty because until just that moment, he had not even had a thought about Annette, and then his guilt was compounded by the fact that he had slept so soundly and peacefully through the night. He scolded himself aloud, "I am such an asshole!" He quickly decided he was not going to wait another second and grabbed the phone on the table alongside his bed and dialed their home phone. As the phone rang, he got a vision of Popsicle still outside on her leash barking wildly because she had been left out all night long, and instantly he felt bad, "Oh, that poor little mutt. He was counting the rings aloud, "Nine, ten, eleven, come on, Annette, answer the phone," when he heard the familiar voice of Doctor Blake behind him, "Good morning, Martin." Marty turned his head to discover the doctor had entered his room, accompanied by two police detectives. He hung up the phone and turned, lying back on the bed, "Good morning, doctor, detectives." Doctor Blake walked over towards him, and the detectives remained where they stood. "How are you feeling this morning?" Marty adjusted his hospital gown, "I feel a whole world better than I did last night, especially since the bloody thumping in my skull has stopped." The doctor reached into his pocket and produced the light, "Let me have a look in those eyes." Marty sat up, "I know the drill, doc, look straight ahead." Doctor Blake talked while shining the light in his eyes, "Like I explained to you last night, the detectives here would like to ask you a few questions." After he finished looking in his eyes, Marty grabbed him by the wrist, "Hey doc, when will I be able to get out of here and go home?" Doctor Blake chuckled, "Not to worry, Martin. After the detectives finish with you, a nurse will be around to escort you down for discharge. It will be just a matter of getting some routine paperwork out of the way, and you can be home as early as ten o'clock." Marty breathed a sigh of relief, "Thanks, doc."

Doctor Blake backed up, "I will let you fellows chat, Marty, I will instruct a nurse to bring you a change of clothes and your personal belongings, because as you know, they were cut off when you first arrived here yesterday." Marty's face turned a little red, for he had almost forgotten having been stripped naked in front of a room full of hospital staff. "Sounds great." The doctor held out his hand, "Well, Marty, in case I don't get to see you again before you leave, let me bid you farewell." Marty shook his hand, "It was nice meeting you, and I don't want to ever have to see you again under the same circumstances." The doctor chuckled, "I second that motion," then turned to the police detectives, "He's all yours, detectives," and then left the room.

After the doctor left the room, the detectives approached Marty, and the closest to him held out his hand, "Hello, Mr. Sooner, I am Detective Brown, and this is Detective Carelley." Detective Carelley then held out his hand, "How do you do?" Detective Brown continued, "We are conducting an investigation into the attempted robbery out at the old silver tracks diner, and during the course of our investigation, it was revealed that both you and your wife were customers at the diner when the robbery took place." Marty nodded his head, "Yes, that is correct." Detective Brown continued, "It is our understanding that you were assaulted by one of the suspects. Is that correct?" Marty nodded once again, "Yes, while I don't exactly remember him specifically doing it, but the heavier one with the rotten teeth, named Fitzy, knocked me out." Detective Carelley interrupted, "You don't remember who attacked you?" Marty nodded yes again, "All I remember is after those guys busted into the diner and started blasting away, they rounded up all the patrons to cuff them to the counter area, the last thing I remember is my wife resisting putting on the cuffs and me urging her quietly to comply with their demands." After that, everything is gone from my memory until I awoke lying in the booth with a paramedic tending to me." "Before they took me away by ambulance, I heard a few of the witnesses explain that the one robber shot the other robber while he was struggling with Annette, and then turned the gun on himself. Shortly after that, Annette apparently took off in our car."

Marty felt a little nervous as he recounted his recollection of the events, and the detectives could sense his apprehension. Detective Brown spoke, "Mr. Sooner, we realize this is probably uncomfortable for you, but we have to collect all eyewitness accounts of the event, so please bear with us." Detective brown continued, "Could you give us some more details about the statement you made about the robbers starting to blast away?" Marty breathed in heavily, "Sure, immediately after the two armed men entered the diner, the one named Fitzy went into the kitchen area, and I was able to see him as he shot one of the workers, and then he herded all the employees into the main dining area." "After a short time, the other guy followed the owner of the diner and his wife to another area where a safe was supposed to be. A few minutes passed before I heard four or five gunshots, and the robber came back without the owner or his wife, and he was bleeding from the top of his head." Marty rubbed the back of his neck, "I have a sneaking suspicion that the owner and his wife were probably shot to death." Marty began to bite his nails nervously, "Once the bleeding guy came out of the office, he went outside and rummaged through the trunk of their car, and returned with a box that contained a bunch of handcuffs, and they distributed them to all the patrons and told us to place an end on each wrist and bind ourselves together." Marty shook his head and looked down, "That is when Annette began to resist their orders. I tried to urge her to go along quietly, but she refused, and I guess that is about the time I got this," he pointed to his bandaged forehead.

The whole time Marty was talking, Detective Brown made notes, "So you have no memory of anything from the time your wife began resisting until you awoke after the authorities arrived?" Marty nodded his head, "That's right." Detective Brown continued, "Have you heard from your wife since seeing her last at the diner?" Marty sat up and placed his feet on the floor, expecting that he would not like what he was about to hear. "No, as a matter of fact, I was hoping you could tell me if you have any information about her." The detectives exchanged glances, and Detective Brown nodded his head, "Actually, another detective in our department arrested a group of teenagers squealing around in your car on the outskirts of town." Marty jumped to his feet, images of brutal gang rape and his wife being left for dead crowded his thoughts, "Oh my god, is Annette ok?" Detective Carelley urged him to sit back on the edge of the bed, "Calm down, Mr. Sooner."

185

Marty collected himself as best he could, "Please just tell me if you know anything about Annette." Detective Brown spoke again, "We questioned all the boys separately, and all of their stories matched. They confirmed that they were hanging out, walking along Deer Run Road, when they stumbled across your car with the keys in the ignition, and could not resist the temptation to jump in and take it for joy joyride." Marty just imagined that the next thing the detective was going to say was that they found Annette's body bound and gagged in the trunk. Detective Brown continued, "Here is where the story gets a little strange. Lo and behold, when we investigated where the boys said they found your car, it was the scene of a pretty massive structure fire, in which two firefighters were injured while trying to extinguish the blaze." Marty shook his head in confusion, "I don't understand. What are you telling me?" Detective Brown turned a chair and sat facing Marty, "That is the reason we asked if you had heard from your wife, because there are some unanswered questions that remain." The detective shifted in the chair, "We discovered a blood-soaked towel in the backyard that we rushed to the crime lab for analysis, which revealed DNA matching the two robbers from the diner, and a third unidentified person." Marty's expression revealed that he was somewhat confused. "Detective, please excuse me for being forward, but I have no idea where this conversation is going." Detective Brown leaned in closer to him, "The fire chief has not ruled out arson as the cause of the blaze, now we are just including Annette as part of the investigation." Marty's eyes widened, "You mean part of the investigation into the fire?" Detective Brown leaned back and crossed one leg over the other, "I wouldn't be overly alarmed at this point, it is very possible that before those two dirtbags went on their killing spree at the diner they stopped off at," he paused and flipped back a few pages. "Here it is, Madam Lydia's Supernatural Consulting Business." He looked back up at Marty, "It could be a simple coincidence that your wife left the car at that location, for some unexplained reason, but we will have to hear her side of things." Marty looked back and forth between the two, "So where is my car now? Detective Carelley snapped his fingers, "That's right, I meant to tell you that your car has been towed to the impound yard, you can pick it up there when you get a chance." Detective Carelley started fishing around in his shirt pocket. "We did swing by your residence last night to chat with her, but there was no answer at the door, and no lights on in the house. Is there some other place else you could think of that she could be?" Marty shook his head, "No, detective, this is really out of the ordinary for Annette, but she has not been herself over the past few days. It doesn't surprise me that with her being pregnant, I am sure you have heard about the whole raging hormones thing before. Detective Brown noticed his partner was not finding what he was searching for, reached into his own shirt pocket, and produced a card with his name and a phone number on it. "As soon as you hear from your wife, we are going to need to chat with her." Detective Brown stood from the chair and reached out to shake Marty's hand, "Oh, and by the way, congratulations on the baby. Marty shook his vigorously, "Oh, thanks so much, Detective Brown. I will be in touch as soon as I hear from Annette."

Both detectives turned and exited the room. Detective Brown turned to his partner, "I get the strangest feeling about this case, and I am not so sure this guy was being completely on the level just now." Detective Carelley looked at him with a strange expression, "I don't get what you mean." Brown just shook his head, "I can't quite explain it other than to say I've got a strange feeling about the husband and wife, and this case, and I think he knows more than he is letting on." Carelley stopped walking and looked at him, but he had an air-tight alibi; he was unconscious from the time he left the diner and through the night at the hospital, the doctor confirmed that." Detective Brown turned around just in time to catch a glimpse of Mary peeking his head quickly out the door and then ducking back in. He reached over and patted his partner on the shoulder, "Take it from me, Carelley, fifty percent of this job is based on gut feelings and instinct." Detective Carelley started walking without his partner, for he felt a little that he was being screwed with because he was fairly new to the force. "Oh yeah, and what is your theory on what the other fifty percent is based on?" Detective Brown stood in place for a moment, looked up at the ceiling as he thought, and uttered a dual-word response as he trotted a little to catch up, "Hard Evidence."

Marty waited until he was sure the detectives were not within earshot before he moved, and then he scurried to the door and peeked his head out quickly to make sure they were still heading down the hall, and as luck would have it, as he did, Detective Brown had to turn around to catch him doing it, "Shit!" Marty stomped his foot lightly on the floor in anger, "What friggin luck, he would have to turn around the moment I peek my head out the door for a second." He returned to the bed and buzzed the nurses' station. A moment, a male voice returned on the intercom, "Do you need something?" Marty pushed the button, "Yes, Doctor Blake said someone would be around with my personal effects and some clothes so I can be discharged." A moment later, the voice came back sounding somewhat disgusted, "Yes, Mr. Sooner, I am drawing up the final release forms as we speak. I will be down there in a little while." Marty caught the sarcasm in his tone, "Oh, sorry for bothering you, but I was not sure if you knew the detectives had gone," and he stuck up the middle finger on both hands and waved them back and forth several times as an obscene gesture to the microphone after he turned off the talk button." The male voice came back sounding very insincere, "It's no bother, don't worry about it." Marty continued his finger antics, mouthing the words mockingly a moment after hearing them. Unbeknownst to him, a nurse had slipped in the door and was standing there watching him the entire time, "Umm, Mr. Sooner." Marty whipped around, startled by her presence, and yelled a little as he grabbed his chest, "Holy shit, you scared me!" The nurse snickered as she walked over to him, "Here are some clothes and your personal effects that you came in with, as you just heard nurse Strauder will be here in a little while to review the final documentation we will need signed before your release, and then you can be escorted to discharge. Marty's face turned a little red when he realized he had been caught mocking the voice at the other end of the intercom.

"Thank you," and he took the items from her hand, and she turned and exited the room. After she left, Marty realized he had no way home, so he placed the items on the bed and approached the phone, dialing the local cab company, directing the dispatcher to have a driver waiting at the hospital entrance.

Marty quickly slipped on the pants and removed the hospital gown as he picked up the receiver of the phone and dialed his home number, struggling to put on the button-down shirt, closing the buttons as he cradled the phone between his ear and shoulder. The thought never entered his head to count how many times the phone rang, but he figured it must have been around nine or more as he closed the final button. He continued to hold the phone to his ear as he recalled aloud the words detective Brown had said earlier, "The bloody towel with the DNA of the robbers is no coincidence." Somehow in the pit of his stomach, he knew something was not right. He wished with all his heart that he could go back in time, back just a few days to before all the craziness began. He missed his wife so very much and longed to feel her embrace. If he could only hear her sweet voice on the other end of the phone, he knew everything would be fine, "Pick up, pick up, please pick up." He stood tapping his foot impatiently, just hoping she would eventually answer and explain that she was feeling really fatigued and must have fallen into such a slumber that she had not heard the phone ringing. Eventually, a pre-recorded voice broke onto the line, "The party you are trying to reach is not answering, hang up, and try your call again later."

A feeling of utter powerlessness and frustration overtook him as he slammed the receiver down, "Fuck..." He closed his eyes and hung his head, "Dammit, Annette, where are you?" A familiar male voice sounded behind him, "Mr. Sooner." Marty turned around, not surprised to see a guy he knew was Nurse Strauder standing at the door with a wheelchair in hand, and a clipboard on the seat, sporting a notable lackluster expression, his voice sounding droll and monotone, "I'm here to finalize your discharge." Marty made a quick mental note, even before

189

another word was spoken, that this man could be the dullest person on earth. Nurse Strauder sauntered in casually and bent slightly, picking up the clipboard, "If you will just have a seat, we can get you on your way." Marty was all too glad to comply and made his way towards where the man had stopped, "Now you're talking my language," he took notice of his name badge reading 'Strauder' as he sat down.

Nurse Strauder handed Marty the clipboard as he began to explain, "What you have in your hands are hospital-required final release forms. I have highlighted where you are to sign." Marty wanted to hurry the process along, "So I sign everywhere you have marked with a yellow marker?" "Yup," was the only response he received. He began scribbling his signature as he was handed each form individually. While he was signing, a distinct buzz sounded in his ears, and the nurse abruptly spun the wheelchair around. His eyes shone black as midnight. "The end is near," the words echoed in his ears eerily as if they were transmitted.

Marty shook his head and batted his eyes, staggering slightly for a moment as he realized he was still holding the receiver of the phone, the recorded voice saying, "The party you are trying to reach is not answering, hang up, and try your call again later." The feeling he had was surreal as he placed the phone on the cradle, "I must be losing my mind," he whispered lowly as he turned to discover the male nurse standing at the door with a wheelchair in hand and a clipboard on the seat. Neither man said a word, and Marty quickly walked towards him, noting the nametag etched 'Strauder', as he picked up the clipboard and sat in the wheelchair. He so wanted to be on his way that he took the initiative, "I will sign where you have highlighted with a yellow marker," and speedily jotted his initials. Within the span of a couple of minutes, he had signed every form that was placed in front of him and was being wheeled through the halls of the hospital and out through the lobby. He was all too happy to load himself into the cab and bid farewell to the hospital, as he gave the cab driver their home address and closed the door.

As the cab swayed and dipped with the contours of the road, Marty once again reflected on his earlier conversation with the detectives and how some of what they said tied ironically close to his foreboding hallucinations at the hospital. He wondered if all this was simply his imagination running wild, or if those delusions may have had some kind of legitimate purpose; he should be taking them more seriously. He vividly remembered hearing the crackle of a fire, and the sounds of Annette struggling, and then the vision of her walking through a wall of flames. He got a chill, as he could not help wondering if she might have had something to do with the fire after all. Marty considered that the detectives may have some of the evidence to implicate Annette's involvement in the fire, but they would probably wait for her to say something incriminating against herself before pursuing further investigation or prosecution.

Marty was sitting there silently staring out the window of the cab as he was considering his wife's possible involvement in this whole scenario, and after a short while, he shook his head and thought aloud, "Stop already," as he slapped himself lightly on the cheek. He noticed the cab was slowing and pulling to the side of the road, and the driver was eyeballing him in the rearview mirror, "You want to stop right here?" Marty had not immediately realized that he had said anything. "Oh no, sorry driver, I apologize for the confusion, I was speaking to myself," he thought a little humor could lighten the situation, "Don't mind me, I am my own best friend," he said, cracking a small smirk, followed by a chuckle. The cab driver rolled his eyes and slowed further until the approaching traffic passed, and then the cab returned to the road. The remainder of the ride home lasted only a few minutes, and Marty gathered his things from the seat and paid the fare plus a small tip through the front passenger side window, "Keep the change." The driver seemed unimpressed with the size of the tip, "Gee, thanks," and drove off, leaving him standing in the cloud of dust that kicked up as the cab pulled away.

Marty felt a sense of urgency to get into the house, hoping that he would find Annette. As he climbed the front steps to their house, he could hear Popsicle yapping from the backyard. He fumbled with the key in the lock and opened the front door. "Annette, are you here?" He did not stay still waiting for a response and searched through every room just in case, but found the house to be empty. "I wonder where she could be?" He went to the phone and noticed there was an unheard message on the answering machine. He pushed the play button, revealing the voice of Detective Brown, "This is Detective Brown. I am an investigator with the local…" Marty pushed the stop button, cutting the message short. He figured the message could be heard later after he figured out what was going on with Annette. He picked up the phone and dialed Annette's parents. Her mother answered, "Hello." Marty did not want to cause alarm in their house right from the start, so he spoke using his nicest tone, "How is the sweetest mother-in-law on the entire face of the planet this morning?" Annette's mom snickered, "Hello Martin, I am fine, and how is everything going with my favorite son-in-law, my daughter, and that sweet little bundle of joy on the way?" Marty stammered for a second, "Um, things are ok, Mom, I was wondering if you have talked to Annette at all lately?" Marty could sense an instant change in her voice, "I talked to her briefly one day last week. Why, Martin, is there something wrong?" Marty thought it best for the time being to minimize the situation because there was no need to cause her parents needless stress, "No, everything is fine, I had to work overtime, and came home early for lunch, and she is not here." He continued, hoping his mother-in-law would not become more alarmed, "Naturally, I thought it was possible that the two of you might be visiting, or shopping, or something, so that is why I figured I would try your house first." Marty could hear his father-in-law speaking in the background, then Annette's Mother covered the receiver to talk to him, her voice becoming nothing more than an inaudible mumble. A couple of seconds later, her voice came back over the line, clear but still sounding concerned, "Martin, we wondered if you have noticed any change in Annette lately?" Marty was hoping to avoid any in-depth conversation and paused for a moment to think, "Sure, I have noticed changes; her belly has grown, she craves unusual foods, and is at times overly emotional, but the doctor has reassured us that this is normal, due to an increase in her hormones and nothing to be worried about." His mother-in-law continued, "That is what I told her, because I too had strange food cravings, and would get all emotional, but her next question caused me to worry, she asked me if the baby made me do things that I did not intentionally want to do." Her words resounded in his ears as a horrible reminder of the ordeal he had been through over the past few days. But he still wanted to steer the conversation in a different direction, "Um, Annette has talked to me about a few concerns, and we scheduled some tests to set her mind at ease. They were completed yesterday, and we have not gotten the results back yet." Marty did not want to remain on the line long and quickly thought of an excuse to get off the phone: "Mom, I don't mean to cut you short, but I only have a little while before I have to be back at work, and I want to grab something to eat." "I will leave Annette a note that I was here, she is probably at a neighbor's house gabbing, give dad my love," Marty said goodbye and hung up without giving her a chance to say anything else.

Popsicle must have been aware that someone was home for her barking became a frenzied mixture of high-pitched yips and subdued howls which trailed off to a low, "woo, woo, wooo.... Marty mused how cute she sounded, and went to the back door and peeked through the curtain to see her hopping excitedly on her back legs, scratching at the door. He turned the lock and opened the door, and the little dog raced in, almost tripping him on her leash, "Ok, calm down." She flipped on her back, stretching out, exposing her belly, while her nub-like tail flicked rapidly. Marty rubbed her belly and chest, "Aw, you must have been lonely out there all night long, you poor little girl," and he removed the clasp from her collar. As soon as the clasp was removed from her collar, Popsicle rolled over onto her feet and darted into the kitchen, her claws clicking on the linoleum as she passed through the room, huffing and sniffing the air, going from room to room searching for Annette. Marty replaced her leash on the nail outside the back door and noticed that her food dish was empty, but she still had some water. He wondered how long she had been without food. He descended the stairs and retrieved her food and water dish, emptying the old water on the grass, and turned ran back up the stairs and into the house. He washed out the dog dishes and refilled them, placing them on the floor where they belong. Popsicle trotted into the room and stood there looking up at Marty, whining lowly to catch his attention. He looked down at her, "What?" She jumped up several times, shoving at his knees while making little grunting sounds, "What's wrong, little girl? Do you miss your momma?" She responded to hearing the word momma by spinning around in a circle rapidly, and stopped tapping her front feet on the linoleum, while making little growling and huffing sounds. Marty reached down and picked her up while rubbing her head, "Don't worry, your momma will be back soon."

Marty bent over and placed the dog back on the floor, and stood up, wondering where his wife could be, when suddenly he got an overwhelming impulse to look out the back door. He raced to the door and moved the curtain to look through. He looked down the length of the yard, but did not see anything that caught his attention. He stood there watching for a little while, but when nothing out of the ordinary could be distinguished, he turned to walk into the kitchen again. But something made him stop and return to take another look through the curtain, and as he looked intently towards the wooded area behind the house, he could make out some movement, and although he could not see what it was, something inside told him it was Annette. Marty flew out the door and ran at top speed down the yard to discover Annette lying on her side in some underbrush a couple of feet from the clearing that marked their property line; she was missing a shoe. He knelt onto the moist brush and pulled his wife until she lay in his arms, "Annette, honey, speak to me," and he wiped the hair back that was stuck to her brow, and he kissed her forehead. The first thing he noticed was what appeared to be dried blood

194

smeared on her face, hands, and stuck in her hair. Plus, he could notice an overbearing aroma of smoke coming from her clothing, and her face and arms appeared a little sooty. Marty picked his wife up from the brush and carried her up the yard towards the house, where Popsicle was anxiously jumping up and down at the screen door. As he began to climb the steps to the back door, suddenly Popsicle stopped jumping and stood there staring quietly as they approached. The moment Marty reached for the doorknob, Popsicle broke into an intense, alarming whirl of barking that startled Marty, for it was quite unexpected. He turned the knob and opened the door, causing the dog to bark even more intently. He waved his foot towards her and scolded, "Popsicle, get back and shut up!" She backed up, turned around, and ran into their bedroom as he carried Annette straight through the house into the bathroom.

Marty gently eased Annette onto the bathroom floor and stood, wetting a hand towel that hung by the sink. He knelt back by her side and began wiping her forehead and face, "Wake up, Annette," as the white towel began to become darkened from the soot and dried blood that covered her skin." He grabbed her with one hand by the shoulder, shaking her, "Annette, honey, come on, wake up." Marty was startled and jumped as Popsicle had appeared in the doorframe and began barking loudly. He turned around to chase her away, and at that moment, Annette's eyes opened wide, shining completely black. He got up and moved slightly in the dog's direction, waving the wet hand towel, "Shoo, take off, you stupid mutt," as he approached, she bolted down the hall, retreating once again into their bedroom. As Marty started to turn back to face Annette, her eyes closed again, before he had been able to notice they had opened, exposing their spine-chilling shade. He returned to the position kneeling at his wife's side and turned the towel to a clean spot, wiping the grime from her skin, "Come on, Annette, it is time to wake up," he said while flicking her nose with his pointer finger. After a little while, that action made her start to come around, and Marty knew it because he saw her eyelid flicker, and she turned her face away from where he had his hand positioned above her nose. He was encouraged by her reaction and pinched her nose several more times, until eventually, she opened her eyes and looked around before looking up at him, "Marty, is that you?" Marty was overjoyed to hear her voice and hugged her tightly, "Oh Annette, I have been worried sick about you, I had no idea if you were dead or alive." He pulled her from his embrace and looked her over intently, "How do you feel? Are you hurt at all?" Annette raised her hands to his chest, pushing him lightly back, "Give me some space for a minute." She looked down at her sooty, singed clothes, grabbed hold of her shirt and pulled it out, and then looked at the back of her hands, which were still blackened, and then felt her hair with both hands, "Whew, I smell like smoke or something." Marty stood and reached for her and helped pull her to her feet, at which point she turned and looked at herself in the bathroom mirror, "Man, I am a mess!" She turned back towards him, "I have got to jump in the shower and wash this stinking smoke smell from myself." Marty shook his head, "I don't think it is a good idea to let you take an unsupervised shower just yet. I just found you unconscious in the woods behind the house."

Annette seemed surprised by her husband's revelation, "How do you suppose I got there?" Marty shrugged his shoulders and turned his hands facing palms up towards the ceiling, "I was hoping you could clue me in." She shook her head no, " I really have no recollection of how I might have gotten back there." Marty pointed to her feet. Well, it appears that you lost a shoe along the way, wherever it is you have come from." Annette could not see past her belly, but she leaned against the sink with her butt and held each of her feet out one at a time until she found the filthy, cut-up, up shoeless one. "I honestly don't remember where I lost my other shoe." After replacing her feet firmly on the floor and standing straight again, her expression looked a little perplexed, "What do you mean wherever it is I came from, wasn't I here with you?" Marty guided her over to sit on the toilet lid, "Tell me what you remember." She sat there for a moment, looking at him with a strange expression, "I don't remember anything. "Now I really feel filthy and in need of a

196

shower. I would prefer to continue this conversation after I am done."

Marty grabbed her by the hands, "See that is why I say you probably should not take an unsupervised shower, you could have another episode and possibly slip and hurt yourself, and we wouldn't want that to happen to you now, would we, my little precious petunia. Annette pulled away from him, "I feel fine, I really think I will be fine enough to shower, and besides, I am not feeling much for some perverted peep show about now, so if you will kindly leave, I am anxious to get started." Marty was a little taken by surprise because she generally always likes it when he played around with her, "Ok, ok, killer, just leave the bathroom door unlocked in case you need me for something, so I don't have to break the door down." She nodded her head in agreement and hugged him tight around the neck. "I am sorry, honey, please forgive me for being short with you, but I am filthy and sore, and would really love a nice hot, long, uninterrupted shower right now." Marty stood up, "I understand, but if you need me for anything, just yell. I will be close by to help," he turned around without another word and walked out of the bathroom, shutting the door behind him.

Marty walked down the hall into their living room and plopped heavily onto the recliner, and sighed slightly as he bowed his head to thank God that Annette was unharmed. Popsicle jumped onto his lap, startling him a little. He noticed she was quivering. "What's wrong with this cute little girl?" he said while caressing her behind the ears. She seemed to respond by looking at him sideways with her crooked eye, as her nubby tail flicked rapidly from side to side. While he rubbed the little dog, he noted the sound of running water as it started in the bathroom. The hot water stung bittersweetly as Annette stepped under the stream, remaining motionless, eyes closed, taking pleasure in the momentary diversion from all that was weighing so heavily on her mind. She remained like that for some time before remembering it would only be so long before the hot water would cease. She opened her eyes and reached for the soap; the sight of her blackened hands streaming with the faded cherry colored water served as a stark reminder that her troubles had only just begun, but had already progressed too far to ignore. Annette hung her head, fixed her gaze upon her swollen belly, and lathered it, wondering how she could feel so disconnected from the presence growing within her. Even then, as she stood beneath the steaming flow, she could feel its cold essence coursing through her entire body like a sinister draft chilling her from within. She wished with every fiber of her being that it could have been possible for her not to have been made aware, **to remain ignorant** of the menace dwelling in her body, but she could not deny and refused to ignore her allotted circumstance.

After Annette scrubbed the remainder of grunge and dried blood from her hair and body, she rinsed and shut off the water. "Ah shit," she realized that she had forgotten to hang a towel outside the shower. "Marty," she called loudly, hoping to catch his attention instantly. He tossed the Popsicle to the floor and bounded out of the recliner, heading immediately for the bathroom, "Annette," and turned the knob, opening the door, "What do you need?" She stood with her arm extended through the cracked open shower door, "I forgot to grab a towel before I started showering. Would you grab me one from the closet?" Marty immediately thought there would not be a better opportunity to give her a hard time, but reconsidered, "You know, under most any other situation, I could torture you like crazy right now." Annette rolled her eyes, for she knew he could never pass on an opportunity for breakin' 'em off on her; but much to her surprise, he laid a towel over her extended arm, "But I will spare you this time," and walked out of the bathroom, closing the door behind him. She opened the shower door and poked her head out, half expecting him to be standing close by, but almost to her surprise, he had really left the bathroom without incident.

Annette dried her body and wrapped herself in the towel, stepped out of the shower, grabbed another towel that she wrapped around her head, and grabbed a couple of cotton swabs to clean her ears. She opened the door and headed down the hall to their bedroom, kicking the door partway closed with her leg as she entered. She opened their closet, pulled out a robe, and dropped the towel she had wrapped around her body onto the floor a moment before Marty pushed open the door, "So did you enjoy your shower?" Annette scrambled to pull the robe on, "Geeze Marty, I think you're trying to give me a heart attack." Marty chuckled, "Oh, I'm sorry, really didn't mean to scare you," his voice trailed off. He walked into the room bearing a wide-eyed expression and approached her; parting the robe she had just covered herself with, "My God, Annette, your belly is huge." Annette looked down briefly before replacing the material over herself, "I know, I know." Marty backed up slightly, still maintaining the look, "No, really, I'm not kidding, you see it in a whole new light when it's uncovered." He reached over and parted her robe again; "It looks like you have a beach ball in there." Annette pulled her robe closed again, sneering at him, "Hah, hah." Marty sensed her displeasure but felt he needed to continue, "No, honey, I'm not bustin' you, since I saw you before the tests yesterday, your belly looks even bigger, and I had not noticed until I just saw it in the flesh a moment ago."

Both Annette and Marty jumped as Popsicle emerged through the door and suddenly began barking furiously. Marty turned around and bent down to grab her, but she was too quick and beat a hasty retreat back down the hall. He turned back towards Annette, "What the hell is with all this damn barking?" Then he paused for a moment, visibly having drawn some sort of conclusion, as he snapped his fingers, "I'll bet she is pissed at us for leaving her tied outside all night long." Annette removed the towel from her head and grabbed the hair dryer, and began styling her hair without saying a word. Marty took her silence as a nonverbal clue and walked back and reassumed his position in the recliner, and grabbed the television remote, clicking on the power, as Popsicle once again approached and jumped on his lap. The sound came from the television before the picture, "Coming up on channel six local news at noon, we give you a glimpse of what it was like inside the scene of the bizarre diner robbery gone

199

wrong, as we bring you several eyewitness accounts of the deadly attack." The picture on the set became clear enough for Marty to see two bodies being removed by stretcher from the familiar diner. The reporter on the set continued, "And we bring you the latest update of the ongoing investigation into the deadly fire on Deer Run Road that injured two firefighters."

Annette turned off the hair dryer, grabbed the brush and can of hairspray, and began styling her hair. She could hear the sound of the newscast that Marty was watching down the hall, but did not pay any attention as the television blared out the news program's theme music. But she stopped what she was doing as she heard the news anchor delivering the report, "In our top story today at noon, arson is suspected in the deadly fire on Deer Run Road that claimed the life of one person and injured two firefighters battling the blaze." Marty put the feet rest on the recliner down as he heard the hair dryer shut off, but was distracted for a moment by the news story on the set. Annette walked to the door and listened closer as the news continued, "Fire chief Harry Caufferman had this to say at a news conference held about an hour ago." The image on the screen switched to a man with a badge and tie, "The investigation into this blaze remains ongoing as we still have many unanswered questions at this time, but we are working closely in conjunction with police crime labs and have not ruled out the possibility of arson at this time." Annette recalled earlier when Marty sat her on the toilet and asked her if she remembered anything from the prior day, and at the time he asked she was having a mental block, which prevented her from recalling anything. However, as she listened to the press conference of the fire chief, she began to remember pulling the car off Deer Run Road and meeting Lydia, and then following her into the house. She remembered the woman confirming her suspicion about the baby, and seeing the book with the illustrations with the scale on which all souls exist. But her memory failed beyond that point, but the smoky-smelling clothes on the bathroom floor made her think she may have been at Lydia's when the fire started.

The image on the screen switched back to the news anchor, "We will keep you updated on the latest developments in the suspected arson fire that claimed the life of one person and injured two firefighters." Just then, Marty heard someone step onto the porch and ring the doorbell. His heart began pounding for instinct warned him that the detectives he had spoken to earlier were standing on the other side of the door. Popsicle was still on his lap and began barking right after hearing the doorbell ring, but Marty just sat there for a moment, extremely hesitant to answer the door because he had not even gotten the chance to discuss anything about the car being on Deer Run Road with Annette. The doorbell rang a second time, and Marty looked towards the hallway leading to their bedroom, where Annette had suddenly appeared. He shot her his most serious look and pointed towards the direction of the bedroom and silently mouthed the word, "Go!" He then pointed to his ear and again mouthed, "Listen." After the doorbell had rang the second time, Popsicle went into a second round of barking. Marty noticed the two figures at the front door were making an effort to see in between the horizontal blinds covering the glass of the door, and he pushed Popsicle from his lap as she escorted him to answer the door. His guess about the identity of the people on the porch was confirmed as he peeked through the blinds and then unlocked and opened the door, revealing detectives Brown and Carelley. Marty yawned and scratched his head while rubbing his eyes, "Sorry it took me a little while to answer, I must have dozed on the recliner while I was watching television." He did not unlock the screen door that separated him from the two men, "Please don't say you have bad news about my wife?" The detectives looked at each other for an instant before detective brown answered, "No, we don't have anything new to tell you about your wife." Marty looked upward, "Thank God, when I opened the door and saw you two standing there, I was almost expecting to hear bad news." Marty continued, "So why am I surprised to see you again so soon?" The detectives paused for a moment, for they were expecting him to open the door and invite them in, and when he did not, it served for a moment of awkward silence. Popsicle interrupted the silence as she began barking at the men; the hair on her back was standing on end. That gave Marty the perfect excuse for not extending an invitation, "I would invite you in, but I'm not always sure I can trust her. Detective Brown nodded his head, "That is ok, we were just in the area having lunch and thought as long as we were close, we would stop by and pay a visit about the matter we discussed with you earlier."

Marty glanced down at his watch, "Well, what do you know, I must have been sleeping longer than I thought. It is already lunch time." He looked back up at the men, "So what's new with the juvenile delinquents who stole my car and set that place out there on fire?" The detectives again looked at each other. This time, Detective Carelley spoke, "Mr. Sooner, we never said the group of kids that stole your car was responsible for the fire at that house." Marty feigned a surprised look, "Oops, was I not supposed to read between the lines this morning, because that was the distinct impression I got after our little chat this morning at the hospital." He put both hands in his pockets, "I mean, really, it seems pretty obvious to me that those kids would be the main suspects in this investigation." Detective Brown stepped forward and put his hand on the screen door, and tried it. "Mr. Sooner, have you seen or heard from your wife yet?" As soon as Popsicle noticed him grab for the doorknob, she ran down the hall barking and squealing like she had been shot at. Marty reached into his back pocket and produced the card they had given him, and was about to speak when Annette appeared from the hallway, "Marty is someone at the door." Marty felt his heart leap as he turned around to see Annette standing there still clad in her robe. His immediate impulse was to scream at her for not staying out of sight, but he kept his cool, "Yes, honey, I didn't realize you were out of the shower yet. It's a couple of police detectives who visited me in the hospital this morning before I was discharged from the hospital." He turned back to the detectives, still holding the card between two fingers in the air, "Annette just arrived, and I was going to call you after she cleaned up, but I guess that is not necessary now."

Detective Brown jiggled the locked handle. "Do you mind if we come in and chat for a while?" Marty unlocked the door and stepped back, "Of course not, fellows, come on in, but hold on for a second while I take a minute to put our killer watchdog behind a closed door." Marty glared at Annette as he walked past, towards Popsicle, who had been peeking her head around the corner of the kitchen wall, huffing and snorting as the detectives entered. As Marty went to grab her, she flipped playfully onto her back and wriggled her feet in the air, and peed, "Come on, grizzly, let's get you into another room where you won't be so much of a distraction." He scooped the little dog into his arms, walked down the hall towards their bedroom, put her in, and shut the door. Annette walked up to the detectives and held out her hand, "I am Annette Sooner, Marty's wife." Detective Brown held out his hand first, "I am Detective Brown, and this is my partner, Detective Carelley." Detective Carelley also shook her hand, "Nice to meet you, Mrs. Sooner." Annette moved slightly back, "Can I offer you detectives something to drink, coffee, tea, or ice water?" Detective Brown shook his head at the same time as Detective Carelley, and they both said simultaneously, "No, thank you." Detective Brown walked in a little way, "Is there some place where we can sit and chat for a little while? We have some questions we would like to ask you." Annette pointed to the kitchen, We can all fit comfortably at the kitchen table if you like." Detective Carrelley nodded his head, That will be fine." Annette led the way, followed by Marty and the two men, "Have a seat anywhere you like, gentlemen."

Within a few moments, everyone was seated, and Detective Brown led the conversation: "Mrs. Sooner, after you left the Silver Tracks diner with your car, can you describe to me where you went and what you did?" Annette adjusted her robe so it covered her legs, "Yes, I was pretty upset after the two robbers shot one another, and I was in a total state of distress and panic when I took off out of the diner and jumped into our car and left." Detective Carelley leaned forward, "Did you know your husband had been pretty severely injured?" Annette reached over and took Marty's hand, "At the time, I was just so distraught and panicked after having to fight off the robber, I really didn't even realize he had been injured." "I just wanted to get as far away from that situation as possible, so I jumped in the car and drove, not really having any particular destination in mind." Detective Brown leaned in, "So where did you end up?" Annette breathed in heavily, and her eyes filled, "Well, I pretty much drove aimlessly, and pulled over on Deer Run Road when I couldn't keep my composure any longer." "I sat off to the side of the road for a little while crying, when this nice lady approached me, I think she said her name was Lydia." Annette was becoming visibly more upset, and Marty reached onto the counter behind him and retrieved a napkin from the dispenser, and handed it to her. "Anyway, Lydia asked me if I wanted to come to her shop and call someone for a ride, because she really thought I was too upset to be driving."

Detective Carelley jotted something down on the clipboard he was carrying, "Did this Lydia tell you her last name?" Annette dabbed her eyes again, "No, not that I recall anyway." "She told me she was some sort of psychic, or supernatural medium, or something to that effect; she even offered to provide me one of her readings as we walked towards her shop." "I declined, and thanked her for the offer, but told her I would appreciate using her telephone if it would not be too much trouble for her." Detective Brown hoped to keep her from becoming overly emotional, so he figured a small diversion would probably be a good thing. "If you don't mind, I am a little dry. I think I would like to take you up on that offer of ice water after all." It worked. Annette stood, "No, I don't mind," and she grabbed two glasses and went to the refrigerator, pouring.

Give them some cold water. As she replaced the container in the refrigerator, Detective Brown spoke again, "So did you use her phone?" Annette reclaimed her seat, "Actually, no, I never got the chance, we entered the shop and I followed her into a back room that she had filled with lit lamps and candles placed all around, where she offered me a towel to wipe the blood off of my face and she told me to stay put for a minute while she got me the phone and left the room." Detective Brown scribbled something on his own clipboard and looked directly at Annette, "How did you get blood on your face?" Annette placed her elbows on the table and covered her face with her hands, then positioned her fingers to her temples, massaging them slightly, "Blood splattered all over me when the one robber from the diner shot his accomplice and then turned the gun on himself."

Detective Brown jotted notes as Annette recounted her ordeal, "Tell us what happened while you were in Lydia's shop." Annette leaned back in her chair, "What I have told you is about it. I was standing in the room Lydia had left me in, wiping the blood from my face onto the towel, when I heard rustling sounds coming from the room Lydia had just entered, and I really have no recollection after that." Detective Brown continued taking notes and looked up at Annette, "What do you mean by rustling sound?" Annette shook her head and shrugged her shoulders, "I don't know, I thought it might be the lady, Lydia, moving boxes maybe to get to the phone, but I can't be sure." Detective Carelley took a turn to interject, "And why can't you remember anything after hearing the rustling sounds?" Annette again shook her head, "I must have been whacked on the back of the head by someone, because I blacked out, and when I woke up, the room was filled with thick smoke, and I could feel the heat of a fire all around me." Annette bent forward towards Detective Brown and placed her hand on the back of her head, "If you feel here, I have a nasty lump where I think someone nailed me." Detective Brown felt the back of her head, "Oh, yeah, that is a nasty lump, he looked over at his partner, "Feel this," and Annette positioned her head a little bit in his direction as he too rubbed, feeling the bump. Detective Carelley sat back down in his seat, "It actually feels like you have more than one lump." Detective Brown nodded his head, agreeing, and he stopped rubbing her head and jotted on the paper, "I was going to say the same thing, Mrs. Sooner. Do you remember anything after blacking out?" Annette placed her hand on the back of her neck and rolled her head around, "Um, I can't say for sure, but I almost vaguely remember opening my eyes for a moment while

I was lying on the floor, and seeing feet rushing about the room and hearing debris hitting the floor and being scattered around." She sat back and rubbed her belly, " I don't remember anything else until I awoke surrounded by heat and smoke, and after that I vaguely remember crawling on my hands and knees towards an open door, but everything is gone from then on, until my husband woke me in the wooded area behind our house."

Marty had been listening silently until this point, chimed in, "It's true, Detective Brown, I just noticed her lying out there a little while ago." Detective Carelley had a perplexed expression. "So why didn't you just drive and get some help?" Annette closed her eyes and rubbed them. "You know, detective, I have no clue, like I said before, that whole time period is gone from my memory; in fact, our car is still parked by Lydia's shop on Deer Run Road. Marty patted her on the arm, "No, dear, the detectives explained to me this morning that our car is at the police impound yard waiting for us to pick it up." Annette shifted herself and crinkled her brow, "Did it get towed because of the way I had it parked on the side of the road?" Detective Carelley leaned in, "No ma'am, your car was pulled over by another officer because it was filled with a bunch of teenagers driving recklessly." Annette slapped her hand on the top of the table, "Shit, of course, I'll bet you a hundred bucks I left the keys in the ignition." Detective Carelley nodded his head, "Well, the driver of the vehicle certainly had the keys in his possession at the time of the arrest."

Detective Brown looked at Marty, "How come you haven't taken her to the hospital, or called us to let us know she was here?" Marty looked up at the ceiling, "You don't know my wife; she can be pretty feisty and stubborn when she wants to be, and she insisted on showering to get all the black off herself before she did anything else." "Hell, she wouldn't even let me stay in the bathroom with her just to make sure she was steady enough to shower." Detective Carelley nudged his partner and looked at Annette, "Can we have the clothes you were wearing at the time all this took place?" Annette stood and pushed her chair out.

"Sure, let me get them; they are still lying in a pile on the bathroom floor." Detective Brown raised a hand and grabbed her wrist, stopping her. "Could you place them in a plastic bag for me?" Marty took the initiative and retrieved a plastic-handled grocery store bag from inside the cabinet by his side and handed it to her. Annette left the room and retrieved the smoky-smelling smelling damp clothes from the bathroom floor and handed them to Detective Brown, "Here you are, all packaged and ready to go." The smoky smell wafted into the detective's face as he took hold of the bag and tied it shut, "Whew, I certainly can smell the smoke on those." Detective Brown tipped back his glass, swallowing the remainder of his water, and standing from his chair, "Well, we have taken up enough of your time, and I would like to thank both of you for chatting with us on such short notice." Detective Carelley also stood and pushed his chair under the table. Both Annette and Marty also stood, and they all headed for the front door. Detective Brown reached for the handle and turned to Marty and Annette, "If we have any further issues to discuss, we will contact you." Marty raised a hand and waved, "Will do, detectives, you know where we live." Then, without another word, the two walked out the front door, down the steps, and hopped into their car. Detective Brown headed for the passenger seat, as his partner started the engine, Carelley turned the steering wheel, and pulled out of where they had parked. "Well, their story certainly seems legit." Brown opened the bag, getting another good whiff of the clothes, and he moved them around slightly, noticing the grass and debris stuck to them and some burn holes in the fabric, "Yeah, you're right, it does, but I still think something is up. I can't explain it, but I feel it."

Chapter 11: The Popsicle Incident

Marty and Annette remained by the door as the detective's car drove from sight. And Marty did his familiar swipe, an imaginary bead of sweat from his forehead, "Whew, I almost shit when you came walking down the hall." He kissed Annette on the top of her head, "I was just going to try to put those two off for a while, saying you had not shown up yet." He walked over and sat on the recliner. "If you had not come out at that exact moment, I would have told them that I had their number, and when I found out where you were, we would contact them." He shook his head and chuckled, "I was hoping not to even let them in, telling them that cockamamie story that Popsicle was some sort of vicious attack dog, I don't think they really bought it at all." "I was really nervous being as we had not talked about any of the details surrounding your disappearance from the diner, and I had the strangest hallucinations while at the hospital that left me with an uncanny feeling that something was not right." Annette walked over to him and placed both hands on his cheeks, bending as best she could with the restriction of her belly, as he leaned forward and kissed her. "But everything seemed to fall nicely into place when you told them the story."

Annette turned from him, went over, and sat on the couch. "Marty, we have to talk." Marty put his feet up on the recliner, "Ok, let's talk." Both Marty and Annette heard Popsicle down the hall scratching at the door. Marty started putting down the footrest, "Hold that thought while I let her out," but Annette raised her hand, "No, Marty, stop for a minute, this is important." Marty could tell by her tone that what she had to say was weighing heavily on her mind, and he put the feet rest back down into a locked position. "All right, honey, what's on your mind?" Annette folded her hands together and fidgeted with her thumbs, "Not all of what I told the detectives is the exact truth." Marty's heart sank, for he knew that what she was going to tell him he probably did not want to hear: "Go on." Annette's chin quivered as she continued, "It's true I was at Lydia's shop, like I told them, but I lied when I said I didn't know the car was stolen." Marty recoiled a little, "Well, how did you come up with that off the top of your head?" A tear rolled down her cheek, and she wiped it away with the napkin she still had in her hand. "When you answered the door, I heard you talk about those kids that stole our car, and it just seemed like a perfect decoy to throw them off the track as to how the fire started." "Actually, those kids were never anywhere near the house, and I heard them roar away when I was still inside the building." Marty had a grave expression on his face. "Well, how did the fire start then?" Annette's voice pitched slightly, and she wiped her nose with the napkin, "I don't know for sure, but I have this feeling I had something to do with it." Marty became a little agitated, "Annette, now what you are saying is some serious shit, you are talking about arson here, and someone died in that fire." He rubbed the back of his increasingly tense neck, "What do you mean you have a feeling you had something to do with the fire, either you did or you didn't." Popsicle began scratching at the door more intently and barking fervently to get out of the bedroom. Annette raised her hands, hoping to calm him down, "That Lydia lady was some sort of clairvoyant or something. When I pulled off the road, she greeted me and told me she might be able to help." Annette's face expressed her feeling of vulnerability, "Marty, she confirmed all that stuff I have been fearing about this baby, everything, without me telling her anything." "She had this old book that told about souls and how an evil soul will attempt to enter the world by filling a vessel without a soul, or something along that line." "She said because I am not supposed to have children, and due to the fertility treatments I have taken has made it easier for the evil soul to take root and thrive inside my body." Marty shook his head in disbelief, "Annette, are you going to tell me you buy into this shit?" Annette shook her head and sniffled slightly, "No, I didn't, in fact, she offered to perform some sort of ritualistic abortion, and I refused, and even got up to leave, that's when I think she whacked me on the back of the head and knocked me unconscious." Popsicle's insistence on getting out of the bedroom was growing to a fevered pitch as she continued scratching and howling from behind the door. Annette continued ignoring the dog, "I think while I was unconscious, the baby was able to take over my body, and somehow the fire was the result. I don't remember anything, but I can't shake the sensation that the fire was a direct result of some action on my part."

Marty could not comprehend what she was telling him, "I can't believe I am hearing this right now, I liked the version you told the detectives better, it sounds sane at least." Annette wiped her eyes again, "I know it sounds crazy, but it's the truth, Lydia told me the soul that fills this child is filled with utter darkness, and must be stopped while it is still at its most vulnerable. Popsicles carrying on became too much for Marty to bear, "Hold that thought while I let this pain in the ass out of the room," and he stood and quickly walked down the hall and opened the door. Popsicle darted past him as he shook his head in disgust, "Damn dog," and she headed down the hall, running right towards Annette and began barking and growling in a frenzied pitch. Annette backed up on the couch, surprised by the outburst from her beloved pooch, "Popsicle, don't be barking at your momma," and she reached down attempting to calm her down, when Popsicle bit her hard on the fingers, laying open a large gash that immediately oozed blood. Annette recoiled and screamed, causing Marty to rush down the hall, but as he started, he tripped over his own two feet, sending him stumbling and flailing down the hall to catch his balance. Try as he might not to fall, he lost all control and tumbled face-first into the living room, right about the time Popsicle had jumped onto the couch and was biting Annette's belly. As he crashed to a halt, what he witnessed in the next split second mortified him. Annette's eyes quickly turned completely black as coal, and she grabbed Popsicle with both hands by the throat and leaped from the couch. The dog gagged and squirmed, fighting desperately to escape her grip as Annette raised Popsicle's body with both hands above her head and slammed her down with tremendous force, shattering the glass top of the coffee table, knocking it off balance enough that it tipped over, landing on its side. The intense impact of Popsicle's body crashing to the floor forced the air from her lungs in the form of a single whining yelp, as her body went completely limp. Annette never took her hands off of Popsicle's throat, and was starting to pick her up once again when Marty screamed, "Annette, no!, He rushed over to her and grabbed her by the shoulders, shaking her violently, "God dammit, stop right now!" Annette gazed directly into his eyes, the shadowy look in her eyes remained for a moment, and a smug grin appeared on her lips before her own eye color returned like two blue balloons floating to the top of a murky black pond.

Annette blinked several times and looked with wide eyes down at her hands as they were still grasped tightly around Popsicle's neck. The little dog's eyes were tightly closed, and her tongue hung limp from the side of her mouth as a trickle of blood ran from her nostrils, down her snout, and over Annette's already blood-soaked hand, mingling with the blood streaming from the bite wound on her fingers. Marty could see the pain in his wife's eyes as she gently placed Popsicle's limp, bloody frame on the floor and sank by the pooch and began to sob, "I think I've killed my precious little girl." Marty stood there for a moment, lost in a feeling of complete shock at what he had just witnessed, before he too sank to his hands and knees on the floor by his wife and Popsicle, and he reached over and placed a hand on both of them, "I believe you, Annette, but I don't know what we should do." Annette looked up at him with tear-soaked cheeks, and she spoke with a voice clear and unwavering, "We have to get rid of this vile influence inside me, before it's too late." Marty looked up, "We can arrange to have an abortion if that is what you really think is best." He hung his head again in shame, for he hated to hear those words come out of his mouth, but could no longer remain in denial. Annette reached over and placed her bleeding hand under his chin, and lifted his head as she looked into his eyes, "We have to do this as soon, today if possible." Marty nodded, "I seriously doubt if we can arrange an appointment today." She shook her head to disagree, "But I think you can, you have connections." Marty could feel the blood from the bite wound on her fingers dripping onto the back of his hand, and he stood and urged her up, "Come on, let's go in the kitchen and have a look at how badly you have been bitten here." He helped her as she struggled to heave herself from the floor, and they both went to the kitchen and placed her hand under running water, which washed the blood surrounding the wound swirling in a steady stream down the drain. Annette winced from the pain and jerked her hand back.

Marty was able to distinguish four or five puncture wounds joined together by jaggedly torn flesh where Popsicle's teeth had punctured the skin on her fingers, and Annette had pulled back in reaction to the pain. His breath hissed as he breathed in through his teeth, "Oh, Annette, I think you need to see a doctor here, this is pretty bad. Marty started to feel woozy looking at the sight of her bloody wound, and her hand went limp as he turned his head away. "Keep your hand under the water while I get you something to wrap that with, and I will call my mother to take us to the hospital." Annette grabbed him by the shirt and stopped him from moving, "No!" I will be fine if we take care of it from here. You have to set up the appointment to take care of this." He turned to look at her as she pointed down to her twitching, swaying belly, "This has gone on long enough and has to be ended without delay; everything else can wait." Marty noticed Annette had a deadly serious look on her face and tone to her voice, "You call your buddy Brett Ludwig at his office and convince him to see us in his office today, and don't let him out of it." Marty thought it best to reason with her, "Annette, he is not going to do that; there are certain rules and procedures that have to be followed, and he could get into some major trouble for not following the proper procedures." Annette opened a drawer by the sink and pulled out a hand towel and flinched as she wrapped it around her wounded fingers, "Fuck procedures, I have to get this thing out of me tonight, before anything else bad happens." Annette untied her bathrobe and exposed her belly, inspecting where Popsicle had bitten, to find there was not even so much as a scratch or welt. She turned off the water and came over to him, "Assure Brett that we are not going to say anything to anyone about this." She began looking frantic, "Hell, I will sign a waiver and videotape myself exonerating him from any liability, and then he can falsify any papers or documentation later on to cover his ass. A tear rolled down her cheek, "I am willing to do whatever it takes to end this now, I can't take it any more." Marty reached out for his wife, "But honey, what if he refuses to do it?" She pulled away from him, "Marty, the two of you have been best friends since kindergarten, and you have been drinking buddies ever since your college days ended. Play the friend card if that's what it takes."

Annette shoved Marty in the direction of the telephone, "Make that call right now, I am going to gather all my energy and ensure this little fuck won't have an opportunity to take control of my body again." A feeling of unparalleled dread overtook Marty as he reached for the phone, grabbed their personal phone book, and dialed the number to Brett's office." A woman answered the North Street women's center How can I direct your call?" Marty hesitated for a moment, and he cleared his throat, "Doctor Ludwig's office, please?" The voice on the other end abruptly said, "Hold please, and the line clicked over to a pre-recorded hold message, "Here at north street women's center are a group of caring, discreet professionals dedicated to offering OBGYN, birth control, counseling," the message was interrupted by a phone ringing once, and then another female voice answered, "Doctor Ludwig's office." Marty looked over and saw Popsicle still lying motionless, and it gave him a renewed sense of what he had to do: "Can I please speak with Doctor Ludwig?" The woman on the other end covered the receiver for a second, and then came back, "Doctor Ludwig is with a patient now. Can I take a message?" Marty looked to the floor, "Yes, have him call Martin Sooner back at home, and please get him the message as soon as possible and tell him it is very urgent." The voice on the other end came back, "I have written it down and will deliver it as soon as he finishes with the patient." Marty thanked her and then hung up.

Both Marty and Annette remained in the kitchen with their eyes fixed on the phone for what felt like a very long time waiting for it to ring, and after about ten minutes, their wait was over. Marty picked it up, "Hello, Marty, old bud, it's Brett returning your message. They said it's urgent, what's up?" Marty once again hesitated, and Brett repeated his name, "Marty, are you there?" Annette nudged him as a prompt to talk, "Yeah, um, Brett, I'm here, I called because I need to talk to you, actually, Annette and I need to see to you as soon as possible in private." Brett's voice lowered, "Marty, what's wrong?" Marty closed his eyes. His face reflected the stress he felt. "Brett, I can't really talk about it right now, but I do have to ask you a huge personal favor as a friend. It involves you performing an abortion." Brett paused for a moment, "Marty, hold on while I pick this up in my private office." The phone clicked on hold, then began ringing until Brett picked it up again, "Ok, now I have some privacy to talk more freely." Brett sighed, "Marty, have you gotten someone in trouble?" Marty gasped, "Oh God no!" He could not even muster a chuckle. "The abortion is for Annette." Brett's voice rang with total surprise, "What?" Marty's tone remained serious. Brett, I wouldn't have even bothered you, but I really need this done fast, and you are the only person I know that can help us out in this situation." Brett's tone remained that of complete shock, "Marty, I don't understand. After the lengths the two of you have gone through to conceive, now you want to abort." Marty interrupted, "I know how it sounds, but please, help me out here, I am begging, you know I have never asked you for anything before." Brett paused for a moment while he considered what Marty was asking him to do, "But Marty, there are guidelines about counseling channels you are supposed to go through first." Marty interrupted again, "Brett, we have considered that, but this situation is urgent; we will sign any waiver you request, eliminating your liability."

Brett lowered his voice to almost a whisper, "I don't have any more patients after the next person I see, all right, dude, you and Annette swing by my office around in an hour or so." Marty breathed a sigh of relief, "Thanks, bro, that gives me some time to get some stuff done first, we'll see you then." Marty hung up the phone and turned to Annette, "I think it could be a go for within the span of an hour or so." Annette rushed to him and wrapped her arms around him. "I will be relieved when this is all over." Marty's eyes fluttered as he fended off tears, for her embrace felt so nice. "So will I," as he kissed the top of her head. Annette rubbed his back, "I just remembered something, we don't have our car here." Marty nodded in agreement, "I have to call a cab and go to the impound yard," as he fished the card that the detectives had given him from his pocket. He dialed the number and asked to be connected to the impound extension, and found out the formalities involved in picking up their vehicle, then called the local cab company and requested to be picked up.

Neither Marty nor Annette wanted to go into the room where Popsicle, for then they would have to face the bleak spectacle of her battered, motionless remains. Marty did not want to face it, but he realized leaving the mess for Annette to take care of would be completely inappropriate. "Honey, do we have some sort of box, or something I could put a Popsicle in?" Annette's breath quivered, and she spun and walked to the back door and looked out, her voice choked off on the first attempt to speak, and she had to begin a second time, "Yeah...um, yes, there is a box in the basement." Her heart felt heavy, and her eyes overflowed, "I can't imagine that our little girl is gone." Marty shared her anguish for as much as he complained about the damn dog, in reality, she gave him a great deal of delight. Without a word, he walked past Annette and went down into the basement to retrieve Popsicle's final enclosure. He grabbed the box and climbed the stairs, and as he emerged into their kitchen, he did not see Annette standing by the door, so he went to the living room to find her kneeling by Popsicle, weeping, and picking up pieces of broken glass. Marty approached them and placed to box on the floor. His knees cracked as he knelt. Annette suddenly stood up, "Hold on a second, we should put something in there to help keep her comfortable," and she went into the nursery and grabbed the blanket she had sewn by hand from the crib. She walked from the nursery and arranged the quilt around the base of the box, "There we go, this was meant to keep a deserving baby warm."

Marty reached for a Popsicle, and as he placed his hands on her, he took notice that she was not cold to the touch. "Annette, I don't think Popsicle is dead." Annette also touched the little dog, and as she did, Popsicle snorted, picked up her head, looked at each of them, and growled as Annette touched her. Annette was overjoyed to see that Popsicle was still alive, "Oh, thank God." Marty placed his hand on Annette's, and then gently rubbed Popsicle behind the ear, "Welcome back, girl, and he tenderly flipped her and picked her up and placed her onto the quilt to inspect her for injuries and remove her from the splintered glass. Annette and Marty noticed that she had received a few cuts on her side, but nothing that appeared as if she would need immediate attention from a veterinarian. Together, Marty and Annette cleaned up the shards of glass that were strewn about the floor, Popsicle struggled to her feet without making a sound, and looked back at them before heading towards the kitchen. Marty quietly followed her and watched as she dipped her head and drank from the water bowl. He stood there watching her for a little while, "It doesn't appear that she has been too badly injured, short of those few cuts."

Just then, a car horn sounded outside, and Annette stood and looked out the window. "Marty, your cab is here." He watched Popsicle for another moment, then went over and kissed Annette, "I will go pick up our car from the impound yard, keep an eye on the dog until I get back, and if she is still fine, we can go get this over with." As Marty spoke those words, Annette doubled over and grabbed her stomach, the cab driver blew the horn again, and Marty opened the door and held a finger in the air to let him know he was coming. He went back to Annette, "Honey, will you be fine until I get back?" She nodded her head, "Don't worry about it, I will be just fine, now go and hurry back." Marty balled up his fist and raised it by her, "Why I oughta, pow, right in da lip." He always got annoyed when she hurried him, because no matter how quickly he got back, she would always ask him what took so long." Annette gestured like she was going to bite his fist, "Yeah, yeah, I'm really scared," and she raised her hand to show him how steady it was, "See, I'm shakin' like a leaf." Marty leaned in towards her, "All right, smart ass, give me a kiss," then trotted out the door and down, getting into the back of the cab. Annette watched as the cab drove away and then shut the door. She turned from the door and was startled to see Popsicle standing just a few feet away, "Ooh, Popsicle, you scared me." Popsicle raised her lip and snarled as she bore her sharp white teeth, "Uh oh, come on, little girl, just calm down." Annette began to kneel, and as soon as she moved, Popsicle rushed towards her, barking in a frenzied pitch, causing Annette to quickly resume the position she was standing in.

The cab pulled up in front of the police station, and the driver turned around, "That will be five dollars and seventy-five cents." Marty exited the cab and pulled money from his pocket, "Here's six dollars, just keep the change," and the driver rolled his eyes, "Thanks, I'll try not to spend it all in one place," and then pulled away. Marty chuckled and shook his head, "Seems like it is time for someone to consider a career change." He dashed up the stairs and into the station, almost hearing Annette's voice commanding him to hurry up. Fortunately, he did not have to wait in any sort of line and approached an officer standing behind a protective booth. "Officer, could you instruct me on the steps I have to take to claim my car from impound?" The officer approached the glass. His expression struck a chord with Marty as being detached, even apathetic. "Got ID and the vehicle title?" Marty produced his photo driver's license from his wallet along with the title and slid it under the slot in the glass for the officer to inspect. He picked them up and looked at the picture on the license, then at Marty, then at the picture again, and casually grabbed the phone and hit three numbers with his thumb, "Don the owner of the Cutlass that was brought in yesterday is here to pick it up," after a short pause he simply said, "fine," and hung up. He slid Marty's license and title back under the glass, "Have a seat over there, Don will pull your car around to the front of the building." Marty took his seat and within a few minutes, he heard the familiar sound of his engine as it pulled in front of the building. Then he heard the car door slam shut, and a short bald man wearing oil oil-stained work uniform ran up the stairs and into the building, "Who's here to pick up the cutlass?" Marty looked around and smiled because he was the only person besides the officer behind the glass in the lobby, "That would be me." The man approached and tossed him the keys, then, without another word, walked away. Marty stood there for a second, then turned to the officer behind the glass, who had picked up a magazine and started reading, "Is there anything I need to sign?" The officer moved his eyes from the page he was reading, "Yeah, sign where it is highlighted," and he slid a form under the glass. Marty signed, and the man tore off a pink page and slid it to him, "For your records."

Marty smiled slightly as he grabbed his copy, "Thanks," and quickly trotted from the station. He thought silently that dude must have ice in his blood. As he walked to the car, he was disgusted to see the mess the kids had left behind. There were drink containers, crushed potato chips, and empty bags strewn about the interior. He was even able to see two distinct bare footprints on the passenger side windshield. "What pigs." He bent over and began picking up the trash when he caught a glimpse of something under the seat. He reached under and pulled out a folding pocketknife. "One of them must have dropped this, and he stuck it in his shirt pocket. He started the engine and headed for home. As he drove, he began to have feelings of extreme guilt for what he was about to do, for even with being convinced that none of what happened was simply his imagination running wild, he was dealing with remorse for having been forced into taking such extreme measures. Within a few minutes, Marty was parking in front of their home and climbing the steps. As he approached the door, he noticed Annette standing by the door. "Hey, honey, I'm home, he wrapped his arms around her and kissed the back of her head. He noticed Popsicle standing a short distance away, staring in their direction. Annette pointed to her, and she bared her teeth and snarled, "She knows about the baby; she has not let me move since you left, and I didn't want her to bite me again, so I have been standing in this same place since you left." Marty moved around Annette and knelt in front of her, "Hey Popsicle," and he held out his hand. Popsicle broke her gaze from Annette and leaned down on her front legs with her butt pointing straight in the air. Her nubby little tail began flicking eagerly from side to side.

Marty picked her up, "Come on, you should go outside for a little while before we go," and he walked with her in his hands to the door, opened it and clasped the leash to her collar, and set her down on the step. She looked back at him, then turned and made her way down the steps to the grass. Marty turned around to find Annette standing behind him, "Annette, are you positive this is what you really want?" Tears became evident in her eyes, and she sniffed slightly, "Yes, Marty, I have never been so sure of anything before." He walked over to her, "Because I was thinking, maybe we were chosen to host this baby for some reason we are not aware of." He put his hand over his mouth and paused for a moment before continuing, "I can't help but think that maybe this is our chosen reality, whether we want to accept it or not." Annette took hold of his hand, "I know what you are saying Marty, right about the time you found me this morning I was dreaming that I was a soldier, at the lead of an army, a voice boomed all around telling me that I am the messenger selected to deliver the bundle into reality, no matter how my brain tried to resist, I could not stop my body from complying." She looked directly into his eyes, "Marty, I don't think I could live with myself if I just ignore what I know." A sad look came over her, "I'm afraid that if I wait any longer that it will be like in my dreams, and I won't be able to do anything to stop it." Marty noticed that as she spoke her thoughts, her belly was actively twitching and swaying. Marty nodded his head, "Ok then, I just had to be sure that you are sure this is what you want," he turned and opened the back door, and Popsicle ran in, and he removed her leash. He closed and locked the door, "We had better get going soon, Brett is waiting for us at his office." Annette headed for the bedroom, talking as she walked, "Give me a minute to get dressed." Within a few minutes, Annette came back from the bedroom fully dressed, "I'm ready." Marty grabbed the car keys from the counter and held them up for her to see, "Me too." he then dialed Brett's private cell phone number, "Brett, it's Marty, we are about to leave." A crackle of interference caused Brett's response to be choppy, "Meet, trance to the main lobby." Marty attempted to communicate that their connection was breaking up, but the line went dead. "Hmm, well, I hope he knows we headed there." Annette walked out of the house first, and Marty followed, as he closed the door behind him.

Both Marty and Annette felt numb as they drove the distance to the North Street Women's Center; neither spoke a word, for they were both engulfed in a raw, unsettling emotional state. The lot to the complex was virtually empty except for a few cars as Marty navigated to the main entrance. He sighed heavily as he parked and turned off the engine, "Here we are." The two of them had feelings of overwhelming trepidation as they walked the distance from the car to the main entrance. Large placards posted at the entrance alerted them of the security measures that were strictly followed with regards to entrance, as the read the signs Brett's voice came over the intercom, "I am going to buzz you guys in," immediately followed by a buzzing sound and click from the door that stopped when Marty pulled it open, and moved aside so Annette could enter before him. Once inside, they had to climb a set of steps and stand at another door. Marty looked up and waved at the surveillance camera mounted in the corner by the ceiling, as another buzz and click sounded from the door. Brett greeted them as they walked through the door with a hug and pats on the back for both, "Marty, Annette, follow me," and he led them through a sitting room and into an office with his name on the door. He motioned towards a set of chairs in front of his desk, "Please sit so we can chat for a while." They both sat, and Brett assumed a position in the chair behind his desk. Marty cleared his throat, "Brett, thank you so much for seeing us on such short notice." Brett rolled himself closer to the desk, "That is what is puzzling me, why such urgency to get this done today?" Both Marty and Annette glanced at each other before she spoke, "You would think we were complete loons if we explained our motives." Brett leaned back on his chair, rocking slightly, "Let me venture a guess...you think you are carrying the spawn of the devil." There was an awkward moment of silence before Marty spoke, "Brett, you know I am

220

not an irrational person, and I realize this seems odd, but we have toiled long and hard coming to this conclusion, and you are the only person who can help us out of this situation." He reached for Annette's hand, "Let's just say we both feel strongly that this is the best solution, and we prefer not to discuss the details that have led us to this conclusion."

Brett nodded his head, pulled open his top desk drawer, and produced a piece of paper, "I have in my hands a waiver of liability. I will need both of you to sign before we begin." He handed the waiver form to Marty, "Normally, I would never agree to rushing into this sort of thing, but because you are such a close friend since we were kids, I am going to make an exception." As Marty took the waiver, Annette bowed her head and grabbed her belly with an obvious expression of discomfort on her face, and without hesitation, after Marty had penned his signature added her own. Brett stood as Annette handed him the form, "Are you ok?" She nodded her head, I'm fine, let's get on with this." Brett continued, "I just want to say briefly that there are other alternatives to abortion available, like adoption, that you might want to consider." Annette shook her head, "There is no need to explain any other options." Brett placed the waiver in a file marked A. Sooner, "I have requested an assistant of mine to stay on the premises to lend a hand; she is unaware of the circumstances surrounding this procedure, so to her knowledge, I have counseled you privately, because you are both close personal friends." He crossed his arms in front of him, "I can get into some pretty big trouble, and possibly lose my medical license for not following the regulations here, so you can't let on to her that this is happening so quickly." He walked around to the front of his desk and knelt in front of her. "If you change your mind at any time before the procedures start, do not hesitate to let me know, and you can walk out of here, no harm, no foul." Annette nodded her head, "You don't have to worry, I am positive about this." Brett squeezed her hand, "Enough said, Annette. How far along do you estimate you are in this pregnancy?" Annette thought for a second, "Umm, I am in the second trimester, probably around sixteen and a half weeks."

Brett's eyes opened wider, making it obvious that he was surprised by her answer, "Wow, if that estimation is true, you are pretty big for being only in the second trimester. He stood and leaned against the desk, "After the first sixteen weeks of pregnancy, the type of procedure that is performed becomes more difficult." "I will be performing a dilation and evacuation, or D&E." Annette and Marty listened intently as Brett explained, "This procedure requires dilation of the cervix, and this will be accomplished by using progressively larger, tapered instruments called dilators." "Once the cervix has been enlarged, tools called a cannula and another named a curette will be used to suction, loosen, and remove any placental tissue, and the fetus will be removed using a grasping tool called forceps." Brett tapped his fingers on the top of the desk. "Annette, I need to make you aware that D&E is somewhat of a complicated procedure due to the size of the fetus and the thinned inner walls of the uterus, which have stretched to accommodate its growth, and there is some risk of internal scarring." "I will administer a general anesthesia to lessen your pain during the procedure, and you will experience some bleeding and discomfort for a few days afterward. You can take acetaminophen or ibuprofen for that." Usually, we do a sonogram before the procedure, but I think that to save time, we can skip that. We can have you on your way home within about an hour. He held his hand up to his mouth, "Not to mention I have a dinner date a little later on."

Brett walked to the door and opened it. "Having said all that, I will need the two of you to follow me." Annette and Marty stood and followed him down the hall and into another room with an examination table covered with medical paper. He handed Annette a blue gown, "Remove all of your clothing, except for your socks, and put this on. I will be back in a little while." Marty stepped outside the room as Annette closed the door and complied with the doctor's request. A few minutes later, Annette emerged, opened the door, and gave Marty the all clear to come in. A short time later, a woman came into the room and introduced herself, "I am Allison, and I will be assisting Dr. Ludwig as he performs your procedure." Now, if the two of you will follow me, I will show you to the examination room we will be using." Allison looked at Marty, "Doctor Ludwig has authorized your presence during the procedure to offer support for your wife." Marty nodded his head, "Ok, if Annette wants me there," and they followed her to their final destination, and she helped Annette onto the examination table, instructing her on the way to position her legs.

Brett entered the room with his wet hands raised in the air. Marty surmised that he was probably in the other room scrubbing in preparation for the procedure. Allison picked up a pair of latex gloves and snapped them over his hands. Brett picked up a syringe from the supply table and approached Annette, "I am going to inject you with a mild anesthetic to help ease any discomfort you might experience during the course of the procedure. As he bent and swabbed her forearm with alcohol without warning, Annette's belly visibly lurched, and she jerked her arm, knocking the syringe from the doctor's hand onto the floor, and her body began to jump uncontrollably. Marty bent to retrieve the needle from the floor, and as he looked up to where Brett was standing in front of him, he noticed Allison's legs advancing from behind. She suddenly began moving towards them faster, and her voice burst forth in a shriek that caused Brett to turn around and face her. He was caught by surprise and did not have time to react, for she was wielding a scalpel that she used to slash the doctor across his throat, laying open a sizeable gash in his flesh, that began where his face mask was tied behind his ear, severing the bottom tie. With lightning speed, the scalpel easily sliced down across his Adam's apple, even slicing through his gown and deeply into the flesh beneath, exposing his collarbone. The force with which Allison had trusted the blade severed the doctor's esophagus, rendering him immediately unable to scream, and blood from his severed corroded sprayed up her face. Brett opened his mouth and grabbed his throat with both hands, wide-eyed and in a state of total disbelief as the blood from his wound gushed forth. He stumbled backward, knocking Marty off balance backwards to the floor, as he was just beginning to stand with the syringe in his hand when she rushed up to them. Annette had noticed Allison as she began walking towards the doctor, but had no clue that she was about to attack him, and as she cut him, Annette began to yell out, "Oh my God!" Marty, having been knocked off balance, fell backward to the floor, dropping the syringe. Brett turned around once again towards him, his hands clutched tightly around his throat, his eyes were bulging and blood coursed from his wound, and he stumbled sideways away from the table Annette was now struggling to get off of, while her belly actively heaved and lurched. Brett collapsed to the floor, and he attempted to crawl, his bloody hands leaving behind red, smeary prints. He was only able to drag himself a few feet before collapsing; his blood continued to gush and spray across the floor, forming a puddle that swelled around his head and shoulders. Marty looked up and noticed that Allison's eye color had taken on that familiar gloomy shade of black, as she quickly advanced towards him. He scurried backwards in an attempt to flee her onslaught, but before he had the chance to escape, she was on him. She jabbed the blade of the scalpel, stabbing him in the chest. He experienced searing pain as a result, and he began screaming for all he was worth, and continued scuffling backwards vigorously with his hands and feet. Allison pulled the scalpel back and plunged the blade again into his chest. The pain from the wounds was so intense that he stopped struggling to back away from her, and he started kicking and flailing his feet in an attempt to fend her off. Suddenly, he remembered the pocketknife found in the car was still in his shirt pocket, and he quickly groped into the fabric to retrieve it. At the exact moment he reached for the pocket knife, Allison lunged the blade forward, aiming once again for his chest, but this time the scalpel blade stabbed him in the forearm. He screamed, writhing in pain, and pulled the knife from his pocket. He quickly fumbled to draw the blade, as Allison drew the scalpel back and punched the blade into the side of his neck, right between his trachea and his collarbone, knocking him onto the flat of his back. In that fraction of a second that the blade pierced his flesh, Marty no longer felt the pain that had accompanied the first wounds; he felt disconnected as the sound of his own screams became a distant, echoing murmur drowned out by an intense buzzing in his ears. Allison moved a step closer and drew back the scalpel again, and Marty reacted by opening the pocketknife and then quickly thrusting the blade in his hand upward, piercing her stomach. Allison backed up, but did not react as if she were in pain, but more as if the force of the blow that had knocked her backwards surprised her. She looked down at the knife jutting from her body and merely looked back towards Marty with a smug look. Without a word, she pulled the knife from her stomach and looked at the bloody blade. An enraged expression came over her as she threw the blade to the floor, sending it skidding behind her. Marty took advantage of the pause and rolled onto his stomach and pushed his body up. Allison lunged forward until she was standing over him and grabbed a fistful of his hair, and yanked his head backwards. Marty screamed out, "No, no, no," and he reached up, seizing her wrist, as she began slicing his throat. All of a sudden, she was knocked off balance as Annette rushed up behind her and shoved with all her might, sending the nurse stumbling a few steps forward as she released her grip on his hair. Marty grabbed his throat, horrified to feel warm blood flowing through his fingers and dripping onto the floor. Allison spun around, her eyes glared a look of seething anger. Annette stood beside Marty, her abdomen still twitching and heaving, holding the pocket knife that the nurse had tossed aside just moments before, pointed towards her belly.

Allison's eyes opened wide, and she picked up a finger, waving it from side to side, and shook her head no. Annette mimicked the evil grin she had come to loathe and nodded yes, then plunged the blade forward, puncturing into the flesh of her abdomen. She thrust with such force that the wind was knocked from her lungs. Annette doubled over, staggering slightly from the intense pain, gasping to catch her breath. She remained for a moment with her hand grasping the handle, feeling it flutter and vibrate. In that moment, the movement reminded her of the way a fish flutters and writhes to free itself when speared. A warming sensation began at the point where the blade punctured her abdomen and continued to spread. She had not experienced internal warmth since conception, when her veins first started to course with its icy essence. Immediately, the presence within her womb ceased shifting and writhing, and Allison's eyes returned to their normal color. Annette threw her head back, her face took on a pain-filled grimace as she held the blade that pierced her skin, then she plucked it out quickly, and plunged deeply into her flesh again, a mixture of blood and amniotic fluid that seemed cool to the touch, spurted from the wounds. Then she ripped the blade from her flesh and stabbed herself again, and then three more times, calling out vehemently, "Die, die, die you fuck, with each thrust of the blade." She paused, as a glazed look appeared in her eyes, and she dropped the bloody pocketknife. She stood there swaying for a moment, and noticed a sudden gush of liquid stream down her legs and puddle at her feet, before collapsing to her knees by Marty's crumpled, bleeding body, and slid herself closer to him. She flipped him on his side and noticed the stream of crimson liquid oozing from his wounds. "Oh, Marty, please hold on."

Allison stood there for a moment, looking dazed as she looked around at the grisly scene, and she picked her hand up that was still holding the blood-soaked scalpel and began screaming hysterically, for she was completely unaware of what had just occurred. She stamped her feet and grabbed her stomach, for the pain from the wound Marty inflicted suddenly rushed in, and looked down wide-eyed at the fresh blood on her hand. Just then, a security guard burst into the room, "What the hell?" his voice trailed off as he surveyed the scene of mass carnage spread out before him. He grabbed his radio from the holster on his gun belt, "Dispatch, this is unit nineteen, I am going to need you to call the police, and paramedics; we have four people that have been stabbed inside the complex at the North Street Women's Center." The guard pulled his gun from the holster and pointed it at Allison, "Drop it, lady." His command did not immediately make sense to her, and she just continued to stand where she was, dazed, shaking her head, and breathing heavily. Again, he yelled out at her, "I said drop the damn blade right now!" Allison immediately complied as he approached and kicked the scalpel away, keeping his gun aimed at her, "Don't you move." Allison kneeled, "I need to know what happened. I don't remember anything." A voice blared over the security guard's radio, "Unit nineteen, we have dispatched police and paramedics to your location. They are on the way, ETA five minutes." Allison continued crying out, her voice rang with a mixture of shock and horror she felt, "The last thing I remember is helping doctor Ludwig into his gloves, I don't understand what happened." A faint sound of sirens penetrated the room, steadily growing in intensity as they drew near. The guard turned to Annette, "Lady, I have to go buzz the police and paramedics into the building. Help is on the way," then darted out of the room. Annette remained in that position and simply nodded an acknowledgment of what he said after he was already gone. Her head began to spin, and the sounds of Allison's wailing and the approaching sirens swirled and mingled together. A wave of nausea swept over her, and she fought off the urge to vomit.

Marty's eyes flicked open and shut a few times, and he looked at Annette. His breathing was becoming increasingly labored, and he struggled to speak as gurgling and clicking sounds were emitted from his throat. He weakly slid his hand across the floor towards her. Suddenly, her mind cleared, and she grabbed hold of his hand and held tight. She spoke softly and caressed his forehead, "Marty, hold on, help is coming." Marty squeezed her hand and tried to speak again. Annette moved closer to him, "Don't talk, save your strength, everything is going to be fine, just stay here with me." The pain from her self-inflicted wounds was intense, and she groaned as a mixture of blood and amniotic fluid spilled from her wounds, soaking her clothing. She adjusted her position to get closer so she could make out what Marty was trying to tell her. Marty struggled to speak again, and a red bubble formed from his mouth, expanded, and burst, sending trickles of scarlet liquid down his cheek. He chuckled slightly, "I was warned." He coughed lightly, and his eyes rolled and shut for a moment, then he reopened them, looking towards

Annette, "I saw my Dad, it was so nice," a tear ran from his eye, "I wanted so badly to let him know how much I love him."

Annette laid down sideways on the floor next to Marty, ignoring the excruciating pain from her wounds, and wrapped her leg and arm around him, as she forced her other hand under his neck, "Just keep your eyes open, stay here with me." As she lay there, she felt a strong contraction in her uterus, causing her to bite her lip and close her eyes, "It seems like it was just yesterday we met, it's really hard to believe we are married five years already." Marty caressed her cheek, smearing a little blood on it, "Yeah, yeah remind me…"his voice trailed off as he struggled to inhale, "five years of weeded bliss." Annette snickered slightly, "You're a prick," then snuggled her cheek close to his, her voice quivered, "It's been the best five years of my entire life, you have been so wonderful." Marty's chin trembled, "I love you so much, my little petunia." Annette closed her eyes tightly, and snuggled closer to him, "I love you more." Annette looked up at Marty and noticed he had taken on a far away look in his eyes, he spoke to her as he stared straight towards the ceiling, "My dad and grandpa are here waiting for me." Annette forced herself to sit up despite the pain from her wound coupled with the lasting contraction, "Marty you can't leave me alone," she grabbed hold of his chin and shook his head, "Come on, look at me, look at me." Marty's eyes rolled and shut, just as her contraction eased, "Open your eyes, stay with me now." Her tears flowed, and she sniffled, "God dammit Martin Allen Sooner open your eyes." She buried her face in his shoulder, "I can't go on without you." The sound of Annette's voice began to fade out and turn hollow, so that Marty could barely hear his wife pleading with him, he had grown weary and confused had the compulsion to no longer resist the overwhelming inclination to depart this life, and he began drifting further and further from his state of existence.

Annette knew without a doubt that she was losing him at that moment and felt desperate to keep him alert. Suddenly, she bolted straight up and slapped him lightly on the cheek, "Ha, ha, asshole got you last." This caused him to revisit, his eyes opened, and he looked at her and smiled weakly. His final words did not sound more than a whisper, "You...got...me..........last," and he went completely limp, staring without expression at her with glazed eyes. Marty could feel his heartbeat slowing, and he realized at that moment his life was ebbing away, and he became filled with sadness in his final moments with his beloved wife. Annette could not bear it anymore and began to shake him, "Marty, don't go, stay right here with me, it's too soon, you owe me a lifetime of happiness, buddy. She pulled his limp body up, cradled him in her arms, and sobbed, for she thought at that moment her heart was surely breaking, "Honey, you just can't leave me, you are the love of my life, my soul mate." Just then, an army of police officers swarmed into the room, with guns drawn. Annette only barely noticed their presence as she wept, rocking her husband and caressing his neck, "Marty, I can't say goodbye, I'm not ready or willing to give you up that easily."

After the police secured the room, one of the officers approached her and noticed her belly oozing liquid. He turned and called out, "Get the paramedics in here, this lady needs immediate attention." He knelt beside her and placed a hand on Marty's shoulder, "Miss, let me lay him down so that we can have a look at you." She looked at the medic, her eyes pleading, "Please help my husband!" The medic gently laid Marty back on the floor, as two more rushed over to Annette. They guided her to lie flat on her back. All of a sudden, another contraction gripped her, sending the room spinning around her, and she breathed in heavily. Her breath hissed as it rushed past her teeth. She closed her eyes and pressed her balled fists into her eyelids, causing bursts of color and light to come into her view. All of her pain had become too much to bear, and she began to lose consciousness; all the hustle and bustle around her became less noticeable, and she simply succumbed.

Chapter 12: Revelation

Annette was suddenly jolted awake as the medics raised her stretcher and locked it into place. She struggled to move but quickly realized she was tightly strapped to the stretcher. A large oxygen mask covered her face, partially blocking her vision, and she had to hold her breath so as not to steam up the clear plastic to see what was going on around her. She could barely move her head and neck, for her body was being restrained by straps binding her in place to the stretcher. The medics began rolling her out of the examination room, where she had lost consciousness. She noticed a group of medics guiding a stretcher directly ahead of hers. A medic knelt on the mattress over top of someone, aggressively performing chest compressions. Annette was unable to see the identity of who it was. She felt desperate to know what was going on with Marty. She began to talk, which steamed the mask, blurring her vision, "Is my husband all right?" The medics who were guiding her stretcher either did not hear her or ignored the question completely and continued pushing the stretcher. The medic closest to her began talking into a handheld radio, "We are transporting a pregnant Caucasian female in active labor, contractions are three minutes apart, estimated to be about seven to eight months, with several stab wounds to the abdomen."

Within a few minutes, Annette was loaded into the back of an ambulance, and the medics climbed in and closed the door. The siren blared, and the engine roared as the ambulance sped towards the hospital. Annette was consumed with worry, not truly knowing if Marty was all right. Another contraction started, causing a grimace to come over her face; she felt a burning sensation inside her belly, but remained unable to move due to the restraints. Annette began to feel very tired and had to fight off the urge to sleep as her eyes flicked and rolled. "Why am I so sleepy?" The medic sitting at her side stood up and looked at her, "You have been given an injection to help ease the pain and intensity of your contractions. We can't have you giving birth in the ambulance; it's probably the reason you feel sleepy.

Just relax, we are almost at the hospital." While he was talking, Annette struggled to keep her eyes open, and without realizing it, temporarily floated into a hazy semi-conscious state. She woke momentarily as the ambulance rolled into the hospital parking lot and screeched to a halt at the emergency room entrance. Her eyes fluttered, for they were sensitive to the sudden burst of sunlight that flooded into the cab of the ambulance when the doors flung open. A team of serious-looking doctors and nurses retrieved Annette's stretcher from the ambulance and quickly moved her towards the entrance of the hospital. She felt disconnected and fuzzy as another contraction clenched her uterus; the flurry of activity around her seemed to be happening in slow motion as she was wheeled towards the emergency room. Annette looked to her right as they wheeled her past an open doorway. She saw a team of trauma doctors working fervently on Marty, but could not distinguish what anyone was saying in the room over top of the bustle of activity going on around her. Just as she passed the door frame of the room where Marty lay, she heard someone yell, "He's going into fibrillation, prepare to shock him." Her stretcher was directed to a room adjacent to the room where he was, and the team of medical professionals instantly began tending to her injuries.

In her hazy state, Annette had not realized that she was still clad in the gown that Brett had instructed her to wear for the abortion, and completely naked underneath. A female nurse slipped the gown down over Annette's shoulders and urged her to remove it, but Annette was not about to lie there totally naked for everyone in the room to see: "I don't have anything on under this." The nurse shook her head, We can cover you with a blanket later, but I have to get this gown off." Annette felt groggy, lay her head back, and closed her eyes, but did not resist as the nurse removed the gown. A doctor wearing a tag with the last name of Rosen OBGYN, without warning, inserted his fingers into her vagina. Annette immediately picked up her head, taken by surprise since she was not looking, "What the hell are you doing?" Doctor Rosen looked at her, "Just relax, I have to do an internal exam to determine if you have if your cervix has

231

dilated." Annette was uncomfortable with receiving medical attention to her female parts by a stranger, "My regular gynecologist is Dr. Sohon; I would prefer if she were here." Doctor Rosen had been a recent addition to the hospital staff as an intern, and his inexperience at that moment was evident. He turned towards a nurse, "Page doctor Sohon to the emergency room, this woman is dilated ten centimeters, and is probably going to deliver very soon." A nurse grabbed a phone, a second later her voice could be heard over the public address system, "Doctor Sohon, please report to the emergency room stat."

Annette began to shiver noticeably as she suddenly became chilled. Another physician present, who was examining her puncture wounds, looked up from the device he had pressed into her belly. "We have to get her into emergency surgery. She has several punctured organs and has heavy internal bleeding. As rapidly as one contraction ended, another began, each becoming increasingly painful. Annette closed her eyes and clenched her teeth as she fought back the urge to scream. Although she was shivering from feeling cold, she was sweating profusely from the strain of the contractions. Doctor Rosen's inexperience in emergencies prevented him from deciding how they should proceed with her treatment, and he looked impatiently up at the clock. "Where is Doctor Sohon?" No more than he uttered those words when another sharp contraction overwhelmed Annette, so much that she yelled out from the pain, and threw her head back and closed her eyes tight. Doctor Rosen removed his gloves and grabbed hold of a clipboard and flipped through some pages, "Well, it appears whatever it is the paramedics administered to stop the onslaught of labor did not work." Just when Annette thought the pain could not possibly get worse, it got worse, causing her to grab her belly, which had transformed into a rock-hard ball of flesh, and howl, "Owww."

Annette looked down to see that she was hemorrhaging heavily from the wounds in her flesh. She put her head back and stared at the ceiling, "I feel the urge to push." Doctor Rosen's voice sounded frantic as he looked around, "No, don't push yet, then looked down wide-eyed and reached towards her, "The head is crowning!" In a flash, a limp, slimy, and blood-covered body of the infant had been expelled from her womb, leaving her with an odd feeling void. A team of doctors and nurses whisked the infant towards a small lighted table and began working feverishly over it. Annette could make out some of what they were saying across the room as they worked on the infant, "There's no heartbeat being detected." Annette felt lightheaded, and the room began to spin around her. A loud buzzing filled her ears, which almost drowned out the physician who had been tending to the wounds, "We have got to get her into emergency surgery now; she is losing a tremendous amount of blood."

The doctor looked at a nurse by his side, I am going to rush to the OR to scrub up, get her prepped to move, and meet me there," and without hesitation, he ran from the emergency room. Annette's eyes rolled back, and her eyelids slowly opened and closed as two nurses covered her up with a sheet and placed a strap over her chest in preparation to move her. One of the nurses turned to the other and placed a hand on Annette's stomach and one on the other on her colleague's shoulder, "Why don't you stay behind and lend a hand to the others here? I can handle transporting her to the OR." The other nurse did not say a word and simply looked back and nodded her head in agreement. A moment later, the nurse, still donning her mask, whisked Annette out of the emergency room and was guiding her down a hallway. Annette slowly opened her eyes and fixed her gaze upon the woman pushing her stretcher, and thought for an instant that she looked oddly familiar, "Do I know you?" The woman offered no reply and continued walking. Annette noticed a small pool of blood had formed on the nurse's facemask just before beginning to fade from consciousness again.

A few moments passed, and Annette was jarred awake as her stretcher banged to a halt against the wall. The nurse had stopped guiding the stretcher and was peering through a small window of a door leading to a room that was dark inside. The nurse looked down the hallway to the left and right, then hurriedly opened the door and rolled Annette's bed in. Once inside, she scurried back and quickly shut the door, but left the light off. Although Annette felt fuzzy and disconnected, she knew something was not right: "What are you doing?" She thought her voice sounded hollow, almost as if she were talking into a plastic tube. The nurse remained silent as she turned from the door and began trying to remove the mask, which had been concealing her identity. She seemed to be struggling to untie the material straps binding the mask around her head. She fumbled to find the point where the straps were tied together. Just as the bindings gave way, a portion of the mask dropped away, revealing a large gash in the skin of her cheek. Even then, Annette still did not fully recognize her. After groping around for a moment, the mask bindings released and revealed to a surprised Annette that it was Lydia standing alongside her in the dark, "Lydia, is that you?"

Lydia had slipped into the hospital completely unnoticed through an unlocked door in the laundry area. While passing through the laundry area, she grabbed a pile of freshly cleaned nurse scrubs. She climbed the stairway leading to level one and felt oddly drawn to the dark, uninhabited room. It was almost as if an unexplainable force had guided her as she traveled undetected. Once inside the room, she quickly slipped on the nursing scrubs over her clothing. After slipping on the nursing garments, she pinned her hair up, placed a sack in a closet, and then walked out.

The heightened level of chaos in the emergency room (resulting from so many simultaneous traumas) allowed her to slip in virtually unnoticed. After entering inconspicuously, she went directly to the unguarded supplies and swiped a mask, gloves, and a cap needed to complete the disguise. She tucked her hair underneath the cap and tied the mask, securing it in place. With her identity concealed, she was able to freely walk around the trauma unit in search of where Annette was located.

Lydia reached her hand out and placed it on Annette's belly, "I am here now, everything will be fine." Annette looked at her with an expression of disgust and anger, "Are you insane? I

don't need your help; I need to be taken to the operating room."
Annette struggled weakly to move, but was hindered by the strap
around her chest, binding her loosely to the bed. Suddenly, a
contraction tightened her uterus, sending a shooting pain through
her abdomen. She gnashed her teeth because of the sudden,
unexpected pain. Her belly began shifting and moving violently,
causing Annette to cry out, "Ahhh!" Lydia quickly reached up,
covering her mouth, "Shhh…we can't have you drawing the
attention of the hospital staff. This will be over before you know
it." Suddenly, to her surprise, Annette could detect the familiar
cold presence writhing within her once again. The contraction
intensified, causing her to thrust her head backward into the
pillow, as beads of sweat formed on her forehead. Annette
realized that she had been duped into believing the threat had
been removed, "Oh no, Lydia, it seems to have survived after
all." Lydia gazed into Annette's eyes, "Yes, it has." Lydia
walked over, walked to the closet, and retrieved a duffel bag,
placing it at the foot of the bed. Opened it and pulled out the
dagger Magda had given her to perform the ritualistic abortion.
She looked at Annette, "You came so close to interfering with
the delivery of this child." Annette's expression was puzzled for
an instant. She suddenly realized that Lydia's allegiance had
changed. No longer did Lydia want to rid the world of the dark
presence, but rather promote its transition.

The contraction reached a pinnacle of pain as it contorted her
abdomen into a rock-hard ball. Then subsided slightly, allowing
Annette's mind to think more clearly. Annette could not believe
that Lydia had changed her mind so dramatically in such a short
time. "Why do you want to help it live now?" Lydia removed
the nursing scrubs and placed them in the duffel bag. She tugged
at the collar of her shirt until her shoulder was exposed. Then
pointed toward a painful-looking, black, pulsating circle of burnt
flesh, "I have been forever marked to fulfill a far different fate."
She pulled the shirt back over the mark, "At first, I was puzzled
as to the reason why I had been spared." "I was tossed down the
back steps safely onto the lawn, instead of being left to burn."
Lydia looked away from Annette, for she was ashamed of what

235

she was about to say, "I remained there on the lawn, cowering, expecting to be finished off." "I willingly succumbed as a trade-off for my life." A tear formed in her eye and rolled down her cheek. "I relinquished my soul to save my ass." "And in that moment I realized I had been granted a merciful reprieve." " I knew as I looked into those murky black eyes that reprieve meant I would be summoned to serve another purpose." "So you see, now I am indebted to serve a new calling." As she spoke, Lydia lifted the sheet exposing Annette's wounded, hemorrhaging belly, "You cannot be trusted with rearing this child, so I have been chosen to take your place."

Annette's head spun and her vision blurred, but she struggled to maintain herself. "The police detectives said a body was discovered in the charred rubble of your shop." Lydia's chin quivered slightly. "I followed behind as you headed toward the end of my property." She looked towards the ceiling, her expression somewhat distraught, "I turned around to get a final look at the blaze and noticed Edna, the nice lady from down the street, rushing in the back door." "I called out to her, but she didn't hear me." "I even ran towards the house to get her, but the flames were too intense; she did not come back out."

Annette became weaker with each passing second. "But I already gave birth, you're too late." Lydia looked at her once again, "Even now, you do not see that you have been manipulated, you have been a pawn, carrying out its ultimate ambition." Annette listened intently as Lydia continued to unravel the mystery surrounding the past couple of weeks, "You carried twins within your womb." Annette shook her head, "No, that can't be…The doctors only found one fertilized egg." Lydia nodded her head, "But it's true, you have been chosen as a vessel for both extremes of the soul scale. One soul, manipulative, dark, and powerful." "The other humble, radiant, and reserved." Lydia moved closer to Annette, "The glowing would counter the gloomy." "Your interference has given rise to an advantage in this struggle. "Now that one has been eliminated, extra time to establish greater influence has been gained by the survivor." Lydia moved close to Annette's ear and whispered, "The dark one influenced you to eliminate its rival, because it would never have been able to by itself."

Annette was mortified at this revelation and became overcome with a feeling of profound sadness, "So Marty was right all along." Tears swelled in her eyes, and her voice quivered, "I should have listened to him and left things as they were!" Her tone became angry, "Why didn't you tell me you knew this?" Lydia shook her head, "I too was deceived...I didn't know until I arrived at the hospital."

Lydia placed a hand on Annette's hard, contracted belly, "It's almost time now." A moment after, Annette began pushing and bearing down involuntarily. She gnashed her teeth from the pain and exhaled hard, a cold sensation accompanied feeling of the infant moving through her cervix. The head crowned, and Lydia guided the infant out of the birth canal effortlessly. She retrieved a length of twine from the bag. Then used the dagger (which was originally meant to end life) to slice the umbilical cord and tied it off tightly. Annette went limp as her uterus relaxed and contracted again as it expelled the remainder of the placental material. The baby cried for just a moment, then quieted as Lydia, looking mesmerized, began cleaning the blood and ooze from the child; a joyous gleam filled her eyes. "It's a boy," her voice rang gleefully." In that instant, Annette realized that Lydia's strength of character was gone, completely enslaved to the child she held.

Lydia continued working feverishly, paying no mind to Annette's deteriorating condition. She finished cleaning the newborn and wrapped him in a blanket. Annette had become depleted due to the massive blood loss and was unable to offer the slightest opposition. Lydia wrapped a scarf around her head, knotting it under her chin, and put on a pair of large dark sunglasses. She wrapped the infant in a small blanket, grabbed the duffel bag, and silently slipped from the room, closing the door behind her.

Annette lay there in the dark, listening to the sound of her labored breathing. She noticed her pulse rate (which had been racing during delivery) had slowed considerably; she felt foolish and defeated. Her heart wrenched with severe regret as she considered that she should have listened to Marty. She anticipated the intense heartbreak the two of them would experience, resulting from the loss of the innocent soul she alone was responsible for extinguishing. She was sinking into a raw emotional abyss as she thought about how much they wanted a family, and how she single-handedly robbed them of that chance. The anguish she experienced was compounded by the thought of Marty not surviving his injuries and his death being her fault as well. If she had only known she was carrying twins, she would have seen the pregnancy through to the end. She closed her eyes and wished that all the pain and torment she felt would be over; she was giving up, having lost all desire to continue. The mere thought of existing without the happy life she and Marty shared was unbearable. Annette's eyes rolled back and fluttered, then stared blankly towards the ceiling.

Suddenly, Annette felt as if she could get up; the pain from her injuries was no longer present. She sat up in the bed, then got to her feet and approached the door. As she opened the door, a bright light spilled in from the corridor, causing her to squint. She looked back and noticed an image of herself still lying on the bed staring straight up at the ceiling. Annette stepped into the corridor, which was illuminated with blazing white light. To her left, she noticed Lydia holding the baby and talking with a nurse. She peered down the hall to her right and noticed Marty standing a short distance away in the shadows. The sight of him made her do a double-take as she noticed he held his arms extended in her direction, a pleading look on his face. A moment later, a pair of ember-red eyes gazed at her from behind him, and then he disappeared backward into the shadows.

Without hesitation, Annette ran as fast as her legs could move, down the corridor towards where Marty had been standing. As she ran, she looked back over her shoulder and noticed a team of people entering the room she had just come from. She ran into the shadow, the floor disappeared from under her, and she fell a few feet onto her hands and knees. She stayed in that position for a few moments, looking around, trying to get a sense of where she was. A thick blanket of fog surrounded her, interfering with her ability to see clearly. The sound of rushing water could be distinctly heard ahead, and behind the blazing white light of the corridor she had just left, projected the shape of a square where she landed. Getting to her feet, she pressed forward. After a few steps, the fog thinned, and she could make out the shore of a body of water. Approaching the water, she noticed a rope tied to a post by the shoreline. She strained her eyes to see where the rope led, discovering it was tethered to the back of a wooden boat about six feet from shore.

Annette felt oddly drawn to the boat, and as the fog continued to clear, she was able to distinguish the outline of a person standing at the front of the boat. Suddenly, her eyes flew open wide when she realized that the person was Marty, holding outstretched arms in her direction. Annette whipped around to grab hold of the rope. As she turned her gaze towards where it was tied, she stopped and gasped to see those amber red eyes staring directly at her. The thick fog had concealed the shadowy figure standing just feet from her, holding the rope tied to the boat.

She backed up a few steps, for a feeling of intense fear had gripped her. Without a word, the shadowy figure smiled and reached towards her with both hands, offering the rope. Annette jumped as it moved, for she was startled and was overcome with fear and apprehension. She refused to take the dark one's offer and shook her head, backing up even further from where it stood. The rope began to slip from its open fingers and slowly moved across one palm. After it dropped from its extended palm, the shadowy figure placed that arm by its side. The end of the rope continued to slip increasingly fast from its remaining open palm. Annette lunged forward and grabbed the rope just before it slipped away. In the instant her flesh grazed the ominous spirit, she sensed the utter evil that was contained within its very

239

essence. In a flash, her mind was filled with visions of all the bedlam and destruction that had taken place over the course of many prior existences. She pulled away, feeling chilled to the core of her soul, realizing the true scope of evil that had been unleashed. Immediately after she snatched the rope from its grip, the dark one turned and walked away, disappearing from her view into the fog.

Annette gripped the rope with both hands and overzealously heaved for all she was worth. The rope slipped from her hands, sending her stumbling backwards. Instantly, the boat began to move from the shore, causing the rope to sink beneath the black water. Annette raced to the water's edge and grabbed hold of the rope right before it disappeared into its murky depths. By then, a swift current had gained an increasingly strong grasp on the boat, causing Annette to lose her footing. She wrapped the rope around her hands and dug her feet into the muddy bottom. She was determined not to let go of the rope and frantically struggled against the current, heaving until the boat began to move towards her. As she pulled it near, she noticed that Marty appeared to be shackled by chains around his wrists at the front of the boat.

Annette guided the boat onto dry land, then quickly climbed on board and rushed to him. She hugged him, burying her face in his chest as her tears began to flow. She became overwhelmed with emotion, for it felt so wonderful to be holding him close once again. It felt like an eternity had passed since she had an opportunity to embrace him. Suddenly, she noticed the boat was moving and turned to see that they were drifting away from the shore. The end of the rope was quickly headed for the shoreline, disappearing under the waters' murky edge. Somehow, it did not bother her to be drifting into the unknown that lay ahead of them. She felt content as long as she was with her darling husband; she was convinced everything would be fine. She watched the last of the rope racing towards the water's edge, "It looks like it's too late to stop it now," and turned her gaze back to face Marty. To her horror, she discovered her arms wrapped around a pole at the head of the boat, not her darling husband. Looking around her in disbelief, she realized she had been manipulated once again, "Nooo!"

As Lydia headed towards the entrance of the hospital, holding the infant close, she became wracked with guilt for leaving Annette behind. Suddenly, a female voice called out behind her, "Miss." Lydia quickly forgot about her guilt, and her heart began to race. She did not acknowledge the woman trying to get her attention and quickened her pace. The voice called out to her again, "Oh, Miss, I need you to stop." Lydia stopped, her mind racing in a panic; surely she had been caught. She turned and pointed a finger towards herself, "Are you calling me?" A nurse, looking about sixty, was waving something in the air as she approached. The nurse, who was out of breath by the time she got to Lydia, "Miss, your wallet from your bag back there." Lydia smiled politely and took the wallet from her hand, "Thank you so much, I did not realize I had lost it." The nurse reached over and moved the blanket from around the newborn's face. "Oh, what a beautiful baby, what is its name?" Lydia looked up in the air, trying to think quickly, "Uh, Raven." The nurse smiled, shifting her eyes from the infant to Lydia, "That's a very nice name." Lydia leaned in to read her nametag to offer a pleasant response. She was interrupted before responding as the nurse reached over and moved the scarf. "Miss, you have a nasty-looking cut on your cheek." Lydia backed away, pulling the scarf over the flesh wound. A wave of panic washed over her. "It's nothing." The nurse moved closer, "No, really, that looks pretty bad. It's bleeding; you should have a doctor take a look at that. It may need stitches." Lydia backed up further, "No, really, don't worry, I'm fine." The nurse's expression told Lydia she was not convinced, as she stepped closer, reaching for the scarf, "Let me get a better look." Lydia was continuing to back away, and the infant began fidgeting, knocking open the blanket surrounding it. The nurse immediately noticed the baby had recently been born and had not been properly cleaned. She grabbed Lydia's arm. "Give me that child," she said, plucking the newborn from her. Then called out to catch the attention of the other nurses nearby, "I need some help here."

Lydia's stomach sank, for she knew there was no way to explain her possession of the newborn. Even though she could have easily outmaneuvered the nurse and fled, instead, she stayed. Suddenly, the nurse clutched her chest, and a pained grimace appeared on her face as she stumbled forward a few steps. Several people dressed in various medical uniforms had already started rushing towards them. Lydia reached for the baby, but the nurse resisted. Another shooting pain in her chest caused the nurse to loosen her hold on the baby, and Lydia quickly reclaimed him. The nurse clamped onto the front of Lydia's shirt. A wild-eyed look of determination gave Lydia the impression that she was not about to let her escape. The tiny infant reached over, placing a hand on the nurse's wrist. Just as his hand touched her wrist, she released her grip on Lydia's shirt, and her eyes rolled back before collapsing to the floor. Lydia quickly rewrapped the newborn in the blanket.

A doctor and two nurses reached the collapsed nurse just moments after she went down. The doctor looked at Lydia, "What happened?" Lydia scooted the scarf further over the gash on her cheek, "She was rushing…to return the wallet I dropped." "And she commented how beautifully my baby is…grabbed her chest, and yelled for help." The doctor was checking for a pulse, then put his stethoscope on and listened for her heartbeat, "I'm not getting anything. Let's get Marion on a stretcher and down to ER stat."

The flurry of activity around Marion, the collapsed nurse, served as the perfect diversion for Lydia to slip away. She went directly to the elevator, pushing the down button. She suddenly felt an uncanny inclination to slip into the ladies ' restroom. As she entered, a couple of security guards got off the elevator and ran past. Something told her they would soon be looking for her. She had to hide the child. Her heart raced as she dumped the contents of the bag (including the dagger) into a trash container. Gently, she placed the infant inside the bag, then zipped it shut. She was amazed that the newborn had not uttered a sound since being born.

242

Lydia exited the restroom and got directly onto the elevator that was waiting with the doors open. Once the elevator opened on the ground floor, Lydia left the hospital through the main entrance, being careful not to look hurried or suspicious. While walking through the lobby, a security guard was ushering a woman away from the exit, as he explained about the hospital being locked down. An ambulance was racing towards the entrance with warning lights all in motion. She managed to slip through the entrance unnoticed as the paramedics wheeled an elderly man into the emergency room. She walked directly to her car and placed the newborn, still in the bag, on the front seat. As she started the car and exited the parking lot, she pondered where to go. She really did not have any idea where she was driving, or why, but she knew wherever they ended up, the dark one was guiding them. She was prepared for whatever revelations remained in store for her.